EMPOWERING THE PAST, CONFRONTING THE FUTURE

CONTEMPORARY ANTHROPOLOGY OF RELIGION

*A series published with the Society for the
Anthropology of Religion*

Robert Hefner, Series Editor
Boston University
Published by Palgrave Macmillan

Body / Meaning / Healing
By Thomas J. Csordas

*The Weight of the Past: Living with History in Mahajanga,
Madagascar*
By Michael Lambek

Empowering the Past, Confronting the Future
By Andrew Strathern and Pamela J. Stewart

Advance Praise for Empowering the Past, Confronting the Future:

"The authors' familiarity with and extensive publications on Duna culture and society provide a 'sufficient ethnography' from which emerges this nuanced account of the forces of change in a contemporary Papua New Guinean society. This ethnography uncommonly privileges the reader with insights into the choices, and their often unintended consequences, made by Duna men and women as they grapple with tradition that is not fixed but constantly shifting, and modernity that is pluralizing rather than homogenizing. The authors capture the texture, ironies, and complexities of Duna society while critically challenging the idea of 'modernity' as a meta-narrative and explanatory concept in anthropology and the social sciences generally. Highly recommended."

—Naomi McPherson, Chair of Department of Anthropology, Okanagan University College, Kelowna, Canada

"This accessibly written book is a very welcome addition to the literature on the Papua New Guinea highlands. It is refreshingly free of jargon, written in a highly readable style, and, drawing on the authors' enormous fund of experience, evidencing considerable anthropological depth and awareness. The focus is on issues of change and the book adopts a commonsense perspective balancing between the timeless ideas of tradition—seen not as static but a constantly shifting perspective—and modernity—seen not as globalizing similarities but as a pluralizing process. It has a particular interest in ritual responses to change that are prominent in Duna culture, presenting some fascinating ethnography on these issues. The book will also appeal to those interested in ideas about the constitution of highland New Guinea social groups, from the early debate on the relevance of African models—a debate to which one of the authors made prominent contributions—to today's concerns with the flexibility of these local entities."

—Paul Sillitoe, Head of Anthropology Department, University of Durham

Empowering the Past, Confronting the Future: The Duna People of Papua New Guinea

by

Andrew Strathern
and
Pamela J. Stewart

EMPOWERING THE PAST, CONFRONTING THE FUTURE
© Andrew Strathern and Pamela J. Stewart, 2004

Softcover reprint of the hardcover 1st edition 2004 978-1-4039-6490-8

All rights reserved. No part of this book may be used or reproduced in any manner whatsoever without written permission except in the case of brief quotations embodied in critical articles or reviews.

First published 2004 by
PALGRAVE MACMILLAN™
175 Fifth Avenue, New York, N.Y. 10010 and
Houndmills, Basingstoke, Hampshire, England RG21 6XS
Companies and representatives throughout the world

PALGRAVE MACMILLAN is the global academic imprint of the Palgrave Macmillan division of St. Martin's Press, LLC and of Palgrave Macmillan Ltd. Macmillan® is a registered trademark in the United States, United Kingdom and other countries. Palgrave is a registered trademark in the European Union and other countries.

ISBN 978-1-349-52850-9   ISBN 978-1-4039-8242-1 (eBook)
DOI 10.1057/9781403982421

Library of Congress Cataloging-in-Publication Data
Strathern, Andrew
    Empowering the past, confronting the future : the Duna people of Papua New Guinea / by Andrew Strathern and Pamela J. Stewart.
        p. cm.
    Includes bibliographical references and index.
    ISBN 978-1-4039-6491-5 (pbk. : alk. paper)
    1. Duna (Papua New Guinea people)—Social conditions. 2. Duna (Papua New Guinea (people)—Kinship. 3. Duna (Papua New Guinea people)—Economic conditions. 4. Mythology, Duna—Papua New Guinea—Aluni Region. 5. Mines and mineral Resources—Papua New Guinea—Aluni Region. 6. Social change—Papua New Guinea—Aluni Region. 7. Aluni Region (Papua New Guinea)—History. 8. Aluni Region (Papua New Guinea)—Social conditions. I. Stewart, Pamela J. II. Title.

DU740.42.S7683 2004
305.89'912—dc22   2003064655

A catalogue record for this book is available from the British Library.

Design by Newgen Imaging Systems (P) Ltd., Chennai, India.

First edition: June 2004
10 9 8 7 6 5 4 3 2 1

Contents

List of Photos   vi
List of Figures, Tables, and Maps   viii
Preface   ix

Introduction   1

Chapter 1
Place and Problem   9

Chapter 2
Flexible Groups   25

Chapter 3
Forces of Change   53

Chapter 4
Leaders and Speech-Making   69

Chapter 5
Myth, Ritual, and Change   91

Chapter 6
The Duna in Regional Context   107

Chapter 7
Concepts of Tradition and Change   121

Chapter 8
Empowering the Past?   139

Chapter 9
Change Among the Duna: A Synopsis and
  Some Wider Implications   153

Notes   163
References   169
About the Authors   179
Index   183

List of Photos

2.1 Settlement at high altitude tucked into hillside in Haiyuwi parish with carefully tended sweet potato garden mounds beside it. Secondary forest and fallow surround the two houses (1999). (Stewart/Strathern Archive)   41

2.2 Two Hagu women. One holds a long cassava root, which will be used for a special pig cooking (1999). (Stewart/Strathern Archive)   41

2.3 Young baby with marsupial fur headband and bead necklace. His father wears a wristwatch, an object much desired. The father has traveled extensively on jobs elsewhere and brought back money used partly for his bridewealth payments (Hagu, 1999). (Stewart/Strathern Archive)   44

2.4 A large pig, which is a centerpiece in the bridewealth to be paid to the bride's kin. It will be claimed by her father or mother as their special prerogative (1999). (Stewart/Strathern Archive)   45

2.5 In hot sun women participants scrutinize bridewealth items being placed on display for a marriage occasion (1999). (Stewart/Strathern Archive)   46

2.6 Two young men hold a Sunday church service at Hagu, playing guitars. They have been trained for this work at the Baptist headquarters in Tangi near Koroba in the Huli area. They are assisting a senior pastor for the parish (1998). (Stewart/Strathern Archive)   48

3.1 A mountainside grave at Hagu, the majestic Victor Emmanuel range in the background. The grave has a special galvanized iron roof, beneath which hangs a piece of the dead man's clothing. His daughter has recently cleared the area of overgrowth as a mark of respect prior to a killing of pigs for his spirit (1999). (Stewart/Strathern Archive)   59

3.2 A set of objects shown to us in the field, including, left to right, stone axe blades, a plastic container holding red ocher used for decorations, round volcanic *auwi* stones, a fossilized nautilus stone *(auwi kendei)*, and a pestle colored with ocher. The bundle at the right-hand side contains a special crystal stone with magical powers (Hagu, 1999). (Stewart/Strathern Archive) — 61

4.1 A view of forest areas devastated by fire in 1997. Swordgrass grows in fallow land in the foreground and the fieldworkers' house at Hagu is visible just beyond it (1999). (Stewart/Strathern Archive) — 84

4.2 Butchering pork for an occasion when leaders will apologize to the spirits for the forest fires of 1997 (1999). (Stewart/Strathern Archive) — 87

4.3 Sides of pork hanging on a pole in a clearing in preparation for a ceremonial cooking. A mother and daughter keep watch over them (1999). (Stewart/Strathern Archive) — 88

5.1 View of Porgera gold mine showing the extensive areas of rock stripped away and the network of roads snaking through the site (1998). (Stewart/Strathern Archive) — 99

5.2 The Porgera mine site showing access roads and some of the installations for refining the gold (1998). (Stewart/Strathern Archive) — 100

5.3 Ekali airstrip seen from the lawn of the Evangelical Church of PNG mission area. The oil-rig site is visible in front of the steep encampment behind it. New temporary homes built by Duna people from the Aluni Valley are visible in the foreground (1999). (Stewart/Strathern Archive) — 102

5.4 The authors at Ekali; airstrip and oil rig in background (1999). (Stewart/Strathern Archive) — 104

7.1 *Anoagaro* man of Hagu with decorations for Independence Day, showing the scenery at his back and the bow and arrows in his left hand. He has a necklace of cowrie shells (1991). (Stewart/Strathern Archive) — 136

7.2 A black-palm bow and a set of arrows with varied points for spearing pigs or shooting birds. The arrow hafts are decorated in black, white, and red. One design conventionally represents "bird's entrails" (1998). (Stewart/Strathern Archive) — 137 and resolves these for the Duna case by showing how the Duna combine two different principles of descent reckoning, the agnatic and cognatic principles. It also engages the contemporary debates about change and globalization by examining the ways in which the Duna have been able to grasp opportunities that have come their way and to internalize the impacts of government, missions, and capitalist enterprise by developing their own accounts of these impacts and their meanings for them. Peripheral as they are to many large-scale processes of change, they have succeeded in viewing the world in their own way: a way that continues to be flexible and always changing, yet recognizably their own. Their past has come to be a resource in terms of which they experience the present and try to envision their future.

Finally, we want to take this opportunity to extend our most sincere thanks to all those persons and agencies from whom we have received assistance in our work, including: the government of Papua New Guinea, for various research permissions; community affairs personnel of the Porgera Joint Venture gold mine, for logistic support; and most importantly our numerous collaborators and helpers among the Duna in the Aluni Valley. We also want to express our gratitude for the extremely perceptive and helpful comments of the anonymous reviewers for this book. Thanks also go to Professor Paul Sillitoe, who has provided valuable comments on our research and supplied comparative materials from his own publications.

Support for our research in Papua New Guinea was given by the Office of the Dean, Faculty of Arts and Sciences, University of Pittsburgh, and by James Cook University of North Queensland, as well as by the Wenner-Gren Foundation and the H. F. Guggenheim Foundation. We are also extremely grateful for grant monies awarded to us from the American Philosophical Society and the Pitcairn-Crabbe Foundation (University of Pittsburgh). We thank also the Institute of Ethnology (IOE) at the Academia Sinica in Taipei, Taiwan, for providing us with facilities as Visiting Scholars in December 2003 and January 2004 to check and revise the copyedited version of our book manuscript. Special thanks in this regard go to Dr. Ying-Kuei Huang, Director of the IOE, and to Dr. Pei-Yi Guo and Dr. Tai-Li Hu. In our text we have sometimes paraphrased translations slightly for clarity of exposition where necessary. Some abbreviations and/or pseudonyms have been used where appropriate.

As with all of our jointly written works, this book represents the equal fusion of our energy, creativity, and collaboration. We remain responsible, of course, for its shortcomings.

List of Figures, Tables, and Maps

Figures

2.1	Haiyuwi parish origins and genealogy	31
2.2	Some residents of Haiyuwi parish and their ties with it	33
2.3	The structure of contributors and distribution of items at marriage occasions	47

Tables

2.1	Duna consanguineal kin terms	34
2.2	Duna affinal kin terms	35

Maps

1	Location of the Duna in Papua New Guinea	10
2	The Duna and Oksapmin Areas	15

Preface

Anthropology has come a long way since the times when its primary ethnographic focus lay in describing how local social systems functioned at a given point in time. Such a focus inevitably involved a foreshortening of historical dimensions in favor of a stress on the supposed synchronic interdependence of institutions and practices. Since the 1960s and 1970s the pendulum has increasingly swung the other way. Nowadays it is common practice to place the emphasis in an ethnographic monograph on processes of change and the wider geopolitical contexts into which those processes are set. This is what we have aimed to do in this book. It is a portrait of a people whose lives since the 1960s have been caught up in patterns of induced change, which they have interpreted, managed, and where possible steered, with reference to their own understandings of their longer term history: understandings that have undoubtedly been at least partly shaped by their experiences of colonial and contemporary changes themselves.

When ethnographers from the 1950s onward first began to describe and analyze the social lives of the Highlands peoples after the earlier colonial intrusions into the region, their initial concern was to achieve an understanding of the basic social structure of groups. An understanding of this sort is still basic to any ethnography; and as it happens ethnographers had difficulties in classifying these societies in terms of their rules of descent governing group membership. The general key to this problem lay in realizing that processes of affiliation to groups, as well as the ideologies defining the groups, were flexible and complex, and were the products of history and change. The Duna people's closest neighbors to their south, the Huli people, posed the problem of group structure most sharply for anthropologists, seemingly following according to Robert Glasse (1968) a relatively rare form of cognatic descent. In order to do justice to this problem, for which the New Guinea Highlands became well known in the comparative literature, we include a whole chapter in this book (chapter 2) on the topic of "flexible groups."

Our main interest, however, lies in historical process, and also in the forms of identity that people forge for themselves through historical experience. Topics of this kind were discussed under the rubric of "modernization" in the 1960s. Today "globalization" has replaced modernization as a popular term of analysis, implying a kind of worldwide network of dependencies and influences and the need to understand this network as an integral part of understanding any given local society or area. Bringing together the global and the local or showing how global influences are woven into local lives has become a major challenge and preoccupation for anthropologists.

Our approach to this newer problem is to stick with our primary local focus as the main line of continuity in our discussion. Thus, we do not describe the entire Duna population but in practice the lives of the people of a small set of local groups in one valley, the Aluni Valley. But the people of this valley have been impacted successively by a stream of outsiders: explorers, mineral prospectors, government officers, and missionaries. Many of the residents have traveled outside of their valley as workers in towns and cities across Papua New Guinea, bringing back cash, material goods, and new ideas and perspectives. "The world" is therefore very much woven into the Valley, so that inevitably a discussion of change implies a broad conspectus of contexts. Nevertheless, our main concern is to show how the local people have *adapted* to change and have altered it to suit themselves.

One of the most dramatic ways in which this process of adaptation is shown lies in the responses people made in 1999 to the activities of a company that came to drill for oil in an area that plays a central part in the Valley people's cosmology, the giant Strickland River, which divides the Duna language area from the Ok peoples to their west. The people developed a new narrative, cast in the mode of their own sacred stories of origins (*malu*) and their general folklore, which explained a particular vision of events surrounding the drilling for oil, their claims on the potential profits if oil were found, and their complex feelings about this latest intrusion into their lives, which was also a major opportunity for gain. The company did not find the oil. But the people did find their own narrative voice about change, which we detail in chapter 5. We conclude our study with three chapters setting Duna history and culture further into the comparative context in their part of the Highlands, and looking at expressions of identity in terms of the theme of "the politics of tradition," of which scholars of Pacific Island societies have recently made considerable use in their analyses.

Our ethnography therefore contributes to anthropological discussions in two ways. It reviews the older debates about social structure

This page intentionally left blank

Introduction

With the increasing complexity and pace of processes of change in social contexts around the world, anthropologists have returned to classic questions regarding tradition and modernity, viewing these in a different way from the earlier literature. The newer viewpoint sees tradition as a constantly shifting, rather than fixed, phenomenon, and modernity as a pluralizing rather than homogenizing process. Historical change and variability are thus the hallmarks of this new perspective in which scholars view the rhetorical deployment of terms such as "tradition" and "modernity" as attempts that people themselves initiate to understand and make use of their historical experiences. In doing so, people may pick on and rework a part of their overall cultural repertoire in order to express their current sense of identity or to adjust to a specific set of changes in their lives. This book explores the efforts of Duna-speaking people in the Aluni Valley of the Southern Highlands Province of Papua New Guinea to achieve such an adjustment.

In our previous ethnographic analysis (Stewart and Strathern 2002a) we have examined in detail one aspect of that adjustment process, involving indigenous ritual and mythology. In this book we make a broader approach to the same problem, incorporating the conclusions of the previous study, but setting these more widely into an exposition of processes of change in the local social structure and in leadership processes. We highlight the impact of mining and the relative lack of smallholder cash-cropping in the area in order to demonstrate the particular effects of uneven development processes within the wider region of the Papua New Guinea Highlands, where ethnographic work has often centered around the emergence of elaborate exchanges, competitive leadership, and subsequently intensive cash-cropping and monetization. The Aluni Duna case differs from this paradigmatic pattern. Large-scale mining projects have greatly influenced the area, while small-scale cash-earning projects are practically nonexistent. Interestingly, although the indigenous rituals for the fertility of the earth have been formally replaced by varieties of Christianity, the people's response to the impacts of mining has been to reassert basic indigenous ritual notions. In the sphere of leadership also, during the 1990s, the preeminent local leaders were all senior men who continued to possess the valued ritual knowledge encapsulated in group origin stories (*malu*). Waves of issues in which the communities were involved, such as sexual transgressions, accusations of witchcraft, suicides, and compensation payments, were all mediated through the actions of these leaders, albeit against a backdrop of generational differences and the inroads of alcohol consumption, new desires born from work experience elsewhere, and political turmoil associated with the provincial and national levels of government. In the light of our analysis of these changes, we explore comparisons with other areas and finally return to the overall questions of tradition, modernity, and local senses of identity. The concluding chapter gives a conspectus of processes of change among the Duna people and relates these to current debates in anthropology on the concept of modernity. We argue that it is the concept of the *contemporary*, and its involvement with both the past and the future, that is effective rather than a standardized set of ideas about *modernity* as such. Modernity, in this view, is not an epoch: it is a shifting and multiple horizon of patterns, expectations, and disappointments generated in the total process of historical change.

A more detailed account of the chapters in the book follows.

Chapter 1 (Place and Problem)

In this chapter we give some basic information about the population we discuss, with a brief description of their habitat, settlement patterns, and mode of subsistence. We follow this with an account of early colonial explorations and their effects on settlement, including the creation of a small government station at the place Aluni, around which cluster a medical aid post, a tradestore, a local vegetable market, and the site of a previous government school. We trace the pathways of a series of explorers and their influence on the people's understandings and imaginations about their world, which involved an idea of the cyclical ending and renewal of the earth every 14 generations through periodic falls of volcanic ash. We depict the early colonial government patrols that brought shell valuables to the people and included an expedition in search of oil. We assess how the colonial administration stopped intergroup fighting and introduced new practices, while modifying others. Finally, we take note of some earlier ethnographic work on the Duna, particularly the work of C. N. Modjeska, who attempted to interpret Duna social life with the aid of neo-Marxist theory, which was in vogue in the 1970s. While we do not follow Modjeska's theoretical approach, his writings provide an invaluable background and counterpoint to our own materials. His interpretation centered on a way of looking at Duna kinship relations, so the next chapter deals with this topic.

Chapter 2 (Flexible Groups)

The key to understanding how kinship intersects with local group organization in the Aluni Valley lies in seeing how flexibility of group affiliation operates. The Aluni Valley Duna practice cognatic descent, that is, persons can belong to named groups, associated with a parish founder, through either male or female links of ancestry. Most commonly people belong through either their father or their mother, and these links are then preserved in genealogies. However, those who belong to agnatic lines of descent through male forebears are the custodians of important ritual knowledge justifying the group's claims to parish land and providing ritual access to powerful spirits of the land, water, and forest, as well as to the spirits of dead kin, which were thought to emerge from the earth after several generations in the form of black, volcanic stones. The agnatic genealogy known to leaders provides the mythical charter for the sovereignty of the group over its land. Agnates tend to be in the minority. Many others accrete around them and are full participants in local activities. This structure, which provides a kind of "backbone" to the group while allowing many people to move around and change their affiliations, constitutes the basic framework of Duna social relations. While agnates hold ritual superiority, they and others all had important roles in communal rituals for fertility, and in kinship-based activities there is a strong insistence on a balanced attention to both father's and mother's side of the kinship universe. Agnation is thus set into a broad network of bilateral kinship ties that are activated whenever marriage payments and compensation payments for injuries or deaths are set in hand. Senior agnatic leaders again play prominent parts in orchestrating these events. Their narratives indicate their keen awareness of the swift changes they have experienced in their lifetimes.

In terms of our overall argument, agnation provides a source of continuity in the Aluni Valley; but the flexible forms of affiliation that complement it allow much movement of people, and especially new influences, to penetrate quickly into any given parish area.

Chapter 3 (Forces of Change)

Christian churches have become extremely important in the Valley since the 1960s. An early Baptist missionary who patrolled the area initiated a wholesale abandonment by the people of ritual objects and practices that previously dotted their whole landscape. In their place people set up churches, in some cases choosing as their pastors the agnatic leaders who previously held the parish's sacred knowledge. Baptist Christianity thus slotted into an existing structure while radically affecting the practices that had upheld this structure in the past. We discuss here some of the partial and awkward adaptations people have made to the new religion, for example in the sphere of funeral practices. One of the perceived problems that vexes the churches is the problem of witchcraft. In precolonial times there were ritual experts who could, under the inspiration of a powerful female spirit, the Payame Ima, perform divinations to identify witches who could then be punished by expulsion or forced to hang themselves. Alternatively they could confess and renounce their activities, in which case their victims, if not already dead, might recover. The churches banned these procedures, but the perceived problems did not go away, and they reached a crisis point during the 1990s. This example indicates the kinds of problems the Valley people have faced since the 1960s. Influence by both government and missions has been patchy. The people have been introduced to new ideas and demands, but without the means to fully grasp these or integrate them into their lives.

Chapter 4 (Leaders and Speech-Making)

In this chapter we look at how Valley leaders have attempted to cope with problems in their areas by their exercise of speech-making skills in general dispute settlements and by their abilities in formal oratory known as *tambaka*, speeches made for occasions of compensation payments following acts of violence. We give examples of such speeches both from the more distant past and from the 1990s. We then move to a discussion of contemporary moots centering on sexual behavior and further to a detailed consideration of records of compensation payments made by men and women of the Valley during their lifetimes. These histories reveal an intersection of relations of enmity and reciprocity over time, incorporating new contexts, such as soccer games that resulted in injuries, as well as older ones, such as those involving sorcery and witchcraft accusations. A discussion of these materials leads into an assessment of the roles of leaders in situations of change. Fundamental to these roles is the leaders' knowledge about the land and the mythology associated with it, which gives them the standing to intervene in contemporary issues as well.

Chapter 5 (Myth, Ritual, and Change)

This chapter explains in further detail the significance of each parish's relationship with its land, including the importance of numerous ritual practices that together were seen as ensuring the continuity and fertility of the land and in delaying what was seen as an ongoing process of decline that could end in the earth "finishing." We highlight the significance of two major spirits, the female Payame Ima and the male Tindi Auwene, both connected to the high forests above human settlement. Ideas about these spirits have fed into the people's responses to incursions by mining companies, both as a way of making claims on resources and as a means of resisting some of the companies' activities. In particular, narratives about the Yuro Ima, a version of the Payame Ima, were brought up in 1999 when the Valley groups were negotiating with the Porgera gold mining company over compensation for what they saw as pollution of the Strickland River by tailings from the company's plant in Enga Province. The Yuro Ima is thought to have had her abode in the Strickland and to have either been killed by the tailings or to have gone away, removing her beneficial influence on the environment. Leaders who know group origin stories linking the river to this spirit figure were able to teach the stories to younger men, enabling them to negotiate with the company. (This topic is dealt with in greater detail in Stewart and Strathern 2002a, but it forms an integral part of our argument here also. For a parallel case see Billings 1998 on the use of myth by an Amungme leader, Tome Beanal, in the context of conflict with the Freeport-McMoran mining company in West Papua, Indonesia.)

Chapter 6 (The Duna in Regional Context)

In this chapter we expand our analytical focus to consider the Duna among other peoples of the Highlands of Papua New Guinea who have experienced rapid processes of colonial and postcolonial change in their lives. The Duna are an interesting and important case precisely because, at least in the Aluni Valley, they have not experienced massive changes in their internal modes of subsistence. But they have experienced considerable effects stemming from mining development in their region. More commonly, anthropologists have reported on areas where the opposite pattern has emerged: a massive switch to cash-cropping (primarily coffee) but only peripheral effects from mining enterprises. Changes have swept into the Valley from outside, causing problems for leaders, but without any huge dislocations of people or growth of pressure on land. It is this circumstance that forms the background to the continuity in leadership and the choice of myth as a means of dealing with mining companies. The replacement of indigenous rituals with Christian church services has probably also reinforced a ritual- and religion-based view of the world. More difficult to deal with has been the issue of witchcraft, as we have seen, and the inroads of violent responses to dispute situations, with a buildup of stocks in guns, both purchased and homemade. By 1999 younger men were parading with guns at brideprice and compensation occasions, in a governmental vacuum caused by a lack of funds for village-level courts and station-based police. Leaders were unable to stem this process either by recourse to government power or by appeals in terms of Christian ideology.

Chapter 7 (Concepts of Tradition and Change)

Much debate in anthropology today surrounds the question of tradition and change. All societies are constantly in processes of change, so that ideas about tradition and modernity represent just the current version of a moving horizon of concepts and practices. In this chapter we review some of the significant literature from the Pacific on this topic, drawing on examples from Papua New Guinea, Fiji, and the Solomons, and then apply insights from these contexts back to the processes of pacification and missionization among the Duna. We show how "the politics of tradition" have come to operate in the Duna case, pointing out that statements about "tradition" have to be understood as statements about the present as much as the past, whether the past is being promoted or rejected. We explore also the connections between rhetorics about tradition and developing senses of national identity.

Chapter 8 (Empowering the Past?)

In this chapter we pursue further the discussion of "tradition" in chapter 7. We do so by looking at four historical ethnographies and comparing these with the Duna case: the Simbu (Chimbu) of the Eastern Highlands of Papua New Guinea (PNG); the Gebusi of the Strickland-Bosavi Lowland area in PNG; the Pangia area of the Southern Highlands Province, PNG; and the Maring of the Western Highlands, PNG. The choice of these four studies enables us to delineate differences in patterns of pacification, church adherence, economic change, and political processes, showing complex correspondences with, and differences from, the Duna case. These studies underline the point that "modernity" is different in different locations, and only historical study can interpret and explain these differences.

Chapter 9 (Change among the Duna: A Synopsis and Some Wider Implications)

In this final chapter we pull together our observations about change among the Duna detailed in previous chapters. We provide a profile of these changes, which helps to identify what we may call the local signature of the contemporary world in one location, multiply criss-crossed by effects from outside of the kind made well-known by Arjun Appadurai's work on "scapes," or flows of influence, but still recognizably formed by its past and able to confront the future partially on its own terms.

This page intentionally left blank

Chapter 1

Place and Problem

Some Basic Information

The processes of change that we discuss in this book are a fundamental part of the lives of people in any place around the globe. From generation to generation, peoples' lives are impacted by new influences, including new technologies, new religious and ritual practices, changing political regimes, and diverse other influences. The degrees of change that take place in particular regions over a period of time vary, as does the acceptance or rejection of introduced ideologies, but change is always taking place among all social groups.

We have only to think of a few examples of how alterations in one aspect of life have ramifying effects on many others. For example, the use of the Internet has changed the way that many people communicate with one another: it allows for electronic publishing, home shopping, e-mailing, and so on. Another example is the use of a common currency, the Euro, among the countries within the European Union, replacing the various national currencies and leading to major alterations in banking transactions. The shared currency and accompanying legislation allowing for the free movement and employment of the citizens of different European nation-states within the Union must over time influence the attitudes that people have toward one another; although in some ways senses of regional identities can also spring up in opposition to homogenizing influences. Hence the European Union becomes a dynamic arena for shifting senses of identity among its peoples, yet these peoples also may retain or develop strong feelings of their local ways of life. Similar processes take place within the small nation-state of Papua New Guinea. Accommodation to outside forces goes hand in hand with reassertions of local values.

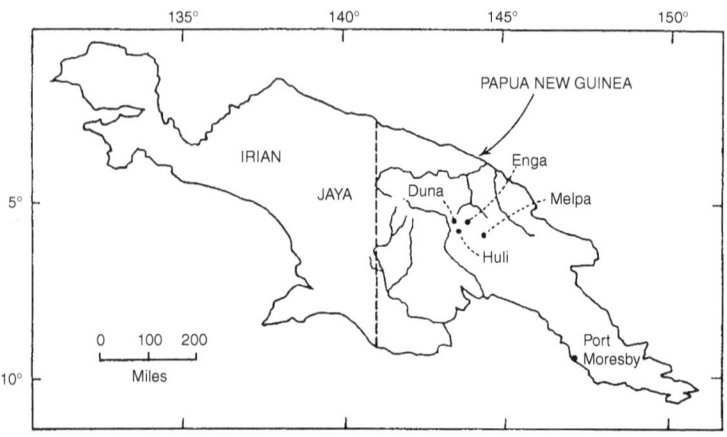

Map 1 Location of the Duna in Papua New Guinea

The people that we are discussing in this book are the Duna people of the Southern Highlands Province of Papua New Guinea (see map 1). We will be discussing the sorts of changes that have influenced the ways in which they lead their lives.

The Duna people living in the Lake Kopiago area are swidden and fallow horticulturalists.[1] Their population is between 15,000 and 20,000. They speak a language that is related to that of the neighboring Huli people as well as to the Bogaiya language, which is spoken by a few hundred people on their southern fringes (Wurm 1964; Foley 2000). The Duna people make their lives in forested, mountain areas where many streams and lakes provide water. Their valley and hillside environment borders directly on the huge Strickland River. The vegetation is lush owing to frequent rainfall, although periodic droughts also occur. Many species of birds inhabit the environment, including white cockatoos, parakeets, and birds-of-paradise. Other animals and birds in the area are wild pigs, cassowaries (large flightless forest birds), and marsupials, all hunted for their meat. These birds and animals also play important roles in the mythological and religious beliefs of the Duna and provide sources of raw materials for body decoration. For example, bird plumes are used in headdresses, and marsupial fur and cassowary quills are also used as ancillary decorations.

The Aluni Valley contains a number of territorial parishes (*rindi*),[2] stretching westward to the Strickland River. The population of this whole valley and its environs is fewer than 1,000 persons. The people build their dwellings on hillsides or within valley pockets at altitudes ranging from 4,000 to 6,500 feet above sea level. Their houses are scattered throughout the area. The entire landscape is peppered with limestone sinkholes and outcrops, which can make walking about rather treacherous unless cleared pathways are followed. In the Aluni Valley, where we worked, there are no functioning roads that motorized vehicles can travel on. The people walk from place to place, visiting people in neighboring parishes or traveling to areas with natural resources such as pandanus nuts and pandanus fruits, which are gathered from trees in the forest. A wide variety of fruits and vegetables are available for collection on these trips within a group's territory.

The Duna intermarry, visit, and trade with neighboring populations including the Huli people to the southeast, the Hewa people to the north, and the Oksapmin and Telefolmin to the west. The Bogaiya people live southwest of the Duna and have over time become considerably integrated into the Duna area through the ongoing processes of territorial shifts in populations. Chapter 6 describes the Duna people's place among other groups, including their immediate neighbors, in Papua New Guinea.

A word may be added here about the Bogaiya, studied earlier by Paul Sillitoe (1994). The Bogaiya are a small, scattered population sharing a single language that shows a relationship with the Duna language, perhaps especially with Duna as it is spoken by people of the Aluni Valley and its points of extremity in Yeru, including Ekali, near to the Strickland River. We conducted some research in the Ekali area in 1999, and found that many Bogaiya speakers had left their hill settlements and come to live near the airstrip run by the local missionary family, who had been there for approximately ten years. In doing so, the Bogaiya had also begun to mingle more with local Duna speakers, and to use Duna as their everyday mode of communication. While interviewing one senior Bogaiya man with the assistance of a younger male interpreter, we found that both men slipped between Duna and Bogaiya almost imperceptibly, and were clearly bilingual. Bogaiya narratives show overlap with Duna ones, for example, regarding the Female Spirit figure, who is important in Duna mythology (see Stewart and Strathern 2002a for a full discussion of the Duna Female Spirit category of the "Payame Ima"). This example shows how pervasively linguistic and cultural usages intermingle in language interchange areas in Papua New Guinea. The Aluni Valley Duna themselves would say of the people living in Horaile parish and beyond it toward Koroba and the Huli people, "no Yuna, ko Karukwa"—"I am Yuna, you are Karukwa"—indicating that Yuna, which is the source of the official name, "Duna," given to their language, is in origin a directional term referring to a cline of perceived differences. Similar directional usages underlay descriptive terms used by peoples elsewhere in the Highlands of Papua New Guinea.

Colonial naming processes sometimes fixed these terms on a map in a way that replaced their earlier contextual reference.

The Aluni Valley abuts stretches of high forest in some areas and low-lying bush in others. New gardens are cut into thick forest or heavy secondary tree growth; while in previously established areas women mound the soil and plant successive crops of sweet potatoes. Men do most of the cutting down of forest trees and they clear garden spaces for their first use. The men also build garden fences in an attempt to keep out domesticated pigs. These pigs are generally cared for by women. The new gardens cut into the forest areas or into regrowth areas may be used for mounding soil to plant sweet potato, or flat expanses of crops may be planted in the area. Once these areas have been harvested and the soil reworked for subsequent planting, mostly by women, the area is planted and harvested as long as it remains in use. Duna practices with regard to rights over land use are discussed more fully in chapter 2, where we describe descent relations between the people of the Valley.

Harvested sweet potatoes are divided into the better, larger ones, which are used to cook and feed to the family, and smaller ones, which are used to feed to the pigs. Pigs are used in various life-cycle activities that are common practices throughout the Highlands of Papua New Guinea: bridewealth payments, funerary feasts, and compensation payments, for example. Although sweet potatoes provide the major part of the vegetable diet for pigs, they also forage in fallow and forest areas for grubs, insects, and worms. Because of the daily requirement to harvest the sweet potatoes, women like to maintain plots of the crop near their dwelling places. These sweet potato plots must be prepared, planted, weeded, and harvested on an ongoing basis. The digging stick is the best tool for preparing the soil for garden mounds.

Sweet potato is by no means the only vegetable that the Duna eat. In addition to forest foods and resources, they grow *Colocasia* and *Xanthosoma* taro, sugar cane, peanuts, maize, pumpkins, onions, ginger, yams, cooking bananas, sweet bananas, and a variety of cultivated green leaf vegetables in their gardens. Both men and women grow these crops with the assistance of their children.[3] From the forested areas other foods can be gathered such as many varieties of edible tree leaves and ferns, earth and tree mushrooms, wildfowl eggs, and large grasshoppers.

Many different kinds of fruit pandanus trees grow in the area. The fruits of these trees vary in their size, time of fruiting, consistency of seeds, abundance of juice that can be squeezed from them after they have been cooked, and the color, taste, and consistency of the juice and pulp of the fruit. These fruits are almost always cooked as a part of a *mumu* (a term used in the lingua franca Tok Pisin), an earth-oven cooking of mixed vegetables and sometimes pork and/or marsupial meat.

The *mumu* is a minor public event, attended by a core of persons who live in the same small hamlet and close relatives or affines who are invited to attend. Everyone participates in preparing the foods and materials that will be needed for the cooking. Various tubers (e.g., sweet potatoes, taro, and yams) and vegetable greens are placed into the oven. On top of this is placed the prepared fruit pandanus. Any meat that is being cooked is also placed over the vegetables. Leaves are packed around the food to protect it from the earth that is piled on top to form the lid of the oven. After all of the food is covered with earth the foods inside steam-cook over a period of several hours.

Early Explorations

Imagine a helicopter flight over a series of craggy mountains, thick forest, and patchworks of settlements spread out below you. You sit in the small cabin, strapped in, ears and eyes protected, straining to take in scene after scene. The pilot has pinpointed your destination on his map and simply asks for a few details. Half an hour or more goes by, then suddenly a grassy knoll comes into view, flanked on either side by steep hillsides. Tiny thatched houses emerge from the greenery. Straight to the west, in a great shallow "v"-shape, lies the dizzying gorge of the Strickland River, and towering over it a castle of mountains, dark blue and hazy, clouds massing at their summits. You have reached the Aluni Valley among the Duna people, the westernmost reach of the Duna population, opened to colonial influence by the Australian Administration in the 1960s, but still without most government services or a passable vehicular road. Arrival by helicopter is dramatic and relatively easy. It also causes a stir of interest among the people, who have been accustomed for some years to such airborne visits from workers from a goldmine in another province to check on the possibilities of pollution in the Strickland River caused by mine tailings. If they themselves wish to travel elsewhere they need to hike out to the government station at Lake Kopiago, a day's walk away, or down to the mission airstrip at Ekali near the Strickland River, and try to obtain a seat to fly out on a small mission or commercial service airplane. This is also the alternative way to come into the Valley: by single-engined plane from Mount Hagen, capital of the Western Highlands Province of Papua New Guinea, arriving after an hour at Lake Kopiago, and backpacking out to Aluni, at first on a rutted, rough, muddy road, and then along pathways where the road ran in colonial times, now covered over with grass and flooded with rainwater in places. The grassy area of Aluni is a welcome sight after such a long walk.

The colonial administration has left its marks on the landscape of rural areas in the shape of such named clearings, around which cluster dwelling houses, churches, and health clinics, places where people muster for elections and gather to sell produce or discuss conflicts. Although Aluni has been a settlement place for several generations, the particular form of the clearing with its tradestore and clinic, and the deserted school and playing field area nearby, are the results of colonial intervention. A hoop-pine tree stands at the edge of the clearing, and in its shade men in the past held debates on the *piki noma*, a grass-covered area which they claimed as their prerogative to occupy in debates. Still today, men cluster in this spot on public occasions, using it to eat small pieces of marketed pork or to play card games beside a tradestore with a meager stock of goods established by a villager who was previously a member of the provincial assembly, having begun as the Aluni clinic orderly. Women sit further over, on a small hump of ground closer to the hut where health workers come to weigh their babies. Often they market green vegetables, fruits, or peanuts, and talk together, netting the strong, attractive bags that they make for themselves and also nowadays for monetary sale.

Up on the hillside of the massive Muller Range to the south of Aluni there are other settlement clusters that belong to the same old parish, Hagu and Sagu in particular. These settlements are perched on breezy outcrops of land surrounded by limestone karst areas with numerous sinkholes. The people make their gardens where they can, skillfully using techniques of mounding to enhance the yields of their sweet-potato crop, and surrounding their houses with introduced *Xanthosoma* taro, banana trees, ornamentals, and cooking sites in secluded hollows. Hagu shows fewer marks of change on the surface than Aluni, though it has its own clearing for volleyball games and its inhabitants have petitioned the Porgera gold mining company for water tanks, hoping to save themselves the long walk over rough limestone paths to fetch fresh spring water for drinking and cooking. The main Baptist church is also there and beside it the dugout area of an artificial pond in which baptisms take place. Nearby is the site of two longhouses built after 1991: one for visiting church people, the other for local men and boys to sleep in, both known as *anda pirapea*, the traditional term for "men's house." The forest fringe is everywhere a backdrop, a world of plants and animals that people use and hunt and the abode of various spirits supposedly, but not definitively, superseded in some contexts by the Christian God as envisioned by various denominations.

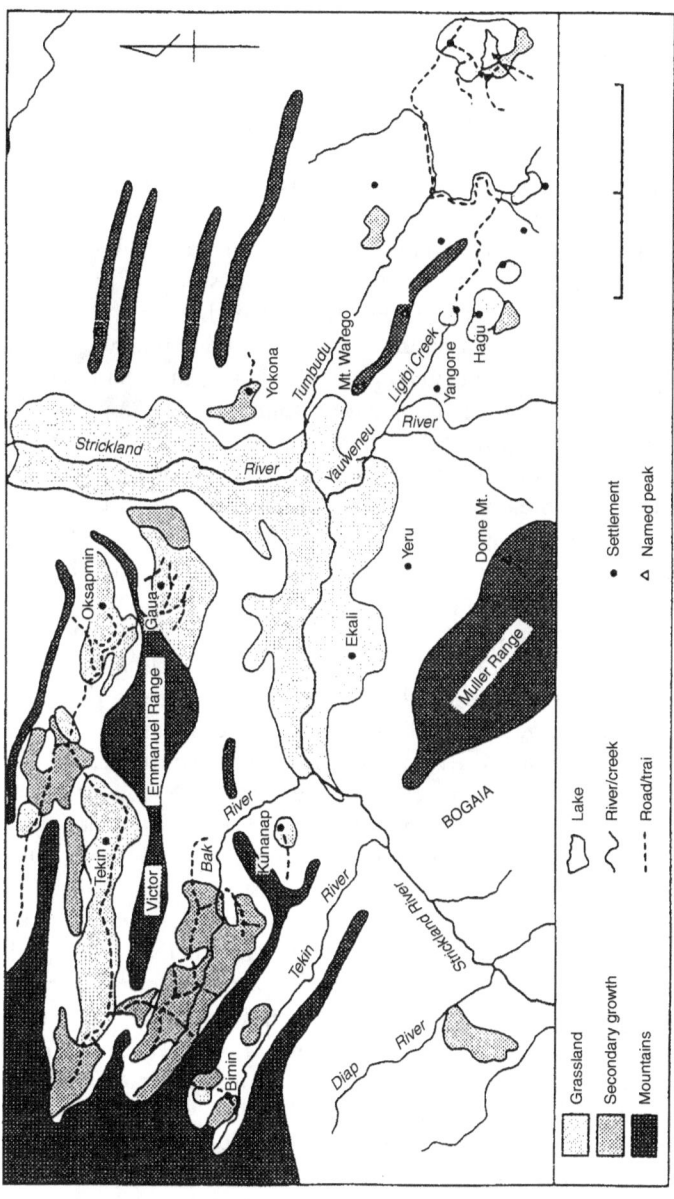

Map 2 The Duna and Oksapmin Areas

The signs of continuity and change blend and mingle with each other almost imperceptibly in the landscape and in the flow of everyday activities. This blending effect is one way in which people adapt to changes in their world, as happens everywhere. It does not mean, however, that people become unconscious of changes around them. It does mean that as time passes, people come to accept as customary, practices that have been relatively recently introduced, and they correspondingly forget how different things may have been before. While the knowledge of change is preserved by an older generation, younger people have a different baseline, founded on their own experiences. Subtle shifts and adaptations in custom mark people's responses to various stimuli, opportunities, and constraints in their life-world at large. In this book we are interested in tracing out some of the patterns of these shifts among the Duna, in looking at their coping arrangements, their ingenious solutions, the impasses they face, their creative reuse of their traditions, and the longer-term corrosive effects of modern changes through which, for example, alcohol, drugs, and firearms have entered into their lives, as they have done more dramatically in other parts of the Highlands more harshly exposed to such changes as well as more involved in economic development through cash-cropping.

The first outsiders from the world beyond New Guinea who directly passed through the vicinity of the Aluni Valley Duna were Tom and Jack Fox, twin brothers who walked out from the distant post of Mount Hagen in 1934, and declared they had searched all the way to the colonial border with the Dutch-controlled part of New Guinea, looking for signs of gold, but returned without success (Souter 1963: 188). They seem to have taken only a few supplies with them, so they must have lived off the country in the main. Older Duna informants remembered traces of the Fox brothers' passage through the Duna area as far as the Strickland River, how they shot game and traded with a leading man in the Kunai parish area; and also how it was feared that their arrival meant a cosmic disturbance was impending (Stewart and Strathern 2002a: 12–13). This pattern of fears was heightened when the second set of outsiders came directly through Aluni on the patrol by government officers James Taylor and John Black, which lasted from 1938 to 1939. Whereas the Fox brothers had carried only a few supplies and had a small band of helpers, the government patrol was impressively large: 20 indigenous police and 230 carriers were employed. Not all of these can have been engaged on each trip, however, because Black and Taylor split up. Black passed through Aluni (Aruni) on his way to Telefomin beyond the Strickland in July 1938, and Taylor also camped there going through to Telefomin on

October 24 of the same year. Both men also made campsites nearer to the Strickland at Yeru (Yeiru) and possibly Ekali. Both crossed the Strickland, constructing cane bridges to do so, and they finally met up at Telefomin on December 2, spending Christmas together there (Souter 1963: 189–192; Gammage 1998: 246–249).

Understandably, the arrival of such large parties of outsiders triggered a mixture of panic, curiosity, and hostility among the Duna, as it did in other parts of the Highlands. Gammage (p. 135) points out that the intruders were thought of as sky beings and the mirrors they carried for trade purposes were seen as "pieces of sky." The carriers took food from gardens when they had to, but at times men brought food for them and even "lined the track, wigs decked in feathers, red sporrans rimmed with pig tails, hands free of weapons" (Gammage, p. 93). Gammage reports this from Black's progress through the Duna area in June 1938. He also notes that people killed pigs and cut their prized red pandanus fruits, planning to feast before they died, because they thought the world's end had come (ibid.). When a leader's pig was shot and he complained, Black gave him a pearl shell in compensation and this seems to have been the first large shell of this kind that local people had seen (p. 94). This fits quite well with the oral accounts we received in the 1990s, which suggested that pearl shells (*kuriapa*) were indeed rare to nonexistent in the Aluni Valley prior to the arrival of colonial outsiders. This same leader then brought out "some foil and paper from a...tobacco tin" (p. 94) discarded previously by the Fox brothers, and showed it to Black. Trophies or prizes of this kind were frequently kept by Highlanders at such times of "first contact." Their actions revealed that they thought the magical powers of the intruders might be encapsulated in the pieces of material culture they left behind. Showing this sign of power to the next white outsider who came was perhaps a way of asking him if he recognized the artifacts of his kinsfolk.

Taylor followed in Black's path, searching for him. Their patrol lines had great difficulty in bridging the 75-yard breadth of the Strickland River and in crawling their way up the precipitous and treacherous limestone hillsides on the other side. Taylor camped in the Aluni Valley opposite where Black had passed. Gammage records that "one man stole an axe. The police caught him and held him handcuffed until his father and brothers paid a pig" (p. 136). Compensation for theft could go either way. Taylor's line was plagued by anxiety over food supplies in this area. Seasonal food shortages do occur in the Valley.

We have recorded elsewhere (Stewart and Strathern 2002a: 14–16, 118) some personal accounts by senior men of Hagu and Haiyuwi parishes of early incursions that probably refer to the Fox brothers and to Taylor and Black. These accounts reveal the trepidation with which the Duna saw these incomers. There definitely were ideas of the possible end of the world in play at this time. Men and women killed pigs and stayed together in the same houses, actions that interrupted the cyclicity of their own rituals and the separate residence patterns of the genders (Stewart and Strathern 2002a: 120). Cautious trading followed the first encounters and episodes of fear. The theme of world's end, reinforced by Christian millennialist teachings, remains with the Duna to this day. One element that has mingled with it is the tradition of the ash fall that is found all over the Highland region (Blong 1982). This tradition records how ash fell from the sky in the past and humans had to take refuge from it for several days. After they reemerged and began making gardens again, they found that the fertility of the soil had been renewed. The world had "ended," but it had renewed itself. When the strange outsiders arrived, it was feared that this event presaged a new disaster, perhaps another ash fall. People's fears and their ritual responses to fear were conditioned by their consciousness of these traditions. The idea of world disaster or cosmic collapse, balanced against the uncertain possibility of world renewal and recovery, is a powerful theme for the Duna, ordering both their hopes and their apprehensions for their future.

Administration

The Fox brothers were explorers looking for gold, although they failed to find any. The Taylor-Black patrol was engaged in basic survey work on behalf of the Australian Administration of what was then the League of Nations Mandated Territory of New Guinea and after the Second World War became a United Nations Trust Territory. The patrol also looked for gold as it traveled. Taylor later established a small gold lease at Porgera, where more recently a huge industrial gold mine has been established, owned by the Australian company Placer Dome and run by the Porgera Joint Venture.

Basic patrols of this kind gave the colonial administrative officers information on geography, population sizes, and potentialities for development in previously unknown areas. After the intermission caused by World War II, the Australians, established earlier in Mount Hagen, turned their attention to the regions west and southwest of Hagen and proceeded to set up government posts at Ialibu, Mendi, Tari, and from Tari further north to Koroba and thence to Lake Kopiago among the Duna. This process of extension of influence took place over the decade of 1950–1960. One of the officers who was prominent in this work of extension was James P. Sinclair, who wrote patrol reports and also published an account of his experiences (Sinclair 1966). Sinclair's own patrols into the land of the Duna were preceded by one led by Desmond Clancy on behalf of the Australasian Petroleum Company. Huli men had brought in gourds of mineral oil to the new station at Tari, stirring thoughts that oil was to be found in commercial quantities somewhere in the hills and valleys between Tari and the Strickland River to the northeast of the Huli. This meant that the patrol would pass through the Duna area. Clancy was deputed to accompany the geologists, taking with him under his control 13 indigenous police of the Royal Papua and New Guinea constabulary (Sinclair 1966: 114). They set out from Tari into the restricted area northward on April 20, 1954, reaching the Strickland, where they found people from the Oksapmin side of the river, on May 24. Like all earlier explorers and later visitors, they were impressed and exhausted by the task of negotiating the huge river and its steep gorge. The patrol lost a dozen men, carriers and police, in the attempt to canoe down the river or swim across it and was then struck by dysentery. The Administration subsequently paid a large number of steel axes and shell valuables as compensation for the deaths of the carriers, some of whom Clancy had personally recruited. The patrol does not seem to have found oil, but its members' reports of the large and flourishing populations in the area contributed to newspaper accounts of a new "Shangri-la" in Papua, echoing the earlier accounts by Jack Hides (e.g., 1935) and Michael Leahy (Leahy and Crain 1937) of their explorations into the interior Highlands region. The interest that this patrol's members showed in oil indicated to the local people that these new intruders were in search of something valuable to them, an impression that entered their historical consciousness in a durable way. When an oil search company came in 1997 to the area of Yeru and Ekali near to the Strickland River at the westernmost end of Duna settlement, its arrival sparked an intense focus of expectations and generated a new narrative linking its activities to the traditional mythology. We will examine these events and their significance further in chapter 5.

Sinclair's own patrol work in the area began on May 10, 1955 (preparations had begun in March of that year). He took with him 50 Huli carriers, who combined their human-hair wigs, decorated with flowers, with the "grey flannel shirts and khaki loincloths" of their new uniform (Sinclair 1966: 119). The aim of the patrol was to set up a new government post to the north of Tari and to explore further as far as the Strickland. Coastal police from outside of the Highlands were partly in charge of disciplining the boisterous carriers, instilling new senses of ethnic hierarchy and colonial control in the people. Sinclair stresses the excitable, self-dramatizing characteristics of both the Huli carriers and the Duna "wigmen" whom he met. He devotes a sizeable paragraph to the appearance and decorations of a particular leader among the Adzugari people, reputed to have six wives, who accompanied him into the patrol camp (Sinclair, p. 123). As they moved north of the Adzugari, the countryside became more rough and marked by limestone, with poor soils and a scarcity of food. He writes, "We fought our way through heavy bush to a high ridge, and there in the distance was Lake Kapiagu [Kopiago], its blue water glittering in the high sun" (p. 125). All of the explorers were impressed by this lake, emerging as something of a surprise in the Highlands, where such large expanses of water are not common. The explorers found that the local people called it *ipa kurupu*, and it seems very likely that this same expression is the source of the name of Lake Kutubu to the south of Huli territory.

Sinclair's patrol notes (see Stewart and Strathern 2002a: 115–117 for more details) indicate the ecological diversity of the Duna area, the rapid thinning out of the population in the limestone country toward the Strickland, and the eagerness of the people to trade for shells and red face paint. Sinclair used this leverage to encourage the people to pay compensation for warfare deaths and to accept the Administration's rule. He noted that people were willing to engage in fractious altercations that could lead to physical violence both among themselves and with patrol members. On one occasion he records that a man beat his wife for digging up sweet potatoes from his plot in order to obtain trade salt. Sinclair interpreted this as a sign of patriarchy, regarding gardens as the property of the woman's "lord and master" (Sinclair 1955–56/1, under date of November 8, 1955, in the Lavani Valley at the headwaters of the Tumbudu River). However, among the Duna, men and women tend to have separate sweet potato gardens, and if a man were to dig from a woman's area he also would be subject to criticism and perhaps physical violence.

On this patrol Sinclair was also interested in obtaining mineral oil deposits from Lavani, but he found the people uncooperative and suspicious, and they protested when the carriers walked too close to their gardens. They were probably concerned that the carriers would steal food. Both police and carriers sometimes stepped over the mark of acceptable behavior on these patrols. Duna people recalled how patrol members killed and ate cassowaries that did not belong to them and burned down a house in Yangone parish near the Strickland, destroying some red crystals used in magic for pig growth. (This was not, however, on one of Sinclair's patrols.)

Sinclair's major efforts were directed to the initial task of establishing administrative control. On entering an area, he would tell those he took to be leaders that the government would forcibly stop their fighting next year. He took with him visitors from an area where a patrol post had been established earlier, Koroba on the southeast of Duna territory. These men wanted to trade with the Duna. A medical orderly, Albert Speer, accompanied the patrol and offered treatments for a range of conditions, such as extracting arrowheads from old wounds or pulling teeth. When deputations from Lake Kopiago visited the patrol, Sinclair gave them presents of axes or knives. He commented that "the people show an extraordinary eagerness for medical treatment that is unique, in my experience, for primitive people" (1955–56/1: 39). Perhaps he was thinking of the kind of interactions an anthropologist, D'Arcy Ryan, observed in Mendi in the 1950s, when men asked health orderlies to pay them for allowing their wounds to be dressed (Ryan 1961). It is true that the Duna have wholeheartedly turned to introduced forms of medicine when these have been available to them. Indeed they give this as an explanation for why certain of their taboos and rituals of the past ceased to be observed. This does not mean that they changed their basic worldview or the frameworks within which they interpret events. In many instances they have adopted new practices on a pragmatic basis, but without rejecting their fundamental ideas about the cosmos and the moralities associated with these ideas (Stewart and Strathern 2001a). Sinclair notes other forms of pragmatic opportunism—for example, people who walked with his patrol but did not carry anything, lined up with the carriers to receive pay. Possibly they saw themselves as helping to protect the party and to introduce it to local people along the way.

Sinclair used cowrie shells for small trade, and the highly valued mother of pearl shells only to pay for large pigs or for land. We see the government here trying to fit into, and to manage, the local shell economy. On a later patrol, no. 2 of 1955–56 from February 25 to April 30, 1956, Sinclair found that a store of supplies he had set up at one place, Kerabo (Kelapo) on the southern edges of the Duna area, had been broken into and approximately 30 pounds of cowries stolen. He accepted three small pigs in partial compensation (February 28). As he approached Lake Kopiago he found that groups were fighting over a bridewealth payment, and that there had been a lot of sickness in the area. Sometimes sickness was spread by the incursions of these patrols. Oral traditions in the 1990s that we collected recalled the period just before and after early contact with the outsiders as times when many people died in sickness epidemics, contributing to the sense of turbulence the newcomers brought with them. At the lake itself his police, who came from the Northern District (later Oro Province) in Papua began making canoes to cross the water. People came to trade food for shells, salt, and paint and watched this new event with great interest, temporarily suspending their fights. Sinclair tried to get them to settle their disputes with exchanges. He established a camp, which became the Lake Kopiago post, and paid the landowners with axes (March 4). On return from patrolling further north he found that a large-scale fight had taken place between the people on the north and the south of the lake during his absence. It might well have been that the fight was occasioned by disputes over the land payments he himself had just made, although Sinclair does not note this possibility. Stories of battles between the lakeside groups are commonly recounted and are tied in with ideas that the spirit associated with a remarkable stone figure known as *tsiri harola* helped the southern groups against the northern ones (Stewart and Strathern 1999a).

Sinclair led the patrol further down the Tumbudu River to Horaile, where he notes that "from here the pale pastel blues of the Strickland were plainly visible" (March 24). This striking view dominates the landscape all through the Aluni Valley. Sinclair camped at Aluni, where there were some large gardens—the same concentration could be seen in the 1990s, indicating the relative fertility of the mound of land on which the Aluni station sits. Sinclair was camping exactly where Taylor and Black had camped earlier on their 1938–1939 patrol. In this way Aluni came to be regarded as the natural site for a government rest station and aid post. Sinclair pushed on to the Strickland and then returned back through Aluni. By April 30 he was back at the Koroba base camp. He noted frequent fighting around Kopiago itself, but not in the Aluni Valley, where population was sparser and food supplies less abundant. On early patrols such as this one the Administration warned fighting groups and told them they should pay compensations for killings. On followup visits the government officers became more exigent, firing shots in the air if necessary and demanding that leaders bring pigs to them for distribution in compensation ceremonies. The kiaps (patrol officers) also themselves paid compensation in axes and pearl shells when air drops of supplies caused local injuries or deaths. The people especially valued the pearl shells and fondled them, laughing, appreciating the high rates of compensation paid. A further patrol by Cadet Patrol Officer R. J. Fairhall, 1958–59/ 7 records that vegetable seeds were distributed and that introduced peanuts were already becoming popular. The trend was enduring. We found in the 1990s that peanuts were a regular and valued cash crop, grown mostly by women on plots otherwise used for sweet potato mounds and sold in small local markets.

From these reports we gain a picture of how the Administration moved to stop fighting and to introduce some new practices or reinforce old ones in the early stages of contact. It is particularly striking to see how closely the Administration interwove its activities with the compensation practices of the area. No doubt in doing so it also transformed or modified those practices themselves. At any rate it is clear that the use of shell wealth helped the Administration to exert influence without always having to resort to force, although force was exercised when it was thought necessary to do so. We pursue the further colonial and postcolonial history of the Duna in chapter 3.

Early Ethnographic Work

Earlier anthropological writings on the Duna concerned themselves largely with classic problems of the analysis and explanation of forms of social structure. The work of Charles Nicholas Modjeska stands out here. Modjeska's ethnographic work provides a fundamental baseline for other studies in the general Duna population area. We concentrate here on giving a brief exposition of the main themes explored by Modjeska.

Modjeska's initial fieldwork was conducted when he was a Ph.D. student with a scholarship at the Australian National University from Canberra. One of the two present authors (A. Strathern) made his first acquaintance with the Duna area in 1970 when visiting Modjeska as his research supervisor in Canberra. The focus suggested for Modjeska's work was the operation of cognatic descent, a topic in vogue at the time as a result of challenges to the "agnatic segmentary" model of tribal societies proposed by E. E. Evans-Pritchard and M. Fortes for the African Nuer and Tallensi peoples (see Barnes 1960). R. M. Glasse, in his work on the Huli, neighbors of the Duna, had strongly proposed that cognatic descent was operative and important among the Huli groups he studied (Glasse 1968). In his own enquiries Modjeska found that cognatic descent was indeed involved as one of the principles of social structure in Horaile, the parish where he stayed for his research. He was not, however, satisfied to use cognatic descent as an explanatory principle for the society, although he accepted it as a descriptive and analytical category through which to understand how the society worked.

Searching for an observer's explanation of Duna social arrangements, Modjeska eventually adopted Marxist theory. He argued that attention to productive processes, particularly gardening, holds the clue to the explanation of Duna social life. He applied the same argument to his understanding of gender relations (see in general Modjeska

1977, 1982, 1991, and 1995). When Modjeska first developed his approach, analyses in terms of "the lineage mode of production," based on neo-Marxist analyses of African agrarian societies, were much in vogue. They had replaced in popularity the earlier, kinship- and descent-based, models elaborated by Fortes and Evans-Pritchard (A. Strathern 1982). Marxist analyses promised to provide insights into the inner workings of societies. Since that time, a variety of more eclectic approaches has entered into anthropology that bring with them different insights for analysis. In particular there has been a renewed interest in interpretive approaches by which the anthropologist tries to understand the symbolic systems of ideas of people themselves and how these relate to their practical actions. In addition, there has been a growing interest in overall problems of historical change. Marxist analyses have been transformed into studies of political economy in general and these in turn have become enmeshed in the "historical turn" of studies in the social sciences at large. It is to this trend of historical anthropology and the study of change that we intend this book to contribute, following earlier work in the same vein (Strathern and Stewart 2000a; Stewart and Strathern 2002a). We stress the adaptations the Duna have made to changes, the transformative effects of these adaptations on their social life, and the larger political and economic conditions that constrain their choices.

The study of change, however, cannot dispense with the analysis of social structure, so in the next chapter we take up the question of group formation among the Duna in the area where we have worked, including the topic of agnatic and cognatic descent. The topic is particularly relevant for understanding how the Aluni Valley Duna people have handled their recent interactions with mining companies, as we discuss in chapter 5.

Chapter 2

Flexible Groups

In the Aluni Valley there are five named territorial parishes, and there is a further parish area, historically associated with those of the Valley, bordering the Strickland River: this is the parish area known as Yeru, in which today the airstrip and mission station of the Evangelical Church of Papua New Guinea are situated. In the Valley the five parishes are Nauwa, Kunai (or Kunei), Haiyuwi, Aluni, and Yangone (or Yangoane/Yangwane). There is a historical separation within Aluni as a whole between the area around the Aluni Station and the hillside settlement of Hagu. From certain viewpoints, Hagu can be considered as a separate unit from Aluni. However the chief agnatic line in Hagu, which in 1991 was centered on the local Baptist pastor who lived there, is the same as that which is recognized as having priority in Aluni, and the pastor served both places. In terms of descent ties, then, Aluni and Hagu are one unit. In terms of practical social relations and senses of identity during the 1990s there was a feeling of an unequal division between them. The feeling perhaps dates only from colonial times, when the grassy knoll now called Aluni was made an administrative center with an Aid Post and school, and the hillside dwellers came to be regarded as ancillary to Aluni "proper." Within the parishes there are several smaller recognized settlement or locality names.[1] "Hagu" may be construed as one of these names that has an enduring historical significance for people's senses of identity, along with the fact that it was a base in the 1990s for the pastor and his son. In fact, Hagu is the earlier settlement of Kepe, the agnatic line in Aluni, and the settlement at Aluni was initiated from Hagu by a female ancestor some five generations ago, according to ethnohistory. In 2001 we learned that the pastor's son had now relocated with his family to Aluni; according to his own account this was in order to help "look after" a new Aid Post and health care building that the Porgera Joint Venture gold mining company based in Porgera donated to the region. He also explained that he wished to avoid the attentions of some witches who had recently returned to Hagu (see Strathern and Stewart 1999a).

Each parish has an extensive tract of settlement and forest lands associated with it, and there is no feeling of population pressure in the area, although there is concern over the perceived gradual declining fertility of the land. This perception may be accurate with respect to certain garden areas, in particular because much of the area as a whole is marked by limestone sinkholes and outcrops, and water drainage tends to carry topsoil away. In mid-1991 Hagu had a population of 34 people, Haiyuwi had 23, Yangone 21, and Aluni 40, making a total of only 118 persons. The whole Valley population, including the residents of Kunai, Nauwa, and the people of Yeru, must amount to fewer than a thousand people in all. Fears of the "land finishing" can in fact equally be interpreted as fears of the population itself dying out, since land and people are closely identified.

In precolonial times these parishes had clear boundaries (*tindi alo*), which could be protected against incursions in times of fighting, and people did not lightly cross these boundaries unless they had some specific purpose in doing so. This sense of separation between the parishes is still expressed today through ideas about relations with spirit entities who are spoken of as looking after, or being the owners of, forest resources. Traditionally, only resident agnatic descendants of the parish founders are held to have the knowledge of the correct way to call out to these spirits (*tama*). The main spirit involved here is known as the Tindi Auwene, the "ground ancestor," a male spirit figure imaged as living in the high forests that flank the settlement areas of all the parishes in the Valley. Each parish claims its own Tindi Auwene figure. Some parishes in addition traditionally have a relationship with a female forest spirit, the Payame Ima, who is said to manifest herself in wind and rushing water and whose abode is in mountain pools and in wild nut pandanus groves. Together the Tindi Auwene and the Payame Ima are held to control access to forest game, such as marsupials and birds. Ideas of this kind have persisted in parallel with the introduced framework of Christian ideas and practices that guides people's daily lives within their settlement areas. The bush is still the domain of the spirits of before.

The Parish and Descent

The invocations to the proprietary and tutelary spirits of the forest that are the prerogative of agnatic parish members are largely directed to the activities of hunting for marsupials and birds. Duna men keep small hunting dogs, and in earlier times they used hunting magic and observed taboos to make their search for game successful. One prominent and knowledgeable man of Nauwa parish (whom we call AH) displayed a bundle of such magic items (*ulupili*) that he had kept. It contained what seemed to be a piece of cinnamon bark, which he said he would burn near the dog's nose to make its sense of smell keen. He said this had come from across the Muller range, from the "Tsinali side," i.e., the sparsely populated and thickly forested Strickland-Bosavi region. When using this magic, he would not eat beans or plant sweet potato vines nor would he roll fibers to make rope or cut stakes to make fences. The rope, he said, might tie up the dog's legs and prevent it from running fast, and the fence stakes might pierce its nose and spoil its powers to smell the game. What these taboos appear to create is a sense of separation, even opposition, between forest-based activities and those of the gardens and the settlement areas. AH added that, since people no longer observe any of these taboos, the power of the magic is broken.

Nevertheless, the basic sense of separation between gardens and forest is preserved. When people cook meat in forest areas they should make a separate offering of it to the forest spirits. If they fail to do this, according to a senior Haiyuwi man (PK), a dog or even a man may go missing, and those who know the resident spirit's name must call this out and entreat the spirit to let the dog go, apologizing for the omission of the required sacrifice. PK gave the names of various spirits of the Tindi Auwene category who might be called on in this way, noting that people of the neighboring parishes such as Nauwa and Aluni were not permitted to know these names and that if they heard them they should stop up their ears. Each parish had its own spirit names and the custodians of these were the parish agnates or, in one instance, a long-standing and trustworthy cognate. Children were not allowed to say the names, PK said: if they did, it was held that the *tama* would kill them. Like AH, PK thought that slippage in the proper observance of these taboos had caused game to be scarce and the harvests from the wild nut pandanus trees of the high forest to be less abundant. One of the taboos involved replacing the ordinary names of items with special names, described as "pandanus language," while traveling in the forest. Both men and women would observe these naming rules, which the *tama* themselves were supposed to have ordained, giving people knowledge of the ritual names to be used. Pandanus language thus equals the language by which humans can communicate with the spirits; it is also a kind of "agnatic" language of the forest areas, in certain regards distinguished from the "cognatic" areas of the settlements, where families with women and children are located. The forest is a domain of magical powers of growth and fertility outside of the sphere of gardening. It therefore was the appropriate place in the past for the location of the *palena anda*, the boys' "growth houses" in which young bachelors were secluded in preparation for their adult maturity. The Payame Ima was the spirit figure preeminently involved in helping the boys to grow, so that they could enter the world of courtship and marriage after emerging from their seclusion. This spirit's consort in the ritual enterprise of "growing" the boys was invariably said to be a male agnate of the parish group, senior and unmarried.

The special knowledge normatively held by some *anoagaro* or agnatic male members of the parish reflects the overall sense that such men are the custodians of the power of the group that is primarily associated with the parish from the time of its founding. The parish can be seen in terms of three different frameworks of identities. In one framework the parish is united by an agnatic genealogy that defines its major subgroups and links it by a string of father–son ties (a descent line) to its mythical founders. These parish founders most often are seen as being *tama*, spirits with magical powers within the cosmos, akin to the Tindi Auwene figures who are still held to be in control of the upper forest environment, or to the *tsiri* spirits of watercourses and pools that sometimes are supposed to attack humans and make them sick but are also said to be responsible for having given pigs and cowrie shells to humans in return for the sacrifice of a woman (see chapter 5 for details). The *tama* who are said to have originated human groups themselves are spoken of in narratives as either emerging from holes or caves in the group's territory or as having traveled underground from another place and then surfaced. In either case the presumption is that they married local women and so began the long reproductive process. Their agnatic descendants see themselves as still connected to the powers of the founding *tama* and their genealogy is intended to show this connection and so to justify their rights over the parish land. In this picture, the parish is essentially identified with a residential, proprietary agnatic descent group.

However, the Duna also recognize genealogical ties through females as providing ties with parish areas that enable people to claim residence and land rights there. Parish members who trace their membership in this way through females are known as *imagaro*. The term *anoagaro*, which we gloss as "agnate," means "man-standing-put," while *imagaro* means "woman-standing put," and we gloss it as "cognate" in relation to parish membership. The *anoagaro* and *imagaro* members of the parish make up its primary membership. Parish rituals joined these two categories together for numbers of ritual sequences of action directed toward *tama*, while giving precedence generally to agnates over nonagnatic cognates. The broader framework of social structure in the parish can therefore be described as one of cognatic descent, that is, descent that can be traced through either male or female links, or combinations of these links. In this framework members of both categories (agnates and cognates) are ultimately linked by descent to the originating spirit powers.

As census materials on persons actually coresident in parishes indicate, the picture "on the ground" is even more complicated, since in-laws (affines) and unrelated people may also be found. Whole sets of kin from other places have also historically migrated from one place to another and have become intertwined with the residential proprietary kin group through intermarriage. Such immigrants nominally preserve their original agnatic identities while effectively integrating themselves into the parish. Over time they become accepted as parish members. Their specific origins are not often referred to, although people know these, and to all outward appearances they are regarded as parish members. Nevertheless their position depends on their continued support of others with help at brideprice and other occasions, and often they are notionally attached to an *anoagaro* family as clients. In terms of actual processes, people make individual and familial choices about where to reside, and with whom to cooperate, based on their personal preferences and situations. A cognatic structure allows for the widespread exercise of choices of this kind; while agnatic lines of descent and succession to leadership provide an ideological framework of continuity and identity within the parish.

In summary, the parish can be seen in three different ways: first as an agnatic descent grouping with patrilineal ties to a founding *tama;* second as a broader cognatic descent group or "ramage," including persons with varying descent ties to the founder; and third as a residential collocation of agnatic and cognatic kin along with others who have joined them as affines, refugees, or friends and who recognize the practical need to cooperate with one another to justify their continuing coresidence and shared use of land. The question here is not which of these ways of seeing the parish is more accurate or "correct" than the others. The three ways are rather different representations of a complex reality that has to be seen in all of its relevant dimensions. To speak of the parish as a "group," then, we must remember that this is a group with flexible characteristics.

The most restricted characteristic is that of the agnatic group; the least restricted is that of the wider residential collocation of people. When the people themselves use the names of parishes, such as "Aluni," "Haiyuwi," or "Yangone," they may have in mind one or the other of these characteristics, or a combination of them. What they mean in any given instance can be determined only by looking at the context of their remarks. A way to understand such contexts is to note that in jural, political, and ritual terms the agnatic model predominates; in terms of overall moral ties of collaboration and cooperation in a kinship framework, the picture is cognatic; and with regard to notions of broader sociable behavior and neighborliness, the idea that the parish is a residential collection or aggregation of individual kin and others prevails.[2]

To give some specificity to these general interpretations, we will adduce materials from one parish, Haiyuwi, drawn from accounts by the recognized senior prominent man in that parish, whom we call PK.[3] In PK's account, his parish began its existence when two *tama*, spirit-men who "did not eat sweet potatoes" (*hina na nayana*), i.e., were not ordinary human beings, traveled from across the Strickland River in the Bimin area and founded the place. One of these two was called Hiwahiwana, the other was Langosula. Notionally, one came to Haiyuwi underground while the other came above ground. The parish line descends from Hiwahiwana, who married a woman called Paiye (this is also the name of a local river). The couple had three sons, but the descendants of two of these went off to other places. The middle son, Pitupelenda, had two sons, and from one of these came the Itake, a subgroup no longer existing in Haiyuwi but with ancestral tracts of land still recognized as belonging to its members living elsewhere. From the other son, Parirua, came Muna, who was in turn the founder of the two main recognized parish subgroups, Pali and Tole, each further subdivided into two. Figure 2.1 develops this pattern, showing agnatic ties of the subgroup to the founding *tama*. We use this as a typical example of how such accounts of descent ties are structured. On different occasions the same informant will give different representations of particular lines of descent, marriage, and children. Figure 2.1 encodes PK's vision of how the main subgroups in Haiyuwi are related through ancestral ties; it does not include his complete knowledge of the various families and their networks of kin and affines.

A feature of this figure that it shares with other depictions of the ancestry of parishes is that in many generations we see how particular antecedents had no issue, or had died out, or moved away, or their *imagaro* descendants are recognized. Agnatic lines persist in spite of the contingencies of residence moves; cognatic kin are recognized selectively. The *imagaro* subgroup in Tole, descending from a woman called Owa, came into being after the woman's descendants returned to Haiyuwi from the distant place of their Huli father. These features,

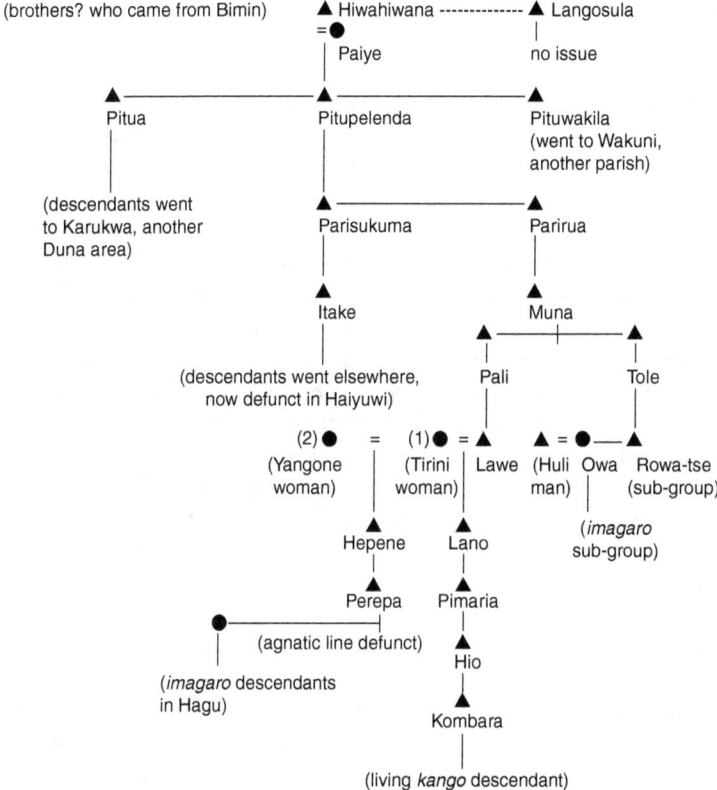

Figure 2.1 Haiyuwi parish origins and genealogy

captured in the narrative, accurately reflect the contingencies of reoccurring historical processes. Nevertheless the model of social structure presented is predominantly one of agnatic descent, supplemented by cognatic ties.

As we have indicated is generally the case, this "actor's model" of the parish does not reveal the complexities of social ties between persons living "on the ground." Figure 2.2 indicates some of these complexities, centered on specific adult residents of Haiyuwi in the early 1990s (September 1991). The *kango* (prominent man or leader) PK gave this account, he himself being a senior agnate of the Pali subgroup, although he does not appear on our list. Two points emerge clearly from the residence histories in figure 2.2. The first is that cognatic links, variously resulting from ties traced through natal female members, are invariably the pathways by which people from elsewhere came to be affiliated. As we will see when we discuss kinship terminology, such persons all belong to lines that are classified as *apa* by the resident agnatic lines: that is, descendants, usually agnatic, of an ancestral female agnate of the group. Second, this general category of *imagaro* members outnumber the actual resident agnates in the parish. Of the ten men listed in figure 2.2, only two are *anoagaro* or agnates. PK himself makes three in total here, compared with eight nonagnatic cognates. In other words only about one quarter of these linking men in the genealogies relevant to the time of fieldwork were agnates, while three quarters were recognized cognates. These nonagnatic families also contained two recognized *kango* or leaders. What this computation of details reveals, then, is that there is no expectation that parish members will be mostly agnates. Most often, they are in a minority in the places where they live. This actually contributes to their perceived importance and status within the local group as the custodians of its most important knowledge and its ties with the spirit world of the environment. We will see the relevance of this point for the study of change when we consider in chapter 5 the Valley people's responses to the challenges introduced into their lives by the activities of mining companies.

Before moving to further topics, we need to take a look at kinship terminology. This is summarized in tables 2.1 and 2.2.

The details in these two tables are given for the sake of completeness and for those who may want to make comparisons with other ethnographic cases. The main point that should be noticed in table 2.1 follows from our discussion of local group affiliations. Cross-cousin terms (*hanini*) are extended over more than one generation, and eventually turn into *auwenene* ties that finally become classified as *apa*. The *apa* are kin at the limits of the recognition of cognatic kinship. *Imagaro* ties tend to become *apa* ties over time within the group also. Perhaps for this reason *apa* kin played an important role in one of the significant collective rituals for fertility held in the past, the *kira pulu* rituals (Stewart and Strathern 2002a). With regard to affines (table 2.2), the in-laws who are a major focus of respect are those classified as *yakane*, notably father-in-law and mother-in-law. A son-in-law must not use his mother-in-law's personal name. To do so would be a mark of disrespect. He should use the term *yakane* as his way of addressing her. On bridewealth occasions there is much focus on the collection of a special sum of wealth, nowadays money, to give to the mother-in-law so that she will agree to her daughter's marriage. This is called *yakane paraiya*, a greeting for or appeasement of the bride's mother. In the 1990s there was much comment at marriage occasions that the sum of money involved here had become inflated, as young men who earned money elsewhere by labor migration came back to

	Name	History of Link
1.	L.	This man's paternal grandfather was from Horaile parish, his father's mother was of Aluni. The father came to Aluni after disputes at Horaile. L. married the sister of a *kango* in Haiyuwi and came to live there.
2.	D.	Recognized *kango*. His paternal ties link him to Mbara near Lake Kopiago. Haiyuwi is his mother's mother's place. His mother brought his father in uxorilocal marriage to Haiyuwi.
3.	KE.	His paternal place is Kakwene parish. His mother's mother was of the Pali subgroup (see figure 2.1) and his father's maternal grandmother was of Itake.
4.	T.	His mother's mother belonged to Pali. After a dispute in his paternal place, Nauwa, his father told him to go and live permanently with Kombara (see figure 2.1).
5.	KI.	His father came as a war refugee to Haiyuwi in precolonial times. The father's father's mother was of Tole subgroup. K. is classified as *imagaro*. The father was a *kango*.
6.	M. (deceased, sons living)	Agnate of Tole subgroup, a *kango*.
7.	J.T.	Agnate of Hirane parish, his father's mother was of Pali subgroup, and the father came to live at his mother's place.
8.	PR. (deceased, sons living)	Agnate of Tole subgroup.
9.	KL. (deceased, sons living)	His father's mother was of Pali subgroup and his mother was affiliated with the Owa section of Tole also. The Haiyuwi people brought KL. back to their parish area after one of his brothers was shot in warfare
10.	TI.	Member of Owa section in Tole, his father's father's father's father's mother was the founding ancestress of the section who married the Huli man (see figure 2.1). The whole section is *imagaro* in Haiyuwi but is also described as *anoa-tsi-ngini*, "the sons of men who came" or the sons of another man taken into the group via their mother.

Figure 2.2 Some residents of Haiyuwi parish and their ties with it

Table 2.1 Duna consanguineal kin terms

Term	Gloss[1]	Ranges of application
mamane	grandfather–grandchild	includes great-uncle and great-nephew
auwene	grandmother–grandchild	includes great-aunt and great-niece
ame	father	includes paternal uncle and classificatory kin
antia	mother	includes maternal aunt, MZ, and FW
auwene[2]	maternal uncle nephew/niece	includes, e.g., FBDS
arane	paternal aunt- nephew/niece	includes, e.g., FFBD
keni	same-sex sibling (male speaking) "brother"	includes, e.g., FBS and MZS
hagini	same-sex sibling (female speaking) "sister"	includes, e.g., FBD and MZD
kane	opposite-sex sibling "sister" (male speaking) "brother" (female speaking)	includes, e.g., FBS or D; MZS or D
hanini	cross-cousin	includes, e.g., FFBDS or D, MFBSS or D
ngini	son	includes, e.g., MZSS
wane	daughter	includes, e.g., MZSD
apa[3]	remote cross-cousin, distant cousin	includes the agnatic descendants of a brother–sister pair in earlier generations (marks limits of recognized consanguineal ties)

Notes

[1] These terms are used self-reciprocally for reference and address except for F, M, S, D (in ref.).

[2] Modjeska (1980: 316) records *auwine* for MB. Our collaborators gave *auwene* for this, making it phonemically the same as the term used between grandmother and grandchild. They did not recognize *auwine*.

[3] Terms associated with *apa* are *auwa* and *auwenene*. *Auwa* can be applied to "child of cross-cousin." *Apa* kin can be considered as "children of *auwenene*." One of our senior collaborators indicated that *auwenene* is used in the same way as Modjeska (1980: 316) reports for *ama*, a term we did not hear. All of these terms indicate an extension of cross-cousin ties over a number of generations.

Key
F = father
M = mother
S = son
D = daughter
B = brother
Z = sister
H = husband

Table 2.1 Continued

W = wife
ch. = child/children
C = cousin
P = parallel
X = cross

Sources: Our fieldnotes (Aluni Valley 1991–1999); Modjeska (1980: 316), based on work in Horaile parish. Modjeska (p. 320) also lists simplified sets of address terms. There may be differences in usages between Horaile and Aluni.

Table 2.2 Duna affinal kin terms

Term	Gloss[1]	Ranges of application
iwane[1]	wife	not extended
noni	husband	not extended
hakalini	co-wife (female speaking)	HW, HBW
kiane	brother's wife–husband's brother	not extended
arane	sister-in-law (female speaking)	BW, HZ
mbaluni[2] *paluni*	brother-in-law	ZH, WB, WZ
aruni[3]	female in-law, daughter-in-law	includes MBW and cross-cousin's W
yakane[4]	mother-in-law, father-in-law, daughter-in-law	wife's cross-cousin
yakini	step-father, step-child	includes also MZH, WZch.

Notes

[1] The verbal root *iwa* means "to plant." This meaning may have some connection with the term for wife. Spouses more often use versions of personal names in addressing each other. All terms other than for W and H are used self-reciprocally.

[2] Modjeska (1980: 324) has *baluni*. In the Aluni Valley people say *paluni*. This is a minor difference of pronunciation. A term Modjeska does not mention is *imanggu*, "woman giving/given." This was frequently used in the Valley as a reference term for affines. Its primary meaning appears to be "wife-giver," used, e.g., for WB.

[3] This term has a wide range of applications. For further details see Modjeska 1980: 324. Women use this term widely for husband's kin, we were told.

[4] This term also has a wide range. It is most characteristically used by a man for his mother-in-law, to whom a special amount of wealth, nowadays state money, must be given in a bridprice payment, in order to appease her feelings at the loss of her daughter and the daughter's removal to the husband's place, which normatively occurs. Asked what the term for FZH was, one informant suggested either *yakane* or *neneke*, "friend."

Key: See under consanguineal terms.

Sources: As for consanguineal terms.

the Valley and the kinsfolk, especially the parents, of girls whom they sought to marry, raised the stakes for the size of the bridewealth's monetary component.

The processes and relationships encoded in figure 2.1 reveal a world of historical contingencies through which people seek to establish patterns of sedimented relationship that are themselves always fluctuating and evolving. The figure does not represent a firmly established set of structural levels in a "segmentary system" of relations. On the other hand it does represent certain structural differences. According to PK's account, all the descendants of the parish founder Hiwahiwana, agnatic and cognatic, are *tsene*, "kin of common descent." *Ramene* are cognates, the dispersed children of sisters of the agnatic lines, who live elsewhere but are expected to come and help by contributing to parish events such as pig-killings. Their original linkage point to an agnatic line may be remembered. In Horaile parish beyond the Valley, for example, Modjeska (1977: 99) remarks on a set of people, called Mone, who originally constituted a *ramene* with respect to the parish of Haiyuwi, from which their ancestors are said originally to have come. As will be evident from our discussion of table 2.1, *ramene* typically contain kin of the *auwa/auwenene/apa* series, the descendants of brother-sister sibling pairs in ascendant generations. In this instance, it appears that Mone was actually the name of a Haiyuwi man whose sister was married to a Horaile man, and Mone himself was given land by his sister's husband. It is his descendants, in turn, who are seen as members of Horaile, now interspersed with those of the original sister's husband. Although these men are therefore agnates of Haiyuwi parish by origin, they have become completely absorbed into Horaile, mingled with their own *apa* kin descended from Mone's sister.

Modjeska reports (ibid.) that these Mone people originally "purchased" land from Horaile some generations earlier, but that now they were accepted as parish members who could make gardens anywhere within the parish territory. In this same passage (p. 99) Modjeska further reports a story he was told that Haiyuwi members had at one time purchased a "block" of land along the boundary with Aluni. Later, however, those living on this "block" were considered to be as closely connected to the Aluni lines as they were to Haiyuwi, so that the group "ownership" of this particular area became moot. From our own information it would appear that this anecdote refers to land on the borders of Hagu, which the Hagu *anoagaro* members say belongs historically to the Itake subgroup of Haiyuwi. Since the Hagu pastor himself is also *imagaro* to the main agnatic line in Haiyuwi, this might give the impression that the land is in some sense shared between the two parishes. In 1999 this whole tract of land was unoccupied, but an Itake man, resident far away in a parish closer to Lake Kopiago station (Hirane), declared that he would be willing to sell it to the government or to the Porgera Joint Venture mining company if they wished to build an airstrip on it. (This man's sister was married in to the agnatic line in Hagu.) This case exemplifies a number of points. First, given the flexibility of the cognatic principle, sets of people can on pragmatic grounds of need and opportunity split off from their agnatic ties and gain entry elsewhere. Second, the "payments" or purchases to which Modjeska refers have to be interpreted within this context of kinship. Third, claims can remain latent and can be taken up again, at least in prospect, if a new opportunity presents itself. Fourth, and finally, a good deal of selective forgetting as well as remembering goes on: PK in his account did not mention the Mone *ramene* at all. It was in his rendition "lost" to Haiyuwi history. The Itake might similarly have been lost to parish memory, but the tract of land in their name and even the vague possibility that this might become a new commercial asset perhaps revived the consciousness of this subgroup's name.

Within the parish itself, then, PK recognized the subgroups of Itake (defunct), Pali, and Tole as *ima-auwa* (women-owners). Pali, he said, are *keni pukwa*, "the big [elder] brother," and Tole *keni tsu*, "the younger brother." Smaller subsets with Pali and Tole are also seen as *keni-keni*, "brother–brother" groups. Lano and Hepene are examples of these smaller sets (only Lano continues to exist within the parish framework). PK used the term *ima-sana* (or *tsana*) for other groups such as the Kunai, with whom Haiyuwi people may intermarry. *Ima-sana* means, appropriately enough, "woman-taking." The cognitive model involved here clearly envisages marriage with residence at the husband's place (virilocal residence) and the major subgroups in the parish as the sets of kin who notionally give and receive brideprice payments in connection with marriage.[4]

Marriage and Cognatic Kinship

Marriage in practice activates complex sets of cognatic kin centering on intergenerational ties of exchange. We have already seen the constant counterbalancing or complementarity of agnatic and cognatic ties in people's representations of parish divisions. This way of depicting the parish as a structured set of relations mirrors the ways in which actual transactions are organized on marriage and other life-cycle occasions. People place a strong emphasis on recognizing both "mother's and father's sides" of a person's kinsfolk for these events. The central aspect of a marriage contract is the payment of the brideprice or bridewealth. On the groom's side, his parents each solicit help from their own kin to help pay the amounts of wealth involved; while on the bride's side her parents are also obligated to distribute this wealth to their kin in turn. Potentially many sets of people from different intermarrying parishes may be brought together by these imperatives of contributing and distributing wealth. Since people are not supposed to marry anyone with whom they recognize a *ramene* tie, marriages do in fact link different parishes together; although, there is some intraparish marriage because, as we have seen, different lines may have "come inside" to live with the proprietary residential group. Dozens or up to a hundred or more people may gather together for a marriage occasion, and their interactions are carefully controlled and orchestrated. *Kango* leaders play a significant role in this orchestration and in the negotiations that go on.

While kinsfolk ultimately exercise control over whether a legitimate marriage takes place, there is also a realistic expectation that young people will seek out the partners of their choice.

This is not a new phenomenon. In the past, courting parties (*yekeanda*) were held at intervals of time, providing opportunities for young men who had graduated from the bachelors' growth rituals held for them to engage in courtship with unmarried young women of neighboring areas (Stewart and Strathern 2002b). *Yekeanda*, by all accounts, were attractive occasions marked by dance performances in which adult members of the community were involved. They were multifunctional occasions at which people performed rituals to divine for the causes of sickness and to bring back to their natal places the spirits of sisters married outside of the group who had died elsewhere and their spirits had indicated a wish to be returned in this way to their earlier homes. A special *yekea* house was built and the young men and women gathered in it. The males played mouth harps and the females played mouth bows, passing on messages to one another by means of words encoded in their music. Youths were said to have sat on the laps of girls at certain points in these interchanges. A boy who befriended a girl might give her a cassowary pinion as an ornament to wear through her pierced nasal septum. The girl might give him a pandanus-leaf sleeping mat to indicate her interest in him. *Yekeanda* were abandoned early in the colonial process after 1960 as a result of disapproval expressed by Christian missionaries from Australia and the United States, including Catholics, Baptists, and Seventh-Day Adventists. They were an integral and vital part of the life-cycle of people's experiences, linking the living to the dead and expressing the transition from adolescence to maturity. People still remember the songs and tunes they performed in those earlier days.

Transition to the married state was, and continues to be, marked by an elaborate transfer of wealth from the kin of the prospective groom to the bride's kin. In many parts of the Highlands region the transfers of wealth at marriage are reciprocal, although not balanced. That is, the wealth given by the groom's kin is met by a reciprocal, but smaller, amount returned by the kin of the bride. This is not the case among the Duna, where the transfer is unilateral, and the aim is to secure rights over the labor and productive powers of the bride in the most general sense. This does not mean the bride is entirely cut off from her kin or incorporated into the husband's natal kin group. It does mean that she is obligated to work at gardening and rearing pigs and later bearing children who will be related both to her husband's and her own natal kin. Given this, it is reasonable to speak of these transfers of wealth at marriage as forms of "brideprice," provided we remember that the groom's side does not "buy" the bride in any total sense nor do her kinsfolk "sell" her. Many anthropologists, however, use the term "bridewealth" in order to avoid giving such an impression. The people themselves understand that the purposes of the transfers are to secure rights, and will translate this process into the lingua franca Tok Pisin, whose vocabulary is based on English, as "baim meri" or "braitprais" (i.e. "brideprice"). Again, such usages do not imply acts of total buying and selling. However, to remind ourselves that rights are being obtained and that the direction of transfer is unilateral among the Duna, it is worthwhile to note the Tok Pisin version of the term "brideprice" here. The term "bridewealth" can also be kept in mind, as highlighting the social aspects of the transaction involved. The important point is to keep in mind what the transfers of wealth actually do.

The transition to the married state was highly ritualized for the incoming bride, in keeping with the fact that she was expected to remove herself from her natal home and arrive as a newcomer in her husband's settlement. After the payment of an acceptable amount of wealth to her kin and its distribution (see further later), the bride came with a pair of netbags, items that women make, suspended at her front and back. She was expected to keep her hands tucked behind the netbag at her chest, and to put special leaves in the one worn at her back to mark her anticipated role as the mother of a child in the future. In addition she was expected to cover her head with a netted cape of a kind commonly worn by married women in other parts of the Highlands. On contemporary occasions of dances to celebrate the national day of Independence or for other festivities, young women may wear netbags of this kind, marking their status as potential brides.

In addition, the sense of liminal danger and importance involved in the bride's arrival at her new place was in the past marked by specific behavioral taboos. She was enjoined not to sleep on the first night after she came but to observe a kind of vigil, in case her own errant spirit (*tini*) might emerge during her sleep and harm the groom. A sense of potential hostility and lack of confidence in the bride's feelings is conveyed by this rule. Girls, however, were not generally coerced into marriage, and might have courted their husbands in the *yekea* house prior to their marriage. The bride was required to observe food taboos also: not to eat sweet potatoes baked in hearth ashes, and to drink only sugar cane broken for her, and potatoes cooked for her, by others while she stayed in the women's house of her mother-in-law. From one viewpoint these rules can be seen as honoring the bride, since others had to look after her. From another viewpoint the rules emphasized the constraints on her, since she had to obey what her in-laws told her to do. And from yet another viewpoint, as we have noted, the rules reflect the liminality of the whole process and its importance in the life-cycles of those involved and in the reproduction of social relations that hinged on marriage as an institution. Interestingly, it does not appear that similar taboos were placed on the groom. His "initiation" would in the past have been completed earlier through his graduation from the *palena* rituals. These rituals putatively strengthened him physically for the "work" of marriage. In the bride's case the emphasis was, by contrast, on her mental and social conditioning for her new role.

The bride's major immediate task in the period following her marriage was not to produce children but to rear pigs. This injunction can be interpreted as a way of requiring her to "pay for her marriage" by replacing the pigs her in-laws had paid as brideprice to her natal kin. A *kango*, or affluent man, might endow the bride with a digging stick for garden work, a female pig, and some pig-growth magic (*palena* plants whose leaves she would feed to the herd from time to time). After the herd had grown, the couple would repay their sponsor. This process was supposed to be completed before the bride had children. The initial emphasis therefore was on the reproduction of pigs rather than on starting a family.

This does not mean that the young couples were not sexually attracted to each other. During courtship, people had the opportunity to playfully express their mutual attraction. Often retained in people's memories of courtship in the past is knowledge of the songs people

2.1 Settlement at high altitude tucked into hillside in Haiyuwi parish with carefully tended sweet potato garden mounds beside it. Secondary forest and fallow surround the two houses (1999). (Stewart/Strathern Archive)

2.2 Two Hagu women. One holds a long cassava root, which will be used for a special pig cooking (1999). (Stewart/Strathern Archive)

sang. One category of song performed by young people was known as *laingwa*. In 1998 we recorded a series of such songs performed for us as examples of the genre by a set of married men and youths, recalling the times when they had sung them for purposes of courting.

A predominant theme in the corpus of songs is an invitation to girls to come and experience the good foods that grow in the youth's parish areas. In one instance the song declares that the singers cannot describe the place, the girls must come and see it for themselves. "Come and marry us and get the greens, pandanus nuts, pandanus leaves for making sleeping mats, fruit pandanus, and other foods that are plentiful here with no woman to consume or use them," the men sing. In another theme they chide the girls of other places for being slow to come and see them. They compare themselves to parrots that come looking for tree seedlings and are wasting their time. They offer marsupial and wild cassowary meat and say they will present the girls with a cassowary pinion as a "bridge" (*tsoko*) for them to cross over on and come to them. (In another part of the Highlands, Mount Hagen, the playful talk of courting is itself described as *ik pol*, "bridge talk.") They express their endurance in waiting for girls to come; and finally they upbraid the girls, saying that many of their age-mates have married already, so why are they delaying? Is it going to school that is holding them up?

> *Kili kipe kawali kipe*
> *Ruku nane pepa kili kipe kawali kipe*
> *Rukupe nane pepa kili kipe kawali kipe*
>
> Some girls carry
> The *kili* and *kawali* leaves in their netbags
> Are you carrying
> The white man's paper in there?

The leaves referred to here were ones used to provide a soft bed for babies to lie on. White man's paper refers to school exercise books.

Netbags are closely associated with women, who manufacture them as a form of wealth as well as clothing, personal adornment, and for carrying children or loads of food. Another category of courting song for *yekea* performances is known as *uuya*. An example follows:

> *Ale sanda ima ndu tana pukwa narai*
> *Ayele sanda ima ndu tana pukwa naraiya pinya*
> *Liwale sanda ima ndu tana pukwa naraiya pinya*
> *Warama sanda ima ndu tana pukwa narai inya*
> *Naraiya pinya hai ai*
>
> She will take the *ale* netbag, but
> The girl does not sit down firmly
> She will take the *ayele* netbag, but
> The girl does not sit down firmly....

And so also for the *liwale* and *warama* netbags. All four terms are alternate words for "netbag." In the song itself the idea of "sitting down," i.e., settling at a husband's place, is expressed in the image of *tana pukwa*, "large bottom." Wives eating the food of their husband's land are supposed to grow large. The singer jokingly teases a girl, saying she is not conforming to this pattern, i.e., she has not married yet. She will take her netbag and go around but she will not settle down, she is still on the move. *Uuya* songs may also evoke the same themes as *laingwa*, offering especially the prized pandanus nuts to any willing takers. In all of these songs it is the youths who must woo the girls by persuading them to leave their homes and come to them. Girls in response may ask the youths if they really have food or really can raise a brideprice.

Once wealth has been transferred and the new wife comes, she is expected to stay with her mother-in-law, make gardens, rear pigs, and not visit her natal home too much. It is remarkable, in the context of the importance of affinal exchanges in many Highlands societies, that the couple are actually discouraged from giving away any further pigs to the new bride's natal kin until the herds of her husband's family have built up again. Equally, the bride's kin do not endow her with pigs as is traditionally done in Mount Hagen with what are called there "the pigs of the house" (*kng mangal*). She is instead expected to work herself to raise the pigs needed, with extra-familial help perhaps from a local *kango*, as we have seen. When the time is right the couple may take one or two pigs over to the wife's kin as *imaloma* gifts, for which a return may or may not be made. If it is, the exercise may be repeated, but it is not expected to build into an elaborate lifelong sequence or to be transformed into matrilateral gifts for children born to the marriage. The marriage payment is a "one size fits all" transaction that establishes the entailments of the marriage in a single event and locks the bride firmly into her new home.

This factor helps to explain why the emphasis in courting songs is on luring girls to come to the youths' places. Once the girl is married she is expected to become *tana pukwa*, fixed in one place. It also helps to explain modern tensions that have arisen around the question of how and when young people may seek to marry. The payment of wealth represents a massive financial investment in the future of kin relationships among neighbors. Entry into this stage of life was in the past carefully channeled through the *palena* and the *yekea* institutions. With the demise of these activities, young people have made their own experiments in courting, by meeting on the road or writing letters to one another; and the senior generation has reacted by a zealous pursuit of their own aims, challenging youths who approach girls and stridently demanding that their parents at once arrange for a brideprice to be paid. This may not suit either the wishes of the young people or the financial capacities of their parents and kin, and acrimonious altercations ensue. Premarital engagement in sexual intercourse is something that the older generation does not condone. They see this activity as a sign of young people not obeying their elders and as a larger indication of cosmic decline in general, as we explain further in chapter 4.

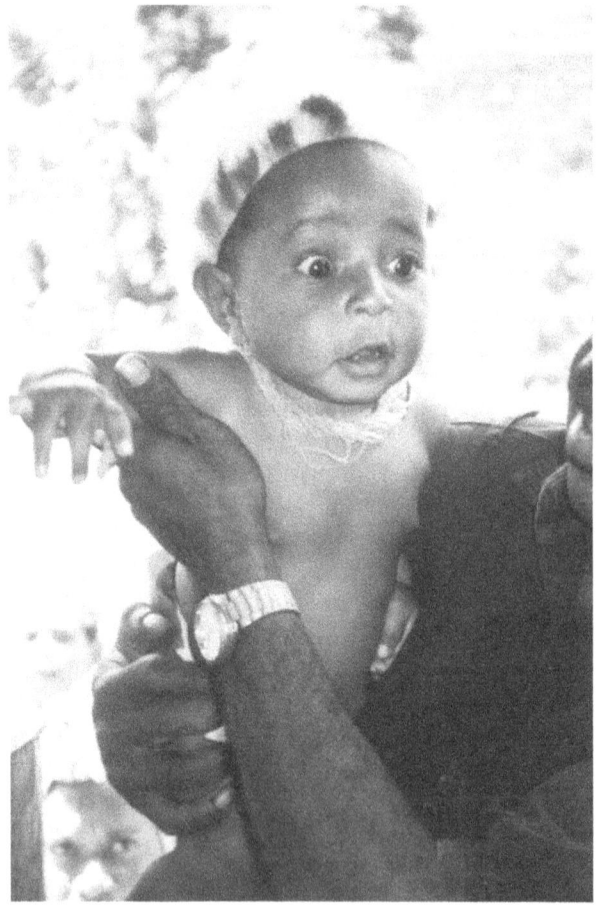

2.3 Young baby with marsupial fur headband and bead necklace. His father wears a wristwatch, an object much desired. The father has traveled extensively on jobs elsewhere and brought back money used partly for his bridewealth payments (Hagu, 1999). (Stewart/Strathern Archive)

Given the importance of the event, marriage negotiations are predictably complex. A further factor makes them more so, and ties them into the intergenerational workings of cognatic kinship and descent ties. The basic idea involved here is that the daughter repays the wealth paid for her mother; or, to put it another way, the father seeks to use the wealth paid for his daughter to repay some of those who contributed a generation earlier to the wealth given when he married his own wife. This means that a contribution to a marriage is a long-term investment, implying and depending on a continuity and stability of relations over time. If a man has a number of daughters he will also in theory continue to repay or reward his own creditors in this context when each of the daughters marries. In practice some of these debts are liquidated in advance, whenever the husband is able to contribute to another category of payment where the creditor needs help. Pigs that are given free from debts are known as *palini*, a term used also for items received in inheritance after a death, without any obligations attached to them. So a father may have some pigs that fall into this category when he and the mother act as principals in the distribution of their daughter's marriage payment. (If a couple have no daughters and only sons, they must seek to repay their helpers nevertheless.)

Given that kin on both the paternal and the maternal sides contribute to marriage payments, it follows that distributions of the valuables

2.4 A large pig, which is a centerpiece in the bridewealth to be paid to the bride's kin. It will be claimed by her father or mother as their special prerogative (1999). (Stewart/Strathern Archive)

2.5 In hot sun women participants scrutinize bridewealth items being placed on display for a marriage occasion (1999). (Stewart/Strathern Archive)

also go to these same categories of kin. Figure 2.3 illustrates this process in schematic form. The father and mother of the groom may receive help from their own kin to gather the wealth goods on behalf of their son. The bride's parents receive this, and the bride's father uses it to repay his kin who had helped him a generation earlier with his own marriage payment. Some wealth items may be given also to the bride's mother's kin but not as a part of this intergenerational clearing of debts. Rather such gifts recognize the mother's role in bearing and nurturing her daughter. A marriage is therefore an occasion that brings together, and both closes and opens transactions between, sets of kin linked by means of it.

It is evident from accounts given by older informants whose memories stretched back into early colonial times or beyond that the size of marriage payments has increased considerably over time. The chief reason for this probably has to do with the introduction of state money into the payment. Senior men who recounted the items they had paid in their first marriages listed between 14 and 28 items (compare Glasse 1968: 54). An "item" would be a pig, large or small, a cowrie shell rope, an axe, or other trade goods from the past such as salt packs. By 1991 cowrie ropes were apparently not in circulation at all, and currency notes varying from five to twenty kina in the Papua New Guinea state currency (valued in 1991 roughly on a par with the U.S. dollar) functioned as items along with pigs, which have remained

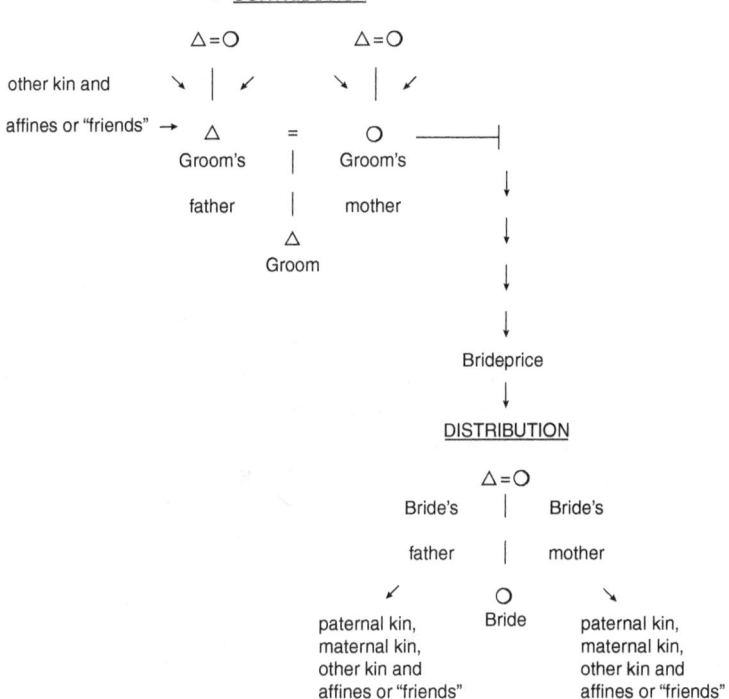

Key: → Direction of contribution or distribution

Figure 2.3 The structure of contributors and distribution of items at marriage occasions

in full esteem as stores of values and media of both exchange and life-cycle sacrifices. The Duna people traditionally count items used for exchanges in sets of 14. They listed former rates of marriage payments at about 2×14 items, and they remarked that now the amounts are double or more what they were previously. This pattern is quite typical for Highlands areas that have been affected in one way and another by cash cropping and wage labor.

The amounts of cash that are given vary with the status and age of those involved. In Hagu a marriage was set in hand in 1999 on behalf of a young man, PE, who had recently taken up a position as a Baptist church worker, working in tandem with another young man to run services and evening prayer meetings in order to help the elderly TK, who had been the pastor there for many years. Both of these young men had been trained at Tangi, the church's headquarters for the

Southern Highlands Province near the government station of Koroba at the border between Huli and Duna speakers. They were literate in *Tok Pisin* and a certain amount of English, and accompanied their services with guitar-playing. They were well esteemed within the community, and this was reflected in the relatively high size of the amount raised for PE, whose natal place was Haiyuwi, the neighboring parish to Hagu. His fellow worker was already married and was the son of the *kango* ML, a Yangone man who lived within the boundaries of Aluni. A local elite network was thus involved in the occasion. PE kept a written record of contributions, which he permitted us to copy and use.

The list contains the names of 71 contributors, including numbers of children whose parents' names as donors are separately recorded. This feature of giving agency to children is related to the point we mentioned above, that the contributors to a marriage payment may have to wait for a generation in order to be repaid when the bride's daughters are married. Ten pigs were recorded, including two designated as large ones, *tangetia*, and one as a sizeable pig designed to be slaughtered and eaten by males attending the event in celebration of the marriage. Robert Glasse (1968: 57) remarks on an identical category of gift among the Huli, "the pig of the wedding," known as *nogo wariabu;* the Aluni Valley people use a similar term, *warepu*. PE's elder brother, married previously, gave this *warepu* pig. Two pigs were listed as small,

2.6 Two young men hold a Sunday church service at Hagu, playing guitars. They have been trained for this work at the Baptist headquarters in Tangi near Koroba in the Huli area. They are assisting a senior pastor for the parish (1998). (Stewart/Strathern Archive)

kipiyasiki, and five as medium size, each worth around K75. In addition, two sets of K100 in money were listed as each equivalent to a *tangetia* pig, and two sets of K50 as equivalent to *kipiyasiki* pigs. This pattern indicates how money can be conventionally made to "stand in" for pigs if there are not enough pigs available to meet the demands of the bride's people. The two largest sums of money, each for K120, came from the *kango* ML and from an immediate sister of PE. All other contributions were made within the range of K10–K40 per person. We, as the fieldworkers, and as coresidents of Hagu, each contributed K10. Thirty-eight other contributors gave this same amount, making a total of K400. Thirteen contributors gave K20 each, making K260. With the two largest contributions, the monetary amounts thus came to K982, just short of K1,000. As we have seen, a further K300 was notionally converted into pigs. The conventional value of the actual pigs handed over was around K775, and if the K300 is added to the previous total, the figure for pigs becomes K1,075, slightly exceeding the monetary amount. The pattern accurately reflects the high value people place on both pigs and money, as well as the tendency for money to "take over" transactional slots. In Duna terms, this payment consisted of around 5 × 14 items, more than twice the number usually listed by senior men for their own marriages. Nineteen of the contributors were listed as females, fifty-two as males. Close kin and associates contributed the most, and the groom himself gave one pig, probably raised for him by his mother. His immediate father was deceased, so the wealth given represents the goodwill of the community at large toward him. His family has ancestral *imagaro* status with Haiyuwi, and his elder brother has lived in both Hagu and Haiyuwi parishes.

Given the fluidity of residence patterns, there is often some dispute about where as well as when a marriage occasion will actually take place. PE's elder brother's marriage took place in 1991, and the venue for the brideprice occasion kept changing. Notionally, the bride's kin should come to the groom's place for the presentation. In this case the bride was from Nauwa parish and her kin were reputedly reluctant to come to Hagu, where the groom, MU, was resident at the time. At Hagu itself, his helpers held numbers of occasions at which they steamed fruit pandanus and discussed how the contributions were coming in. Men and women shared in these deliberations. People enjoy these occasions, which give them a reason for cooking food together and talking generally. Visiting men retired to the communal men's houses at Hagu when night came and sometimes included those who were expert in balladic song performances (*pikono*), which may hold the attention of their listeners until daybreak, making them prepared to stay for further discussions the next day.[5]

The groom's people generally prefer to offer the payment near their home because they often find it difficult to catch, rope, and truss pigs for transport elsewhere. In this case, however, in the end they had to do this. On succeeding days the Nauwa people sent word about more items they wanted, especially a sum of K100 for *yakane paraiya*, the gift earmarked for the future mother-in-law. They also asked for a further K100 as a "fine," alleging that MU had said something disparaging about the bride herself. He denied this. They sent word first that the pigs to be given should be brought to the pathway between Hagu and Haiyuwi. And on the actual day of the event the contributors came as far as a clearing between Haiyuwi and Nauwa but then received word to go all the way to Nauwa itself. Sweating and panting up steep slopes and along muddy tracks, shouldering or dragging their pigs, the Hagu and Haiyuwi people went, complaining that Nauwa was distant and that in the past things were not so friendly between themselves and the Nauwa people. Apparently the various kin on the bride's side had not agreed among themselves about the locale. There was also an underlying cause for awkward feelings, since it had turned out that bride and groom were related as distant cousins on their respective mother's sides. Such a relationship is considered a bar to marriage if it comes to light. The bride's side's demands for a higher payment stemmed from this problem, which went deeper than the earlier suggestions about disparaging remarks. The groom's side had assembled two separate *warepu* pigs, one for the father's and one for the bride's mother's side; four *tangetia*; eleven *kipiyasiki*; and about K300 in cash. In their reckoning this came to $4 \times 14 + 6$ items, a large amount. Yet on their arrival they were not offered food as guests and were given only a cramped space in which to set up their display of pigs and money, without any certainty that their offer would even be accepted. After much argument, however, the marriage went through.

The *kango* ML played a crucial part in this negotiation, as he also did on a number of other occasions of this kind over 1991–1999. He acted as an active, senior *kango* on behalf of Aluni and Hagu people who lacked such a personage among them. He held a bundle of small sticks, each one representing a pig or sum of money. He used this as an aide mémoire in reciting the amounts to the bride's people, and after doing so he walked over to them where they were congregated and discussed things separately with the bride's paternal and maternal kin, who had not made joint counsel about the event in advance. It was the mother's kin who were annoyed about the cousin tie, which was likened to siblingship, and it was they who increased the demand for the size of the *yakane paraiya* gift.

At every marriage we observed, a *kango* played a similar role to that noted here for ML, sometimes in concert with other *kango*. Every marriage occasion has its problems, which are basically caused by the pressures on the bride's kin to obtain a large amount in order to pay off debts and satisfy people's feelings. Given the close geographical range of most marriages and the small size of the overall Valley population, it is also highly likely that a distant kin relationship of one kind or another can be traced between the partners. Whether this is made a problem or not may depend on contingencies rather than being subject to strict rules. Desire for money has also exacerbated these problems. The traditional shell valuables cannot be used as a backup. Money has completely replaced them. Since only limited amounts of money come into the area and since it has so many potential uses, this circumstance is productive of conflicts. The circle of persons drawn in as contributors has probably increased as a result, which will lead to further problems later in time. The perceived value of money in relation to pigs has also changed. In one instance a father distributing his daughter's marriage payment tried to pay for a small pig he had received a generation earlier for his own marriage with a K10 note, the amount such a pig would then have fetched, only to be told that now K50 was required. Obviously this "index-linking" of past gifts leads to increased monetary needs today.

A further extra expense may be incurred if a young man decides he does not want to marry a girl to whom he has become affianced. Courting songs from the past, which we have quoted earlier, play on the idea that a youth and a girl may exchange presents. They may also today make such presents a mark of their intention to marry. Glasse (1968: 52) notes that a similar practice existed among the Huli. The betrothed pair among the Huli would address each other as *lawini*. Glasse writes that if the betrothal was broken by either side, no compensation was required. However, in the case of PE's marriage described earlier, he had been friendly with a local Hagu girl who had assisted him in thatching his new house, in anticipation of sharing it with him. Later, it was rumored that the girl's mother was a witch, which meant that she also might turn out to be one later. Although this was never brought up as a reason in any public context, it may have contributed both to PE's decision to break off his relationship with her and to his payment of a sum of money to her, ostensibly to compensate her for her work on his house. Hagu in 1998 and 1999 was a theater of strong feelings and fears regarding witchcraft; and a Baptist church worker in particular would try to steer clear of being embroiled in ongoing conflicts about it.

The introduction of money has also meant that a groom is more likely to be directly involved in his marriage arrangements than in the past, since he may have access to cash through employment and travel. Senior *kango* were emphatic that this circumstance was contributing to the turbulence that often surrounded issues of sexual relations, preference, and courting. They basically thought that their sons were getting into escapades too young nowadays. PK commented on PE's marriage as follows:

> These two who have married here are really very young. Previously, a girl could marry if her breasts had fallen down and she had menstruated many times. But a boy like PE and [he named another youth of the settlement in which we were staying at Hagu] would certainly not be married. They would not even be thinking of it. They would not be living in the men's house. They would not go around seducing women. They would work along with them and prepare earth ovens of food with them.
>
> The marriage payment is also very high now. It used to be 14 items. They would give stone axes and nassa shell headbands and cowrie ropes and salt packs with perhaps five pigs.
>
> Young boys would be sent into the bush [to take part in *palena anda*]. We called them *kilini kando raiya*, the boys who cut pieces of the *kilini* leaf as a decoration and wore it in their hair to make it grow big. Their bodies would grow large and later they could put on the *manda kalu* wig [an upturned wig with horns at either side, colored with red ocher]. Until that time we called them *kuni tse* ("the root of the bone"). Experts spoke *palena kamo* ("growth magic") over them. They were expected to wake up in the morning with the birds. They used special words to greet the morning dawn and for marsupials which they hunted.
>
> Their seniors would also consider a young man's ability to work before they would allow him to marry. With girls, too, they would watch their work and how obedient they were to their parents. People were keen to make a marriage with girls like that. In fact, we still think this way.

PK's observations catch well the keen sense of change that all senior people expressed. This highly developed historical awareness is a result of the swift alterations that have occurred in their lifetimes since the 1930s and, more especially and clearly, the 1960s when colonial administration began. We review some further aspects of that history in the next chapter.

Chapter 3

Forces of Change

From the mid-1950s onward the Duna were affected by a rapid series of changes brought to them by the Australian colonial administration and by the waves of Christian missions of different denominations whose personnel entered their area and set up stations, outposts, and rudimentary roads or patrol tracks. Prior to this time of colonial influence the Duna had belonged to an extensive network of interregional traditional ties and relationships based on circulating ritual performances aimed at ensuring the fertility of the earth and the life it supported. These rituals are discussed further in chapter 5.

This elaborate panoply of indigenous ritual practices has been replaced by Christian rituals of prayer and worship, but the people have creatively incorporated Christian prayers into the sacrifices of pigs that were so significant for their religion in the past.

Another factor of change in the area, as elsewhere in Papua New Guinea, is the presence of gold and oil mining companies that come into the region from various countries. There is a lengthy history of mineral prospecting in the area. As we have seen, the earliest explorations and government patrols were driven wholly or at least partly by the wish to find sources of gold, oil, and gas.

The various agents of change—government, missions, and commercial companies—operated partly independently of one another and partly in concert or under mutual constraint. This chapter discusses in general how the Duna have responded to the constraints and the opportunities that change has brought to them and how they themselves have reinterpreted and managed their own history as it has intersected with the outside world.

Missions

Missions of different Christian churches established themselves early on during the colonial period in the Duna area. It was the practice of the churches to wait for the moment when a newly administered area was "derestricted," that is, expatriates other than administration officers were allowed to travel within it, and then at once send in a patrol of their own, led by a missionary attached to the nearest church, with the immediate intention of proselytizing and setting up local church branches, effectively staking out territory for their own denomination in competition with others. Sometimes the missionaries were camped out right on the borders of such an area, just waiting for the "word to go" in the race to find new church adherents. The enterprise of converting people to the Christian faith was, and is, one of the major means by which the churches solicited support from their home congregations in North America, Europe, Australia, and New Zealand.

One Duna Patrol Report by Neil J. Grant (1956/7) records that the priest of the Catholic Mission based in Tari within the Huli area, accompanied the patrol, presumably to assess prospects for the extension of his mission's work. On this patrol the government officer continued the work of intervention in fights and in urging groups to pay compensation for killings. He also heard court disputes and consigned offenders to prison or ordered compensation to be paid. We see the tasks of pacification proceeding; and the gradual introduction of sanctions as well as incentives. Patrols continued to be large, impressive affairs. Sinclair himself led a further patrol (no. 8 of 1956–57) on which an accompanying Australian filmmaker, R. Maslyn Williams, filmed extensive footage (18,000 feet of Eastman color film). Some of the filmmaker's supplies were brought in by a seaplane, which landed on Lake Kopiago. Another plane, a Norseman, crashed while making a supplies drop. The work continued to be hazardous and uncertain. The filmmaker filmed footage of the patrol moving through the Strickland gorge. Apart from the brief reference to the priest of the Catholic Mission in Tari, the government's reports do not appear to have been greatly concerned with mission impacts or with policy issues regarding missionization. The presence, or future activities, of missions appears to have been taken for granted for the most part.

It is likely that there was a tacit acceptance by the government that mission work was a part of the larger project in which the Patrol Officers were themselves engaged. If this is correct, there is little doubt that mission and administrative objectives generally did go together quite well. Missionaries were dependent on government permission to enter and remain in areas. If they broke laws they could be removed or deported either by their own authorities within their churches or by the government itself. While some government officers, as a part of their official duties, took an interest in recording aspects of "traditional culture," few saw it as a part of the government's task to support, preserve, or help to develop that culture. Most of what fell under the heading of culture at that time related either to local social practices such as polygamy or separate patterns of adult residence for men and women or, most prominently, to ritual and religious institutions of the local people. For example Cadet Patrol Officer Fairhall's report, Koroba no. 7 1958–59, notes that old men were reluctant to speak about forms of burial, but told him that coffins were built from bark and light timber and placed on sharpened stakes in the dead person's garden with a swordgrass roof above the body on the platform. Family members would not eat sweet potatoes from that garden for two years. After the body had been on the platform for several months the kinsfolk would remove the bones and bury them, wrapped in leaves, in a hole near the deceased's old home. The skull of the deceased might be placed separately in a tree hollow.

Practices of this kind were exactly those targeted by the Christian churches, whose missionaries wanted people to adopt Christian forms of burial along with the belief system that went with them. Government patrol reports thus helped to point missionaries and evangelists to avenues of custom, which the missionaries then observed and sought to change into those conforming to their own churches' rules.

Shortly after derestriction, then, a number of missions moved into the Kopiago area. Catholics, South Seas Evangelicals, Lutherans, and Seventh-Day Adventists were among those who entered early on. The Catholics were operative at Horaile in the 1970s when Modjeska worked there. There was still a small Catholic church in the main village center in 1991, and nuns resided at the Kopiago station, where they ran a school for young children, beside the government primary school. Lutherans had a residence and station on the way to the Health Centre east of the station, but their operations did not appear to be vigorous, although they maintained a precious radio by which their other stations could be contacted through a mission network. The Catholic nuns at the station also maintained their own time slot on this network, which linked the whole of the Southern Highlands Province together. Mission workers could obtain flights on Mission Aviation Fellowship planes that flew the dangerous routes between small airstrips where the churches had their various outposts.

The Administration permitted missions to enter newly opened-up areas that came under administrative control, in part because the available government funds were not sufficient in all cases to provide schools and health care. Missions were required to supply these benefits in addition to what the Administration itself could provide. From the viewpoint of the missions, the acts of giving schooling and health care would fit in well enough with their aims of proselytizing the people. The Administration also recognized a "civilizing" role played by the missions in the process of acculturation. The relationship asserted here between civilization and the Christian religion is classic to European colonialism. (See McPherson 2001 for an excellent discussion of colonial practices and ideology in Papua and New Guinea; and Robbins 2001, n.d., for comparative materials on indigenous reformulations of Christianity in the Ok region.)

The South Sea Evangelicals (SSEM) and the Seventh-Day Adventists (SDAs) had smaller establishments, also near the administrative headquarters. While the former seem not to have expanded as far as the Aluni Valley, the latter had gained a significant footing at Aluni by the late 1990s. The most influential churches in Aluni, however, were the Apostolic mission, and the Sovereign Grace Baptist mission. The Apostolics had their main center at Tirini, about a mile out from the station. Walking past there on the road to Horaile and Aluni, the most striking evidence of their activities lay in the concourses of young people playing basketball or volleyball. This is one way in which churches try to gain the attention of the youthful generation so as to establish themselves. The Apostolics are also in a general sense Pentecostalists, embracing the ideas of divine healing and ecstatic worship with speaking in tongues. During the 1990s there was a long-established Apostolic church at one corner of the Aluni settlement area, looking toward Kunai territory. Its quiet custodian was skeptical about speaking in tongues, explaining that there is always a problem with regard to getting someone who could interpret its meanings to the congregation. One of his leading members was a man whose wife and daughter were under suspicion of being witches in the community.

The Baptists in Aluni clearly regarded themselves as the "mainstream" church. This was surely in part because the church's pastor, based in Hagu settlement as we have noted, was the sole senior representative of the agnatic line of Kepe in Aluni. It was also, however, because of the historical impact of a single early missionary (and subsequently also his son) who came from the United States (Ohio) and patrolled vigorously in the Aluni Valley soon after derestriction. To a remarkable degree people's oral accounts of this figure attributed the foundation of their church and its practices to his words and actions, including his comments on their own customary practices (Stewart and Strathern 2002a: 121). He is said to have told people that the pigs slaughtered and consumed to celebrate a marriage (the "wedding pig," see chapter 2), should be consumed by both men and women rather than only by men. This was an injunction, however, that was not greatly followed in practice in the 1990s, since men tended to consume most of the meat and it was they who did the slaughtering, carving, and cooking of the animals. Another pronouncement the missionary was said to have made had to do with the observance of menstrual taboos. Asked (no doubt by men) if these taboos should be continued he supposedly declared they should, perhaps giving some health rationale for this advice. We can see here both the "scatter shot" effect of the missionary's prescriptions and proscriptions and the kind of "founder effect" that he engendered in the area. People refer to his sayings as canonical for their contemporary practices. What he may have regarded as improvisations in response to questions, or as *obiter dicta*, have been caught in the web of oral history and been given authority on a par with the messages in the Bible itself. The missionary's son has a less secure reputation. He was said to have been rough and authoritative when running church services.

The importance that people give to this particular missionary is perhaps related to two factors. First, he came from Tangi near Koroba in Huli territory, which the Valley people still regard as their "headquarters." The Baptists do not maintain a station at Lake Kopiago itself, so the Aluni people do not have a contemporary authority figure in their vicinity to whom they can look for guidance. Second, and concomitantly, the Valley Baptists have to a remarkable extent been left to run their own affairs since the early founding days of the church in their area. Their isolation has had interesting correlates. They have had to improvise some of their own solutions to problems as these emerged. We discuss this point further in chapter 6 when we consider the topic of witchcraft. On the other hand they have developed a tendency to cling to the few words of guidance they received in those early times, which inhibits their responses to some forms of change. A good deal of confusion results from these somewhat contradictory circumstances. The confusion applies to both practices and doctrines. For instance, people told us that the reason they did not perform Christian-style wedding ceremonies was that they had not yet been taught how to do these. This state of affairs gave them a carte blanche to continue their brideprice practices, but without any occasion to sacralize or bless the marriages in their Christian churches.

One leading man, PK, who himself had been a pastor at one stage of his life until he married a second wife, noted that there was confusion about where a person's soul goes after death. Christian doctrine says that the soul goes to Heaven or Hell. This conflicts with the traditional idea that the *tini* or spirit tends to stay near its former habitation and has to be encouraged in funeral laments to depart for the place of the dead in limestone hillside areas where the bones were formerly placed in secondary burial. The call of a bird (*pirori*) near to the grave site is seen as a mark of the *tini*'s presence and possibly also as a sign of witchcraft. PK, using mission terminology, called the *tini* a "Satan," reflecting teachings he had been given that the spirit that stays at the grave is a "bad" spirit, whereas the "good" soul goes to Heaven. Such a notion may have its origins in the early Christian church in Italy and Europe. Theological fragments of this kind find their way to places such as Papua New Guinea, where they find an awkward place for themselves in juxtaposition with previously existing notions of body, mind, and spirit. In practice Duna women continue to address the *tini* as the soul in their laments and to direct it to fly away to the limestone shelters in the mountains cared for by the Payame Ima female spirit, who is the custodian of the dead. They do so not because the spirit is seen as "bad" or "evil," but because it has painfully to learn that it is dead and must leave its living kin and go to join the world of the dead. In their songs the women express both their grief for the death of their relative and their wish to help the *tini* reach its proper destination. Sending the *tini* away is also a part of people's adjustment to the death, of realizing that the person is really gone from the living world. An unquiet *tini* near its former home can make people sick, so it must be sent on its way. This idea is no doubt the indigenous equivalent of the idea that the *tini* can be potentially dangerous, promulgated by the Baptist missionary. Also, the Christian churches in the area did not want the people to believe in the existence of any spirits other than those defined in the churches' teachings.

The Duna have in general used their isolation creatively in the realm of ritual practice. Forbidden to make above-ground burial platforms, they make a platform for the coffin underground, covering the grave with slats and a roof of grass thatch, replaced by corrugated iron if possible when the thatch rots. Sometimes they quietly remove the slats after the coffin has disintegrated and place the bones in one or the other of the traditional ossuaries that each parish territory has. People contribute money and pigs for a cooking of food (i.e., a sacrifice) to go with this occasion. They do so on a low-key basis and refer to such events as a "little party." An important ritual in the cycle of

3.1 A mountainside grave at Hagu, the majestic Victor Emmanuel range in the background. The grave has a special galvanized iron roof, beneath which hangs a piece of the dead man's clothing. His daughter has recently cleared the area of overgrowth as a mark of respect prior to a killing of pigs for his spirit (1999). (Stewart/Strathern Archive)

life and death is thus camouflaged by verbal relabeling, making it seem modern and innocuous. Such usages were probably developed as a means of evading and quietly subverting outsider diatribes against traditional burial practices (see Stewart and Strathern 2002a: 131 on *tini*, and 133 on burial sites).

Less easy to deal with have been the *auwi* or "stones of power," which used to be the focus of elaborate ritual activities among the Duna. We have dealt with these at length elsewhere (Stewart and Strathern 2002a: 69–91). The founding Baptist missionary is said to have told people to destroy these. One type of stone is round and black in color with rust-colored insets: volcanic ironstone. This kind was most frequently described as the petrified organ (heart) of an ancestor of some generations ago that had decided to "come up" and announce itself to a descendant, empowering its finder to set up a ritual site and make sacrifices to it. Officiants rubbed the stones with pork fat to please them, and asked for prosperity and curing of sickness (see Modjeska 1977: 98, 280–284). Another kind of stone is called a "hat of the sun" (*hewa sangi*). These are classified by archaeologists as "prehistoric mortars" and are found in many parts of the Highlands, where they are universally regarded as the abodes of spirits. Prehistoric pestles, presumably used with mortars, are described as the penis of the *tsiri* bush spirit, and could be used as a focus for sacrifices. A further kind of stone is a prehistoric petrified nautilus fossil. All of these stones were regarded as associated with particular spirits and cult practices; and all of the spirits were held to be capable of causing sickness or death if people's actions displeased them. Conversely their goodwill was solicited as a foundation for fertility, prosperity, and health.

Invariably, people declared in the 1990s that in the preceding years they had thrown away or burnt all of their *auwi* stones. However, they were able to produce examples of these stones for inspection once they learned that there was an interest in them and that they could serve as a useful adjunct to an interview in which a person wanted to explain or describe a practice from the past. They would say that they had found the stones in a rock crevice, or an abandoned garden site, or in an old log of a tree, or that they had kept them in their houses as ornaments. In one instance TK, the Hagu pastor, himself brought a reddish colored stone that he said must have "jumped sideways" and rolled out of a fire when they were burning all their *auwi* at the orders of the Baptist missionary many years earlier. He added that he had just found it by chance and brought it to us because he knew of our interest in such things. He suggested that the *tama* (spirit) associated with it could have made it jump in this way. His remarks revealed the idea that *tama* could be still operative and resistant to the missionary's teachings at the time. Prior to the arrival of the missionary, the whole landscape of each parish was thickly dotted with named ritual sites, each dedicated to a particular spirit and marked by *auwi* stones. Senior men continue to hold this knowledge, and it is reasonable to suggest that they think the *tama* are still there and capable of acting but that the *tama* are afraid of the power of the new religion. This seems to explain, for them, why new ancestral *auwi* do not come out of the ground. Perhaps they are biding their time, but in the meantime are pursuing a policy of noninterference.

Missionaries seem to have given two different messages to people. One was that the *auwi* stones were "bad" because they could kill people. Another was that people's souls went elsewhere and did not stay in the ground, so that *auwi* were in fact just stones, without any powers. It is possible that different churches took different lines over this issue. Catholics may have simply said that people's souls went elsewhere on death and that the *auwi* stones were harmless; while Baptists may have taken the line commonly found in fundamentalist Christian practice, that the stones were evil and must be destroyed. One idea is that it is the spirits of those not baptized that remain in the ground; another notion, however, is that these have all gone to

3.2 A set of objects shown to us in the field, including, left to right, stone axe blades, a plastic container holding red ocher used for decorations, round volcanic *auwi* stones, a fossilized nautilus stone *(auwi kendei)*, and a pestle colored with ocher. The bundle at the right-hand side contains a special crystal stone with magical powers (Hagu, 1999). (Stewart/Strathern Archive)

Hell, because they were not "saved." People can maintain a state of uncertainty about them, while being very concerned about what will happen to themselves when they in turn die.

The local Duna pastors make up their own conjectures. Some follow the views of the older generation that the spirits of those who died before the missionaries came are still around in the environment. Others suggest that they have gone to some place other than the Christian Heaven or Hell. Where they do go is not a trivial question because people are still concerned about what causes sickness. For instance, they think that if a rat or other creature disturbs their parents' bones in an ossuary, this can cause the dead parents' children to become sick. In the past, when skulls of the dead might be brought out and painted in black and red or white and red earth colors as a part of funerary or celebratory cult practices, people thought that various birds could represent omens or signs. A red or black parrot (*kango*) flying in could indicate the parish whose members were responsible for the death of a villager; a red and green parrot (*yaluma*) could indicate the same. If a grassland bird (*kutiki*) called out, this was a sign that a woman's *tsome* (blood magic) had killed a villager. And the call of the *pirori* bird, as we have noted, could be taken as a mark of witchcraft activity. There was a roster of ways, then, of linking a death to its putative "mystical" cause in sorcery or witchcraft. The disappearance of above-ground platform burial (*malia*) at the behest of the missionaries has truncated the contexts in which such signs might appear. Interestingly, only the *pirori* example was regarded as contemporary. This is most probably because fears of witchcraft are very real, whereas we did not find a single case where a death in the 1990s had been ascribed to specific acts of sorcery.

Nor did we find instances in which sicknesses or deaths were overtly attributed to the actions of ancestral *auwi* stones. This may be because the stones were thought of as either dormant or as destroyed; and no new stones were being brought into the ritual scene via discovery. Since the *auwi* stones were also closely tied in with the exercise of leadership in rituals by *anoagaro* men, the loss of rituals directed toward these stones has probably contributed to difficulties in the maintenance of control over others by the senior agnates in the parish areas. To a certain extent, pastors as agnates of their parishes have been able to take on the mantle of authority afforded them by teachings about God. And certainly, the stress on building small churches, reminiscent of stone-cult houses, in every settlement where the Baptists have penetrated, has provided an aura of continuity within change.

Pastors have also been able to seize on certain church practices in order to reinforce their own power. The Baptists at Hagu began in 1999 to reimpose on female church members the rule that they should keep their heads covered while in church (see 1 Corinthians 11: 5). They also used the tool of temporary "excommunication" to punish people who broke any rules of morality or practice the church endorsed. The Hagu Baptists took communion seriously, going to the length of obtaining real wine and wafer bread either at their headquarters in Tangi or far away in Mount Hagen to use on the occasions when communion was to take place. They disparaged the practice of some other churches in which dry biscuits and "cola" were substituted for these "real things." The pastors kept books of names of communicants and struck off from the list anyone who was found to have engaged in sexual misconduct or to have been involved in business to do with witchcraft, either directly as a witch or in praying or receiving compensation for a death said to have been caused by witchcraft. On the other hand a witch who confessed and repented could be brought back into the congregation. In exercising influence over matters such as these, pastors appealed to Biblical texts. The reference here is to Revelation 20: 12, in which there is a prophetic image of the dead standing to be judged before the throne of God and the scroll of "the book of life" is opened and the dead are judged according to their deeds recorded in this book. Revelation contains a number of passages on this theme of the book of life (e.g. 3: 5; 13: 8; 20: 12). The Hagu pastors likened this book to the book of names they maintained on their congregation, implying that if they cut people's names out, the same was done in Heaven.

Such a form of discourse could clearly enhance their power if people took it seriously. Since rumors of the possible end of the world at the impending millennium were very strong in the late 1990s, this circumstance also tended to enhance the pastors' powers. On the other hand they were quite willing to reinstate those who returned to the fold of the church and declared repentance.

The Baptists in Hagu were careful to avoid any definite pronouncements on the return of Jesus and the end of the world, themes built to heights of considerable fear and interest by the Pentecostal churches throughout the Highlands during the 1990s (see Stewart and Strathern eds. 1997, 2000). Their pastors were aware that New Testament texts were the basis of this position (e.g. Matthew 24: 36, 44; Mark 13: 32–33); and they consciously distanced themselves and their church members from any hint of millennial rumors, although news of such ideas regularly entered the area, probably in the first place via followers of the Apostolic church, but also as a result of people visiting urban areas and returning with input from the outside world. This conservative approach of the Baptists to ideas of world's end has probably helped to keep the Aluni Valley people away from the ecstatic forms of revivalist teaching that have swept the Ok peoples to their west, beginning in the 1970s (e.g. Robbins 2001 on Urapmin).

Neither the Baptists nor the Evangelical Church of Papua New Guinea established at Ekali near the Strickland favor the ecstatic forms of worship or speaking in tongues that usually characterize such revival movements. In spite of this, at a more muted and less overt level, a sense of cosmic unease, stemming from rumors about world's end, was pervasive in the 1990s. This was because people tended to interpret aspects of change as indicating the processes of genealogical time encapsulated in their own traditional mythology and ritual system. A full cycle of time from the period of the first ancestors was seen as 14 generations. Genealogies of links to the founders of groups tended to be some 10 or 11 generations in depth (for an example, see figure 2.1). Given some uncertainties and variations, this could mean that a cycle of growth and decline was soon to be completed. The idea that young people would no longer listen to the words of their elders was built into this notion of a cycle. Also involved was the idea of environmental decline and the need to combat this with defensive and creative rituals (*rindi kiniya*). Since the *rindi kiniya* cycle had been disrupted by Christian influence, and since Christian teaching itself contained visions of world's end, destructions by fire and flood, and the apocalyptic return of Jesus, the stage was well set for the play of imagination and fear among the people in general, whether the pastors dwelt on this issue or not. People nevertheless went about their business without much daily reference to these problems.

Seventh-Day Adventists (SDA) in Aluni took up this concern in a proactive way, also with the sanction of the same texts that declare humans cannot know when God will decide to send Jesus back into the world. They enjoined people to be prepared at all times for the return of Jesus (the Parousia), and to live their lives in constant readiness for it, so that they would be among those saved and would go to Heaven. A local pastor, who in 1991 had lived in Hagu, was able to set up a successful compound of SDA adherents at Aluni in 1997–99 on the strength of this motto. He encouraged people to leave the Baptist church and join his movement. He organized youth activities and a display of youth gymnastics and games at Aluni on the site of an abandoned playground of a primary school that had existed in Aluni. He persuaded the Porgera Joint Venture Gold Mining Company to donate money for t-shirt uniforms the youths and girls wore for this occasion. Internal disputes in this little community broke out after he was posted elsewhere by his church authorities. One of the attractions his compound had offered to women from Hagu was refuge from accusations of witchcraft and freedom from involvement in raising compensation payments. But the pastor's prestige was partly affected by the confession of one of his own sisters that she had been involved in witchcraft activities (Strathern and Stewart 1999a).

In sum, the experience of change among the people in the Valley has been both pervasive and at the same time patchy. They have been heavily socialized into new practices, and yet have been left to fill in many gaps with their own bricolage. Modjeska (1977: 97) tells an anecdote in passing that reflects this same process in a Catholic context. He depicts a traditional idea of a spirit who keeps waters flowing at the edges of the world by using his fighting pick to disperse logs jamming the rivers. This spirit is clearly a version of the *tsiri*, and the image is reported also by Goldman (1983: 199, 224) for the Huli of the Koroba area. Modjeska reports that his informants told him that the spirit had a flowing white beard and was now identified with St. Peter. This image of the long beard and the identification with St. Peter are clearly accretions on the complex of *tsiri* ideas improvised by the Horaile people with whom Modjeska worked. The process of assimilating local spirits into a Christian pantheon is also characteristic of Catholic ways of thinking. Baptists at Aluni never made any comparison of that kind in conversations with us. They tended to keep the pagan and the Christian worlds apart, while expressing unease about the relative power of God vis à vis indigenous *tama*.

Government and Development

In the early days of administration, government patrols were frequent and intensive. The airstrip at Kopiago was built with local labor and paid for with shells. Australian patrol officers were replaced or accompanied by indigenous Papua New Guineans from other areas at the time of national Independence in 1975 onward. From that time also Kopiago was involved in national parliamentary politics. A Local Government Council had been set up earlier but was short of funds owing to the lack of any imposition of a head tax on the populace. Another problem for development in the area has been the slow progress on road construction. Wherever roads exist, cash cropping and the building of commercial tradestores can develop. In 1972–73 there were only nine stores in the Kopiago area (compare this with 503 in Ialibu, on the main road south from Mt. Hagen). In Aluni in the 1990s there was a single store, cargo for which had to be carried on the backs of villagers from Kopiago station, a day's walk away. By the late 1990s the road between Aluni and Horaile was impassable for motorized vehicles and in places had disappeared due to vegetation growth and disuse. The state of the road was a major bone of contention and concern in the area. At one time in 1991 a rumor came that a new government project had been approved to extend the road from Aluni all the way to the Strickland. People began to talk enthusiastically about getting their shovels and axes ready for the work. But nothing came of it. No money was allocated.

Indeed shortage of money for projects is a major burden mentioned in reports in government files since the 1970s. A business development officer for the Southern Highlands Province, Daniel Opa, was also apologizing in the 1980s for his inability even to visit Kopiago to assess things there: he cited lack of transport. Certain amounts of money were from time to time allocated for road work, e.g. K5,000 in 1976–77 for the Tumbudu road; but such sums were sparsely distributed and insufficient. A single sum of K20,000 was made available in 1990 for the Tumbudu road through the efforts of the Provincial Member, Simon Arawe. The Officer in Charge (O.I.C.) at Kopiago, Owen Lora, placed frequent requests for funds for transport and to mount patrols. There was only one constable on the station for a population of 11,000 people, Lora noted.

He requested a staff of five police, a vehicle, and a functioning radio transceiver. The police headquarters in Mendi seems to have ignored these requests, citing lack of funds, and the O.I.C. noted that as a result there was low morale.

From the point of view of the people, the lack of government patrols and the insufficiency of the police on the station itself was, and remains, a major problem. There is no effective process of hearing court cases available at the station. The situation is confusing for the people. On one hand, they are expected to settle their conflicts peacefully and with authorized procedures. On the other hand they are not able to call on effective sanctions to back up this process. In 1991 the provincial government in Mendi was interested in the prospects and conditions for establishing Village Courts, staffed by local magistrates and operating in terms of customary law, in the Kopiago area. But this project also did not come into effect during the 1990s, probably again for lack of funding. The government reports also indicate by 1989 that holdups were taking place on the road between Kopiago and Pori on the way to Koroba. In one instance a Patrol Officer was held up and asked for K500. Politicians, or ex-politicians, also sometimes caused problems. A letter of March 4, 1990, from Mr. Luke Segowa to the Provincial Police Commander (Jeffrey Kera) in Mendi complains that a politician had been selling liquor and dice at Dilini (Tirini) marketplace, and had hit someone on the head and instigated a fight near his house, on other occasions firing his shotgun in the air and stirring up followers over a claim to a piece of land that the land mediation committee had awarded to the Peragoiya people. One of the problems involved was that the police officer at the station was a brother of the politician, by the same father.

Another, underlying, factor was the removal, in 1985, of police powers from the government administrative officers themselves. They became dependent on the police, and understandably complained when police work seemed ineffective. Already in the late 1980s, as a result of vehicles coming in from Tari, the Kopiago station was unsafe, with drunken residents and visitors inebriated from liquor consumption at the local club and a general aura of danger and potential aggression. While a remote area like the Aluni Valley was relatively free of these trends, it was certainly vulnerable to them and to the spread of guns and liquor that elsewhere in the Highlands has created massive problems and difficulties for the government and people alike.

A further part of the problem lay in the disrepair of housing for public servants at the station. Competent officers were reluctant to stay in Kopiago, even if they were committed to their jobs. In 1991 no officers were resident from Forestry or the Department of Primary

Industry (Agriculture) because of a lack of housing or an unwillingness to live away from home areas. As a result the area was almost devoid of projects by which cash could be earned. The only two government services that appear to have been functioning to some extent in the 1990s were the primary school at the station and the Health Centre or hospital. The school had some 300 students. The Health Centre mounted some patrols to outstations and carried out immunizations for tetanus, measles, BCG, and polio. A total of 500 patients were treated for pneumonia and 350 for malaria. These were by far the most frequent conditions dealt with. The Centre had a staff of 16, and 15 Aid Post Orderlies (APO) were based in village areas. One of these was at Aluni. The records the Aluni APO kept for October 1991 showed a total of 109 persons treated, 61 males and 49 females, with 13 treatments for respiratory infections, 52 for infected sores, 5 for scabies, 13 for malaria, 20 for miscellaneous wounds and aches, 5 for eye, ear, or tooth conditions, and 1 case of mumps. Seasonally, these patterns alter.

In other months stomach upsets or conjunctivitis in children may predominate. The preponderance of sores as a category of treatment reflects tropical conditions and minimal access to hygienic measures. A chronic problem was always shortage of medicine at both the Health Centre and the Aid Posts. Newspaper reports since 1999 indicate that this problem continues to be endemic and significant. Lack of finances, poor organization, and difficult road conditions, compounded by criminal holdups and corruption at various levels, explain the problem. In 1999 the Porgera Joint Venture Company was setting up a new health center at Aluni, but its future at that time was uncertain. One of our correspondents wrote to us that it was due to be opened in 2002. Staffing and supplies were likely to be a major problem for it in the absence of road access.

Little cash income is generated within the Aluni Valley. As we have implied, agricultural development was nonexistent in the 1990s. People grew minor cash crops such as peanuts and these were marketed locally, mostly by women. The single trade store was often out of goods. Cash came into the Valley through the return of its residents from wage labor elsewhere or by remittances such laborers sent from time to time to their kinsfolk at home. A sprinkling of younger men were employed at the large Ok Tedi mine in Tabubil in Sandaun Province, a relatively short journey by plane to the west of the Valley. Others worked in Mount Hagen in the Western Highlands Province or further away in the national capital, Port Moresby. Interviews with men now entering middle age showed that many of them, prior to their marriages, had spent time as contract laborers on plantations or urban workers in other provinces. One young man explained to us at length his peregrinations and adventures in a number of places, one the distant location of Bougainville Island. He spoke in detail of his relations, good, bad, and mixed, with expatriate employers, and of his constant attempts to amass money to take home. When he did return, he said, he distributed the greater portion of his savings to his local kin in Hagu. Such acts are investments for the future. Not coming from a prominent or numerous family, his aim was to secure goodwill and assistance in a brideprice payment, which eventually came about.

This short survey of some main lines of change indicates how patchy the whole process is and how contingent it is on multiple factors. The basic problem for the Duna people in the Valley is that they have been introduced to a world of potential new opportunities and have been subjected to many new constraints. While the constraints remain real, their chances to realize the benefits of "development" have not improved. The Duna, however, are in many ways "satisficers." They manage to make lives for themselves and to improvise responses to change. In this regard they are greatly helped by the basic adequacy of their own agro-forestry practices.

Chapter 4

Leaders and Speech-Making

Duna male leaders are expected to be "men of speech" (*anoa hakana*) (Stewart and Strathern 2000c).[1] They are called upon to use this skill in a variety of contexts, largely having to do with conflict resolution. This is especially the case in regard to their ability to make ceremonial speeches to mark the payment of wealth in compensation for killings and deaths that provoke, or can involve, further conflict between sets of people, particularly those of different territorial parishes. This category of speeches is known as *tambaka*, a shortened version of *tamba haka*, "speech for compensation." In the neighboring Huli language area, the linguistically cognate term *ndamba bi* is translated by Laurence Goldman as "talk for closing down," i.e., to finish a dispute (Goldman 1983: 62). Such speeches are still performed, and are carefully prepared in advance. The leader delivers such a speech in a rapid stylized and rhythmic form that gives it an almost musical quality, employing condensed metaphorical expressions, repetitions, lists of places, and aphorisms that give it a gnomic and ritualized aura suitable to the occasion. The aim is to achieve closure by definitely marking a settlement; or to open up an issue by making a strong claim. Speakers on either side of a dispute answer each other in this stylized way, after listening to debates and consulting with their peers.

In the precolonial past, leaders made *tambaka* for settling or ending bouts of intergroup fighting. This was called *wei wiya*, "putting the fight to sleep." Leaders of the senior generation in the 1990s retained a knowledge of such speeches and provided examples. In one instance a leader adopted successively the roles of both sides in a dispute that was about the enforced death of a woman who had been accused of witchcraft. In this case, an autopsy was performed and indicated that she did not have the signs of being a witch (an engorged area of dark blood around the heart) within her. Her kin thus demanded compensation for her death. Leaders had to be adept at negotiating and attuned to nuances of public opinion, all of which they tried to express in their choice of words. They have to show the same facility today in the regular disputes that emerge between people and that are heard in public moots. In Aluni these take place most often on Saturdays beside the Aid Post in the clearing originally established by the Australian colonial Administration that has since become a marketplace and general place of gathering. We consider some of these disputes later.

Compensation for offences of various kinds constitutes a cultural focus for the Duna. Disputes of many kinds, but in particular those involving physical injuries or deaths, can be mediated by the giving of wealth in the form of pigs and/or state-introduced money (the Papua New Guinea kina and toea currency), and in the past by payments of shell valuables, notably the cowries that were a hallmark of the position of leaders in the society (Stewart and Strathern 2002c). Before people agree to make these payments, they engage in considerable debate about the facts of the case, culpabilities involved, and the amount of compensation that should be paid. Strong feelings may come into play and people may threaten one another physically. The words of the leaders are important in either escalating or modifying and managing these feelings. Similarly, they play an important role on bridewealth occasions when they help to negotiate the payments between kin that must fulfill a complex set of obligations spanning two generations and involving extended sets of relatives on the mother's and father's sides of both the groom and the bride.

In the Aluni Valley each parish in the 1990s tended to recognize just one or two senior living men as having this role of the leader as speech-maker. We give here an example of the kind of speech used to end a period of fighting, given by P, a prominent older leader of Haiyuwi parish, followed by the speech another such leader (ML), of Yangone parish, planned to give for an occasion in 1991 that did not in the end eventuate.[2]

Speech 1

This speech begins with a conventional metaphor: "the *yawa* greens do not have bones." A bone is equivalent to a cause of enmity between groups, and the meaning here is that the two groups do not have such an enmity. The speaker goes on to suggest that there was no deep reason for the fight, it was just something they entered into. The speaker next says that he will plant blossoming trees near his house, trees to which parakeets will come and cluster. The meaning is that the speaker's group will raise many pigs to pay a compensation for a death the other side says they have caused. The magic for pig-rearing draws on the image of parakeets that flock to blossoming trees. Parakeets are a manifestation of the female spirit, the Payame Ima, who has a general beneficial role in relation to fertility and prosperity. The speaker warns the other side not to start fighting again. Meanwhile his own allies are coming to him like marsupials that eat leaves and roots with their requests for compensation. He promises to make the *wei wiya* payment soon: "you must swallow your saliva, later I will give to you" (*nanokone ndu potya uwanda na*). Swallowing saliva is a mark of anticipatory desire. The speaker says he will not forget, but will keep working to satisfy this desire. The speech overall consists of 48 lines of text, each line spoken as a separate unit but flowing into the next. Its speaker had delivered many such speeches in the past at peace-making ceremonies between sets of fighters from different parishes.

Speech 2

The events detailed here began when one night persistent sharp cries reached the settlement of Aluni conveying the news that an Aid Post Orderly (APO), who was related as a sister's son to one of the subgroups in the parish, and who had been posted to a distant village, had been attacked there and killed. The cries were going out to rally people to march over and claim the dead person's body, so that they could bury it at Aluni and claim any compensation that might be owed as a result of the death. The village involved was not friendly to Aluni and people feared that the confrontation might lead to a further fight. At the same time they felt it was imperative to claim the body. Struggles over bodies are quite common among the Duna. Competing claims arise from the fact of cognatic descent, which gives people access to more than one local group. As a result the members of more than one group may also seek to bury a person in their own ground. On this occasion leaders emerged with bows and arrows and women began to wail for the supposed death. Tension and excitement ran high, and many people set out at once. In the morning, however, some returned with the information that the APO was not dead but had been beaten up in a dispute with an erstwhile friend of his. They said that the APO had shot one of this man's pigs that had been trespassing in his garden and had not paid compensation for this act. Angry, the pig's owner had waited for him at the doorway of his health clinic and had struck him on his way out, leaving him unconscious but alive. The Aluni people joined with their neighbors of

Horaile to threaten counterviolence if compensation was not paid for the attack. The APO was taken to the hospital at Lake Kopiago and himself later downplayed the event, saying compensation was not necessary; the man who struck him was being held and would be taken to Tari in the Huli area to be prosecuted there for this attack. The court would also decide if an order for compensation should be made.

Three of the prominent leaders in the Aluni Valley area took part in the discussions over the next two days on this event. ML was one of these and he had prepared a speech to request compensation. Although it was not delivered in the end, he had memorized it in advance and recited it as an example. He broke it into three parts.

Part 1: in this part ML first declares that they must settle the dispute by gathering together and "closing" it at all the little settlement places in the parish where the APO had been working. Next he notes that the close kin of the APO (mother, father, sister, brother) want to "eat": that is, they want to receive compensation for the attack on their male relative. Finally, he says that the APO had been "given" to the village people in the place where he was working, for them to look after, but instead they had killed him, broken his bones and removed his heart, liver, and kidneys (seats of strength): a piece of dramatic hyperbole to reinforce the claim for compensation.

Part 2: ML took on the role of the father's kin of the APO. In all public events centering on life-cycle processes there is a sustained effort to recognize both father's and mother's kin. This is another feature that fits with the Duna emphasis on cognatic descent and cognatic ties in general. In this case the speech is interesting because the APO's father's kin came from Oksapmin, west of the Aluni Valley Duna across the Strickland River. ML describes them as men who wear a different form of clothing and decorations, cane belts, penis gourds, beetles on their noses, white cockatoo feathers on their heads; and who do not sleep but are active at night. He implies that these people, different in their customs from the Duna, could take aggressive action over the injury done to their son. Their decorations could also mark their intentions to make sorcery against their enemies. The overall impression is that the father's kin will threaten force against the other side to back up their demands.

Part 3: ML switches to the perspective of the mother's kin, and he makes a contrasting set of claims, based on the morality of nurture. *No antia heyana kili auwa*, "I come as the mother, the owner of the pearl shell fragment" (given to her child as an ornament), he says. He proceeds to add images of leaves used to line the netbag for the boy to sleep in and of medicinal ground rubbed into his skin to treat him when he was ill. The mother's breast was always available to him, no matter where or how late in the day it was. For all these contributions to his body the mother's kin want to be paid in pigs, which they will kill and cook to consume in return for the damage done to the flesh of their nephew.

ML's speech here perfectly reflects the two facets of the ideology of compensation based on bilateral kinship: the father's side threatens violent revenge on a political level, while the mother's side makes their stand on the claims of morality and nurture. Force and morality together make up the substance of the demand.

As we have noted, the speech was not actually delivered. One of our field collaborators, an agnate of the Aluni parish who saw himself as playing a role in deciding whether or not to fight over the injury, reported that ML had arrived late on the scene, after the attacker and his victim had both been taken away to the government station. A rough, stony road constructed by voluntary labor in colonial times leads up to the village where the incident took place, and at that time the road was still in repair so that an ambulance and police vehicle were able to make their way up it. At the Lake Kopiago district office, where the administration for the Duna area is located, the Officer in Charge determined that the attacker had broken the government law in several ways, including by his assault on a public servant as well as trespassing on a government area, the Aid Post, in order to make his assault. He refused to have the case discussed in a moot, locked the offender in a police cell, and took steps to have him transported to Tari, since no court magistrate is stationed at Kopiago itself. Compensation, as a civil issue, would also have to be considered in a hearing separate from the criminal trial. The categories of introduced law were thus imposed and the elaborate rhetorical skills of ML were not brought into play to mediate the conflict in this instance. In addition, it would probably be a long time before the court case was heard and the local people could not easily travel so far away to monitor the event.

This situation encapsulates neatly the processes of change that have undermined some of the powers of leaders at the local level while establishing state law through a centralized administrative apparatus. In practice this apparatus has itself been relatively weak at the local level, for a number of reasons. Lake Kopiago station consists of an all-weather airstrip beside the large lake that gives the district its name, flanked by a set of government offices and houses for officers, and further along the road by a row of tradestores. A government school and a Catholic mission station stand a little further back, and there is a Local Government Council guest house near where planes land. In the 1990s the station was plagued by a lack of funding for its administrative functions, poor standards of housing, and drunken and criminal behavior by both passers-by and residents. Local leaders constantly called for more funding and a stronger government presence. There were few government patrols to places without passable vehicular roads, and the roads themselves were deteriorating further through the lack of maintenance funds. The ideas of government control, of "development," and of "law" had been firmly implanted in people; but the realities barely corresponded to such notions. Village leaders in 1991 were expecting that the system of locally controlled but government-sponsored Village Courts, which had been in place elsewhere since the 1970s, would be introduced in their area, giving them a more definite range of sanctions to employ in handling disputes. In Village Courts, locally elected or chosen magistrates, assisted by literate court clerks, sit regularly to hear disputes and apply fines or imprisonment of offenders. Peace Officers help these courts also by bringing in disputants and watching over them; and the rural police are supposed to be available to see that fights do not erupt and prisoners are taken away. Village Courts require funding and commitment of personnel. In 1999 the Aluni Valley leaders' original hopes had not been realized, and few even thought they later would be. One man, voicing popular feelings, also commented that there seemed to be no proper "law" against witchcraft and asked us what could be done about this. We answered that he had to work through his representatives (Councillors, Members of Parliament). When he was himself elected a Councillor he was involved along with others in a moot dealing with accusations of witchcraft and assertions of threats of violence involving the son of a senior leader of another parish.

In the effective absence of other means of handling disputes, leaders convened these local moots regularly. They most often took place on Saturdays, when people came to the marketplace at Aluni, as we have noted. People would drift in gradually and a plaintiff would begin stating an accusation against someone in the presence of whoever was there. Leaders were almost always on hand and usually had discussed the issues, or knew about them, in advance. Gradually they would intervene with questions, and supporters of either side would informally line up. When a man was accused he usually sought refuge with the other men in a space previously reserved for males in the meeting area. When a woman or girl was the object of an accusation she was often awkwardly thrust out on her own under public gaze, separated from the rest of the women. Women on these occasions tended to work at making netbags or to look after market produce for sale. They followed the proceedings with interest but tried not to look too involved unless they were called as witnesses. The atmosphere at these moots was often intense. Leaders had a difficult and complex task in mediating between the parties, recognizing their own complex webs of cognatic ties, which could extend to both sides.

One reason for this prevalence of tension in disputes had to do with the character of the disputes themselves. Often they had to do with sexual behavior and, in particular, but not exclusively, with control over sexual activity among young unmarried people. Adultery, and disharmony between newly married spouses, also frequently occasioned disputes. In many instances the same cases came up again and again at moots, with successive efforts to clarify facts or to secure compensation for admitted offences. In one such case the then prepubertal daughter of a woman inmarried at Aluni was taunted with being a witch by three slightly older girls. Her father, who was recognized as a minor leader and who "looked after" work at the local Aid Post, brought a complaint on behalf of the girl against her accusers, who eventually were required to pay compensation for what they had said. Interestingly, the point that the case turned on was that, while the girl's mother was well-known as a witch in the community, the daughter could not be one, because witchcraft is said to develop in a woman only after she becomes sexually active, marries, and usually has a child. In subsequent years after this case, concerns over witchcraft grew more severe (see chapter 6). A further issue that disturbs people and rouses strong tempers is the theft or killing of pigs. Theft destroys trust between kin or neighbors, while the unauthorized killing of a pig represents a serious destruction of value. In either case plaintiffs tend to be indignant and to insist on restitution. Leaders try to ensure that this happens, but defendants must agree if they are to pay for their supposed acts, and, if not, then all that people can say is that the matter will have to go to a government patrol officer or to the magistrate's court in faraway Tari. This lack of local sanctions explains why leaders are frustrated by the government's failure to inaugurate Village Courts in their area.

The concern with young people's sexual behavior is clearly a product of recent historical change. Asked what was done in the precolonial past when young people transgressed rules of sexual conduct, the senior leader PK said, "We shot them with arrows." While this was probably a partly humorous exaggeration, it contained a grain of truth. Rules regarding the spatial separation of males and females, which implied also constraint on their sexual interactions, were strict in the past (see chapter 2). Sexual intercourse prior to marriage was discouraged. Boys were enjoined to participate in growth rituals for their own physical maturity in bachelors' houses (*palena anda*) presided over by ritual experts who themselves were senior but unmarried and notionally were "husbands" of the Payame Ima (female spirit). For boys, intercourse prior to completion of the proper growth rituals was held to stunt them and curtail their maturation. After they had passed through the cult they were decorated and they paraded themselves in readiness for courtship at *yekeanda* occasions and for their subsequent marriage.[3] With the early demise of the *palena anda* cult and the somewhat later disappearance of the *yekeanda*, youths in the colonial and postcolonial periods have increasingly attempted to enter into sexual liaisons of their own volition and at various stages of their growth. Young men have traveled to other places, worked on plantations, stayed in towns, learned new ways of looking at the world. Thus "initiated" into a wider world, they have returned home with ideas of their own. Girls have on the whole had less opportunity to travel; but some have been to primary and secondary school, have frequently visited Kopiago station, and regularly walk on the roughly constructed public roads in order to visit the Saturday market that is held at Aluni. Along the way they meet youths and may exchange pleasantries with them. Schooling has brought literacy and with it the ability to write letters. Accusations that a boy had "written a letter" to a girl sometimes came up in moots, with the implication that a letter, like engaging in conversation, implies an inappropriate attempt at intimacy. Clearly, the senior generation, accustomed to arranging marriages as a way of managing networks of relationships, felt threatened by these activities. It fell to the leaders, themselves all senior men and some of them with a history of polygyny and their own management problems, to deal with these accusations and sort out their results.

These same men also perceived a cosmological dimension in the problem. According to Duna ideas of the cosmos, rituals of repairing the earth (*rindi kiniya*) were in the past performed in order to appease spirits and renew the fertility and prosperity of the land and the people bound up with it. The cessation of these rituals and the adoption of the ritual forms of the new religion of Christianity, along with its associated ideas about world's end (its millennial eschatology), have left people with a profound sense of unease about their own physical state and that of their environment. Action that is out of its proper time and place, such as precocious sexual activity, is held to stunt the bodies of young people, and this process in turn is thought of as pointing to a general decline of the forces that keep the world in order. For this reason accusations against youths, including against the sons of the leaders themselves, portended this greater process of decline as well as being trouble cases that required an immediate solution. The parents, especially the fathers, of girls sometimes pressed marriage on boys said to have made advances to the girls. Embarrassed, the boys' fathers were likely to plead that they had no pigs or money on hand with which to pay an adequate brideprice. Nevertheless, they recognized that only by such a marriage could "order" be restored. The boys themselves, however, were just as likely to refuse to be coerced into a marriage they did not want. A way out was available by paying some kind of compensation for the supposed or actual offence.

Compensation is the regular way of resolving many disputes, and leaders are prominent in it. We turn now to this topic.

Compensation

Compensation payments to allies and also to enemies for deaths in warfare provided an important arena for leaders in the past to demonstrate their wealth as well as their speech-making capacities. But the payment of compensation for offenses is an enduring aspect of social relations that is pervasive in many contexts today as well and involves both young and old, men and women. A survey conducted in the early 1990s of more than 30 persons, mostly but not exclusively men, indicated that all of those interviewed had been involved in making compensation payments on their own account and as helpers of others in their networks of kin and neighbors. Their involvement tended to be continuous over time. Compensation is still an important activity in the maintenance of social relations. Those interviewed mostly belonged to Aluni parish, and it was clear that people of the parish regularly assisted one another in this arena. Predictably, leaders produced the longest list of occasions in which they had been involved. Perhaps their memories were more copious and accurate than those of others. But it is likely that their objective participation is also greater.

For example, we take the list of compensations made or contributed to by two brothers, both senior men of Haiyuwi parish. The elder brother, PK, is a *kango*, while the younger, W, is a man of moderate status, a widower, who in 1991 lived in Aluni. W had taken part, according to his account, in ten compensation occasions. On all of these occasions he had acted to help others who were principally responsible. He had not initiated any compensation payment himself. Those he helped were all of the parishes within the Aluni Valley. One was his elder brother PK. Six he listed as simply friends or neighbors whom he had "assisted" (*piasaiya*). Two he described as his classificatory sons (*ngini*), and one as an affine or brother-in-law (*imanggu*, literally "woman giver/given"). Only one of the ten was a woman, belonging by marriage to Hagu settlement. In nine of the ten cases he gave small amounts of money, ranging from K2 (two kina) to K10, with an average of K5. In helping his elder brother, he had contributed three pigs, a considerable investment. The occasions he listed tended to be ones that turned up typically in other people's accounts also. For instance, a young man had shot another with an arrow by mistake; a woman had accidentally trodden on a child at a public event; a boy had hit a small girl; a man from Nauwa had struck a prominent neighbor of his. The interweaving of friendship with wide-spreading bilateral kinship ties within the Aluni Valley as a whole tends to ensure that many people are mobilized to make small contributions to help on these occasions. Reciprocal obligations are built up and fulfilled in this way. W's account gives us a cross-section of these regular involvements that ordinary people have in the process of repairing social disturbances.

PK's list was longer than W's, although not by any great margin. He cited 12 occasions, of which 6 were the same as ones that W mentioned; this shows the overlap of involvements between brothers. He helped other *kango* men four times. On four occasions he gave pigs, once on his own behalf when he paid K20 and eight pigs for killing one of his wives. Most of the instances he cited referred to times when he helped others with amounts of money ranging from K2 to K10 (average K5.60). One of the *kango* he helped came from his own parish, and the other three were all from within the Aluni Valley. Two of the occasions when he helped another *kango* involved compensations paid to people further away, in Oksapmin or the Lake Kopiago vicinity. PK's record, then, resembles W's in general, but shows a greater linkage with the activities of men comparable in status to himself. In terms of his own categorization of people to whom he had given compensation (or had contributed to such a payment), he described two as his cross-cousins (*hanini*), two as his in-laws (*yakane*), one as his "son" (*ngini*), one as his cross-cousin's child (*auwene*), one as his "brother" (*keni*; this was the *kango* of his own group whom he helped), and four as "friends" whom he had assisted (*piasaiya*). The remaining payment was the one he undertook on his own behalf, given to his wife's kin. This spread of kin and affinal ties is comparable to that in W's list. In both cases the list reflects a relatively dense network of relationships within the parishes of the Aluni Valley. This shared feature is a result of the practice of marrying largely within the Valley, although there is certainly no rule to this effect, and as we will see next, the pattern is modified when we consider the Kunai parish people.

Asked how people repaid one another for "helping" gifts (*piasaiya*), PK replied that such reciprocity was not confined to compensation occasions, but could be exercised also if there was a brideprice that had to be raised, or pigs were being killed for another purpose (funerals would be an example). It would not, he said, be necessary to ask, since people would hear news that a person who had helped them was in need of assistance for an occasion and they themselves would think about this and bring a contribution. A debt (*yano*) is thus created by these transactions, but such debts are met in a very informal and flexible way, without special sanctions, and they belong to the moral sphere of interactions that again is diagnostic of a close mesh of local intermarriage and kin ties.

We may compare PK's list with those given by two other *kango* men, K of the Kunai parish and AH of Nauwa. K listed 17 occasions, AH listed 21, both rather more than PK. K's connections link him significantly with the Kopiago area, so we find him leading or assisting in events centered there, as well as in the Aluni Valley. K also listed two occasions whose roots lay in the precolonial past. A Kunai man's father had fought against someone in Kopiago and shot him. The arrow stayed in the man and later he died. In these circumstances the owner of the arrow is considered responsible for the death even if it occurs many years later, and K had helped the son of the man who did the shooting to pay a compensation for his father's action. The son also had to pay some of his father's allies and friends for their help in this same fight because the father was considered to have been the *wei tse*, "the initiator" or "the cause" of the fight, and whoever helped him could claim compensation again for the long-term effects of wounds they had sustained. Here we see how physical injuries can become the basis of long-term relationships of obligation.

K described one compensation in detail, in which he was the primary giver. This was for a girl who was drowned in the lake at Kopiago and K's group was held responsible. He contributed a set of 14 pigs, including one very large one, for this occasion. His mother's kin, who live near the Kopiago station, brought a further 14 pigs to help him and he killed a male pig and presented it to them to thank them for this. People from another nearby parish, Mbara, collectively contributed a set of 14 and another 4 pigs, making 18. His father's mother's people, the Yakuni of Arou parish, brought him another 14 pigs, and received also a male pig for this. He purchased a pig for K200 and gave it plus K120 in money as a funeral gift to accompany the return of the girl's spirit (*tini*) to her natal place. When he returned from the event he killed a further pig and gave half of it to the people of Hagu and half to the Aluni people. Another pig he gave to the people of Yeru near the Strickland and the Bogaiya area; and a further one to his three wives; all these for the contributions they had made to the event. He also killed a pig for the young men who had helped him transport pigs for the event. This detailed account shows that a leader needs considerable resources to be a center person in a compensation event. Calling on help from the mother's or father's mother's people, or other cognatic kin, is also a standard way of gaining assistance, all of which the *kango* may need to repay later. The term for pigs killed to reward those who help is *ita kiapa kliya*, "the pig to clean off the mud from the leg": a phrase that appropriately reflects the condition of the forest pathways between settlements around Aluni and Kopiago.

AH's list, which was the longest of the 30 collected, also provided a microcosmic snapshot of social relations, and his cases spanned from precolonial times to the time of the interview in the 1990s. Examples of compensations stemming from sorcery and witchcraft entered in. For instance, he contributed a "rope" of cowrie shells (numerous shells sewn onto a long backing of twisted plant fiber) to a compensation made for a killing by *tsome* sorcery ("poisoning"). In another case, a *kango* of Haiyuwi killed an Oksapmin man whom he suspected of making *tsome* sorcery, but this man's son claimed his father was innocent and asked for a compensation payment, to which AH contributed. On another occasion, an Aluni leader had accused a woman of witchcraft and she had hanged herself, but an autopsy showed she was innocent, so the leader had to organize a compensation for her death, and AH helped with this, describing his role as that of a "brother" in a general sense. This particular compensation ran through a large number of accounts people gave. It clearly constituted a part of local public history. A speech dealing with an occasion of this sort was given by PK as an example of compensation rhetoric (Stewart and Strathern 2000c: 37–45). Clearly, such an event could produce a crisis in social relations with its putative revelation of a wrong "verdict" followed by a suicide. This record shows that in such a case a wide set of people mobilizes to rally round the leader and makes sure that a compensation is paid to stave off retaliatory hostilities by the woman's kin.

In another case a man argued that his wife had been killed by a set of assault sorcerers (*tsuwake tene*) who had come over from Oksapmin, and that her own father had been involved in assisting the murderers. By the time the husband made his suspicions known, his wife's father was dead and the onus of paying compensation now fell on her mother's second husband, whom she had married after her first husband's death. The Duna people from time to time evince considerable fear of these marauding sorcerers from Oksapmin, who are supposed to stalk the bush areas at the edge of settlements. As with witchcraft (*tsuwake kono*), ideas and fears of this sort are strongly embedded in people's minds, which explains why those accused find it difficult to combat the charges against them and why someone might shoulder a liability for actions he had nothing to do with, just to keep the peace and avoid revenge.

AH's account of these kinds of cases was mixed in with examples of physical injuries, illicit sexual approaches, and suicides. Verbal insults did not figure in his list or in the bulk of cases others gave. Compensation tends to be focused on physical injuries, in which illicit sexual behavior is included, and actual deaths. AH himself was involved in 1991 in a long drawn-out case in which he was claiming compensation from another *kango* of his own parish for injuries to his chest sustained in a fracas. He visited Aluni often and complained that he had various bodily pains, which he thought would not heal properly until his attacker had paid the compensation to him. This stress on compensation is a typical feeling for the Duna, and one they share with the Huli (Goldman 1983: 283). The idea operates as a sanction encouraging people to pay compensation for injuries, since this, it is thought, may prevent the victim from sickening and dying, in which case a higher compensation would be demanded. "A pig in time saves nine" could be the Duna motto here; or rather it could save 14, since this is the minimum number of items that should be given in any compensation.[4]

Payments of wealth for compensation in cases of injury are thought to act directly on people's bodies. Wealth in this context itself has magical powers of healing. A quick payment of a pig to a wounded ally could, it was thought, heal the wound, and also stop the man from dying. Failure to pay for a wound inflicted could, on the contrary, result in the victim's death even after the lapse of many years, as we have noted; in which case the kinsfolk of the victim could still demand compensation. "Pay early and often" could, then, also sum up the Duna attitude to these predicaments. It was an attitude that had remained strong throughout many changes and had long outlasted the context of intergroup hostilities into which it had been typically set in precolonial times. Perhaps the practice of settling all kinds of disputes with compensation payments had continued to be strong in the Aluni Valley partly because of the area's remote location, which made walking to the District Office in Kopiago an all-day enterprise, and partly because the provincial government, based far away in Mendi and Tari, had never introduced the long-awaited Village Courts system. As a result people continued with their own informal solutions, adapting and applying them to new situations as these came along. The terms of engagement or dialogue sometimes intersected with introduced elements. In one case leaders said they would need to wait to see the results of an x-ray taken at Tari to determine whether a plaintiff's bone had been broken. Often leaders complained that they had no government support for their work. In relation to the perceived problem of witchcraft, in particular, as we have noted, they were uncomfortable that there seemed to be no government law that specified how to deal with it. Yet they managed well enough on their own. It was less clear whether a further generation of community spokespersons, who had not grown up with superior knowledge of ritual and magic, would be able to wield the same authority, and show the speech-making capacity, of the senior *kango* who were still active in the 1990s.

In his dispute with a fellow parish member in 1991, AH received a total of 56 wealth items, expressed as 4 × 14, since wealth goods are counted in symbolic sets of 14. AH's antagonist in this dispute was H. A pig in H's care broke into and ate food from one of AH's gardens in 1990. H claimed that AH's fence was inadequate but three informal adjudicators (*Komiti* men) said this was untrue and H should pay K400 for the garden (a large sum of money). H said he would not comply because the pig's true owner was far away in the capital city of Port Moresby. The adjudicators then found that two pigs were involved, one of them H's own, but he still would not pay. Both parties then went away and at this time the pigs broke in again and destroyed the garden entirely, according to AH's account. On return, they fell into dispute again and H struck AH on the ear, then they fought and fell into a ditch. H fell on AH and one of AH's ribs was broken, and the *Komiti* men said that now H must pay compensation for this injury. AH's kin on his mother's and his father's side all supported this claim, understandably, since they would stand to benefit in any distribution of the compensation AH would subsequently make. The *kango* from Yangone and Haiyuwi (one of them ML) backed up this claim further, and in May 1991 H paid. AH is of the Songwa group from Yeru and has ties with Nauwa parish through his mother's mother's people. H's tie with the parish is also through his mother's mothers' people, and his own agnates, the Yaliya, belong to the Kopiago area. Neither man, therefore, is an agnate of Nauwa.

In due course AH distributed the wealth gained from this compensation, giving to the following categories of people:

1. His mother's mother's husband's son, the Baptist pastor at Hagu, a prominent old agnate of the parish. AH called this recipient his *auwene* ("uncle").

2. His father's mother's people of Haiyuwi parish. The recipient here was PK, a *kango*. AH called this man *ame antia* ("father's mother's kin").
3. His fellow Songwa of Yeru, in particular a senior recognized man, whom he called *amekeni ndu* ("paternal unlce").
4. His co-parish kin in Nauwa, the immediate recipient being a recognized man of status who is of AH's mother's mother's group.

In this way AH distributed wealth among four out of the six parishes in the whole Aluni Valley area, concentrating on *kango* or other recognized community members. The case shows how a single event may come to involve leaders on a Valley-wide basis. Compensation payments, like brideprice and pig-killings for funerals, are an important focus of social networks and their mobilization on an interparish basis. AH in particular, living away from his agnates, seeks to spread out his ties so as to secure his local position.

As we have earlier noted, women are active in contributing to compensation payments. They have, and had in the past, independent access to wealth by making netbags, which could be exchanged for pigs, and by rearing their own pigs. One woman, for example, cited two occasions when she had helped men whom she called "brother" (*kane*) with a large pig (*ita tangetia*). Another woman noted that she had also contributed a large pig for one of these occasions and that she called the man she helped "brother-in-law, husband's brother" (*kiane*). Both of these women indicated that their contributions were separate from those of their husbands to the same events. When asked about this, and on hearing the lists of occasions the husbands had contributed to, they said, "Those were the things the men did in their communal men's house (*anda pirapea*)," i.e., separately from their wives. These two were middle-aged women. An older woman reported three contributions, totaling nine pigs, five of them large ones, and one half-side of pork. One of these occasions was to pay compensation for the death of the mother of a younger Yangone man, who had been hit on the head years previously. When this woman died in 1991, her death was attributed to this blow and so compensation had to be made. The largest contribution made by the older woman was for the death of another senior woman who was the grandmother (father's mother) of a prominent man of her group. The grandmother came to stay at her grandson's place and became sick and died there. Her kin asked for compensation (presumably claiming neglect, perhaps failure to protect her against sorcery or witchcraft), and so they paid. These women listed only pigs. A younger woman listed four monetary contributions to events, amounting to K12 in all.

Leadership and Change

Two fundamental capacities defined the *kango*'s position in the past: wealth in resources, principally pigs and cowrie shells; and ability to speak on public occasions of conflict or ritual when such wealth was given away, to create and maintain social order. These two requirements are found prominently in many parts of the Highlands. Their respective weightings, however, differed from place to place. In Hagen, for example, the position of the *wuö nuim* (leader) was defined primarily in terms of wealth, but those who were able to speak effectively were those who wielded the greater influence over others. Indeed, talk and wealth were bound up together, since leaders in Hagen were those who persuaded others to help them in their enterprises and then represented their support group in public negotiations over an event. There was a feedback effect between wealth and ability to talk with influence. In the Duna case there was an especial emphasis on ritual knowledge. This was because of the pronounced Duna ideology that the state of the land, seen as part of a whole cosmos, depended on a great cycle of rituals to maintain health and prosperity, the *rindi kiniya* cycle. *Kango* ought to be at the center of these rituals, not only contributing to them, but embodying the proper knowledge of them and their associated dances and origin stories that encapsulated their power.[5]

4.1 A view of forest areas devastated by fire in 1997. Swordgrass grows in fallow land in the foreground and the fieldworkers' house at Hagu is visible just beyond it (1999). (Stewart/Strathern Archive)

This capacity of knowledge about the land is still shown in senior *kango*'s *malu* (origin stories) regarding the tutelary spirits of the forest and its pools and lakes, principally the Tindi Auwene and the Payame Ima. It is also shown in their sheer knowledge of the names of different localities and the ritual associations of these names. Such names are the record of the powers of local spirits to whom rituals were in the past directed. On one occasion of a pig killing in 1999, the *kango* ML made a speech in which this kind of knowledge was demonstrated (Stewart and Strathern 2002a: 133). He and others of Hagu and Aluni were killing pigs as a sacrifice to spirits of the forest, especially the Payame Ima, for the disturbance of their abode that had happened in 1997 with a forest fire that some young boys had accidentally started during a time of drought. The fire had destroyed large stands of trees, causing wildlife to flee elsewhere. These same areas contained the bones of the dead or had previously been used as ritual sites. ML had sponsored the occasion because two boys of his own group had set the fires that led unintentionally to this desecration and endangerment of the local cosmos.

ML began his speech with a superficial reason for the pig killing:

> I killed pigs before because I was sorry for my mountain. I told my boys [he has many sons] to make fences and keep the pigs out of gardens, but they said I did not share the money with them when the pigs were sold, so I am killing them again here now. And since the rest of you have also brought meat from pigs you have slaughtered, let us cook them and eat them together.

This opening statement contained a recognition of the sorts of tensions between the generations that can exist today as a result of monetarization in general and in particular perceptions about returns for labor. Elsewhere in the Highlands, too, older people frequently complain that young people have become reluctant to do the work of looking after pigs (Strathern and Stewart 1999b: 92; 2000c: 162). They say this is because young folk prefer to wash and keep themselves clean and to go to town and find ways to earn and spend money there.

After this brief commentary on change, ML launched into his major theme:

> Our mountainside was burnt by fire. We have come together here and many agnates and cognates of the place Apuka and the place Minda are here [here he refers to people of the Songwa group whose *malu* associates them intimately with rituals for the order of the cosmos in the Aluni Valley and beyond it]. Some of our people have left and have

gone to Paiya and Apaiya [in Haiyuwi] and Ayumu [an old term for Nauwa parish]. Or they are at Tani [Horaile], Irauwa [Aluni], Yamongwa [Yangone], or Kwaia [Kakwene, a distant parish].

ML's words here bear witness to two things. One is the tendency in cognatic systems for people to move around, leaving their agnatic or natal places and staying with other kin. Kinsfolk scatter, but some come together for special occasions such as pig killings to spirits of the land. Second, ML shows to his listeners that the parishes of the Valley have ancient names, known only as esoterica to a few *kango* such as himself. These ancient names encapsulate a sense of the indigenous spirit powers associated with the places themselves. ML's own parish is Yangone. His personal settlement is called Sagu. Yamongwa stands for Yangone, but is probably also the name for an old distinct settlement within Yangone parish territory, separate from Sagu.

ML now launched into a recitation of the names of areas that were burnt in the fires:

> We do not have two or three men together to kill pigs , I am doing this by myself. I killed three whole pigs and cooked also six further sides of pork for the mountain. Over there the hills of Yaki and Konowa [in Yangone] were burnt. Before I was not sorry for these hillsides, but now I am, and you have all come to help me. My own hill is called Kare Luki. My father's skull rests on its slopes. All these hills were burnt, and all the skulls of our ancestors with them.
>
> The skull of Waini was burnt
> The skull of Pele was burnt
> The skull of Hanguya was burnt
> The skull of Kiya was burnt
> The skull of Yokona was burnt
> The skull of Kauwa was burnt
> The skull of Hayako was burnt
> The skull of Timberia was burnt
> The skulls of Kili, of Koli, of Kone, of Peya, of Apeya, all these were burnt.
>
> When my kinsfolk die nowadays I make Christian prayers for them and I throw flowers into their graves [meaning, that ritual practices have changed and sacrifices to the ancestors have ceased]. But now I am sorry for the mountain and so I am killing these pigs here.

Here the mountain and the skulls that rest on it are fused together as parts of the land (*rindi*) as a whole in its cosmic sense. At the same time, by separating the mountain itself, in another sense, from the ancestors, ML is able to reconcile his new Christian practices with piety toward the dead and the past. His contemporary "environmentalism" can also be seen as reintegrating past with present ritual practice. His brief reference to current Christian rituals led the way for his son, who is a Baptist church worker, to make specific Christian prayers over the meat that was laid out in a ceremonial row in the forest clearing where the event took place.

This kind of symbiotic approach to indigenous and Christian forms of ritual is one that the Valley people had developed over the years since the first Baptist missionaries came to their place, baptized people, and left after Independence. Left to themselves, leaders like ML have firmly maintained that they are Christians, while seeking ways still to pursue their fundamental values expressed in the relationship with their environment, which remains crucial to their daily life. Introduced positions, such as that of Local Government Councillor, have not impinged strongly on the people, largely because the Kopiago Council raises no tax and does not receive many resources from the Provincial headquarters in Mendi. When in earlier years the Provincial Member for their side of Kopiago came from the Kunai parish, the Valley people experienced some benefits, chiefly payments for road construction and the maintenance of the Aid Post (the Member had begun his career as an Aid Post Orderly himself). However, after the system of Provincial representation was discontinued by decision of the national government in 1995, this advantage

4.2 Butchering pork for an occasion when leaders will apologize to the spirits for the forest fires of 1997 (1999). (Stewart/Strathern Archive)

4.3 Sides of pork hanging on a pole in a clearing in preparation for a ceremonial cooking. A mother and daughter keep watch over them (1999). (Stewart/Strathern Archive)

ceased. The position of the national-level parliamentarian had always been held by a representative from the more populous eastern parts of the electorate. (In 2003 a new Member was elected, whose home was near Lake Kopiago station.) The station Officer in Charge rarely comes on patrol except at the times of national elections, and visits by health officials to examine and vaccinate small children only occasionally occur. The Aid Post was chronically short of medicines in the late 1990s, but a new Aid Post funded by the Porgera Joint Venture mining company was pending. The *kango* remained effectively the only leaders with any enduring local presence in community life as a whole.

As is the case elsewhere in the Highlands, one category of personnel was increasing in significance. This was the category of Christian pastors serving the various churches. Such pastors tended to act as moral arbiters in relation to rules of behavior their church advocated. Their principal instrument of control was that of removing people's names from the rolls of church communicants in cases of perceived misconduct or rule-breaking. The Baptist pastor was based at Hagu in Aluni and by the 1990s he was very senior, having served since the 1960s in that capacity. Two younger men, trained at the mission center, had begun to take over his effective work in 1999. One of these was the son of ML whom we have mentioned above. They were literate, spoke the lingua franca *Tok Pisin*, and played guitar tunes.

Young men like this have the potential to become significant in local affairs, especially if they are agnates of the parish in which they are working. One man, previously resident in Hagu, established a flourishing Seventh-Day Adventist compound in 1998 at Aluni, where he instituted strict rules of allegiance. By 1999, however, issues over witchcraft and compensation had fragmented his followers. Part of his success had lain in people's fears of world's end at the coming millennium. But when more pressing and—for the Duna—tangible matters such as deaths from witchcraft and compensation payments came up, it was once more the *kango* who reasserted their ability to handle trouble in the community.

This page intentionally left blank

Chapter 5

Myth, Ritual, and Change

For the Duna, as for many other peoples of the world, myths and rituals form a vital part of their ongoing adaptations to historical change. This is particularly the case in relation to changes that impact their environment, as mining projects do in a dramatic way. The reason is that Duna religion largely had to do with maintaining a balanced relationship with the cosmos as a whole, seen in terms of a symbiosis between people and the land. We have noted earlier how one term for a parish group is *rindi*, literally "ground," and how ancestral stones, *auwi*, were believed to emerge out of the ground a number of generations after persons had died. At death, funeral arrangements involved the dripping of bodily fluids from the deceased back into the ground, contributing to its ongoing fertility; while the *tini*, or soul, was thought to fly like a bird up into rock shelters in parish territory above the level of cultivation of gardens. The parts of the person after death were thus seen as distributed into different regions of the environment. They were not entirely lost to the parish but remained as influences within it.

Moreover, within each parish there were numerous sites where sacrifices would on occasion be made to a whole range of spirit powers. These spirits included the ancestors of current parish residents, but they also included "nature spirits," for instance the male *tsiri* spirits, who were thought to have their abodes in low-altitude places beside river courses. *Tsiri* could throw ashes at people who intruded inappropriately into their domains and could make them sick. The ability to cause sickness is a common denominator among all spirit categories. Such sickness is always seen from within a perspective of restoratory sacrifice. It is a sign of something that has gone wrong in the relationship of people with the spirits. Since the spirits are also those that can grant wealth, health, or fertility to people, sacrifices are seen as required in order to regain their favor. Sickness is therefore not a neutral, physical event. It is always seen as a sign of some social or moral problem. This way of looking at the world is common to the Duna and many other people of New Guinea. It is a mistake to see spirits that were thought to send sickness to people as simply "malevolent." Sickness has to be interpreted as a part of the whole process of ensuring the stability and survival of the *rindi* by means of reciprocity. People made sacrifices in order to appease spirits and enlist their powers in a positive way, so as to reestablish balance in their overall cosmos. It is in this sense that sacrifice has to be seen as "restoratory."

Each local parish tends to have its own traditions and narratives about spirits associated with its land. Older *anoagaro* leaders in the 1990s were still highly knowledgeable about these narratives. Marks of the spirits were invariably thought to be special kinds of stones that people found within their parish areas. These were either black volcanic stones, crystals, or prehistoric artifacts such as mortars and pestles. People rubbed fat from sacrificed pigs on these stones as a way of pleasing the spirits. For instance, they would rub grease on a stone identified as the *ngunuma* or heart of a *tsiri* who had died, and the *tsiri*'s spirit would then give them plenty of healthy pigs. One *tsiri* was said to have been the source of the valuable cowrie shells that people employed in brideprice and compensation payments (Stewart and Strathern 2002c). The man to whom this *tsiri* first gave cowries was reported to have shot his own sister and given her body to the spirit. He was said to have done this while he was possessed by the *tsiri* himself. He then cut some lengths of bamboo and put them just outside his house. During the night he heard noises and in the morning he found that the bamboo tubes were filled with cowries. He and his relatives were able to use the cowries to pay ritual experts who came to oversee important cult events in their parish (Stewart and Strathern 2002a: 56).

The reputed act of the man, shooting his sister as a sacrifice prior to receiving wealth, reveals how pervasive the ideas of sacrifice and reciprocity are in the thought-world of the Duna. From one viewpoint, the act can be interpreted as an analog of reciprocity in marriage. A woman is "given" in order to receive wealth. From another viewpoint, the act falls into a class of sacrifices Duna traditions record, in which human substances and body parts are offered to spirits as a part of an overall cycle of renewal and maintenance rituals, which are called *rindi kiniya*, straightening out or repairing the earth. Narrators of the story did not elaborate to us what the *tsiri* was thought to have done with the body of the sister sacrificed to him: whether he ate the body, for example, or rather took the woman's *tini*, or spirit, as his bride in the spirit world. The story does not focus on this issue. It is concerned with how people gained shell wealth, and it expounds what G. W. Trompf (1994) has called a "logic of retribution." Everything must be paid for. The Duna theory of sacrifice corresponds to the popular maxim, "there is no such thing as a free lunch."

This fundamental idea explains why Duna rituals were triggered by adverse events in people's lives and always took the form of sacrifices. Pigs were the vital medium for these sacrifices, and one Duna narrative explains how in early times the people of one group, the Poli, used to mourn the death of their pigs and kill people (children in one version) as sacrifices at the pigs' funerals. A hero from another group, the Songwa, came upon an occasion when this was about to happen, and he instructed the Poli to reverse the order of things and instead kill pigs as sacrifices at the death of humans. He made his point by butchering and roasting a pig that had been set up for mourning on a funeral trestle after its death and offering its meat to the Poli, garnished with salt to make it more palatable. The Poli overcame their shock, took the hint, and became consumers of pork. The hero, named Kepepa, is thus credited with introducing the era of civilization to the part of the Duna area that was home to the Poli, close to the Strickland River.

This area also holds considerable cosmological significance for the people of the Aluni Valley as a whole. It is the place of origin of several of the agnatic lines of groups whose members live in the parishes of the Valley as far as Nauwa. These include the Songwa, Poli, Laiye, Yangone, and Kopetei groups. The stories of origin link these groups to particular places, to spirit beings (*tama*) with miraculous powers, and often to wild creatures such as snakes, which they recognize as ancestors of humans. Stories of this kind therefore strongly reinforce the notion of an intrinsic link between people and their environment, whose powers are represented in mythic logic as animate beings. Typically, a creature such as a python can appear also in the shape of a man. These ancestors are thus seen as something elemental, midway between humans and creatures of the wild, but endowed also with superior powers.

One category of spirit stands in counterpoint to the *tsiri*. This is the figure of the Payame Ima, a female spirit of great power who is thought of as having entered into a marriage-like relationship with a chosen bachelor in a given parish. She would grant her partner the powers of a ritual expert, able to use a divining stick, the *ndele rowa*, to discover witches in the community. She would also show him magical plants (*palena*, "ginger"), which were used to help young bachelors grow into manhood in a special seclusion house in the forest (*palena anda*, "ginger house"). Inspired by her, her partner presided over the maturation of these bachelors as an honored senior ritual expert. As long as he remained with her, he was obliged not to marry a human wife. In some versions of Payame Ima stories, the spirit is also said to have made magical gardens in the bush for her partner. If others looked at this magical source of food, it would vanish: a detail that emphasizes the relationship as private and special, yet beneficial to the community at large.

Not all parishes had traditions of this spirit. Narratives about her are prominent in Yangone, Aluni, and Haiyuwi. The experts whom she favored tended to be *anoagaro* members of their parishes, closely related to *kango* men. This was certainly the case in Yangone, where the spirit was known as the Hoyape Ima, the "light-skinned" or "red" woman, believed to have had a sister. Here she was also said to have died by falling into a river, a story that perhaps grew up in the wake of local Christianization and abandonment of earlier forms of ritual. Memories of and notions about the Payame Ima's importance are nonetheless highly tenacious, and in some areas she is still thought of as looking after forest wilderness areas. In 1999, as we have noted earlier (chapter 4), a Yangone leader, ML, made a special invocation to areas of the forest where fires, accidentally lit, had spread and may have disturbed secondary burial sites and areas associated with this spirit. ML is of the same lineage as the ritual expert of the past, who was said to be married to the Hoyape Ima.

Another version of this spirit, known as the Yuro Ima, the "woman who swims," is closely associated with the Strickland River itself. She is thought to have swum up and down the river and when she raised her arms lightning flashed and thunder sounded. She was identified also in the form of lights seen moving on the water of the river. As in stories about her in other locations, she is said to have had a brother who accompanied her. She made a magic bridge over the intimidating expanse of the Strickland and used to help people trying to cross the river on human-made cane bridges or to save those swimming in the water from drowning. Finally, she is said to have controlled the wild game, mostly pigs, of the extensive grasslands around the Strickland, directing them as she pleased into the pathway of hunters, thus enabling them to be shot.

As a spirit of the wild, the Payame Ima was thought to hold sway over two different ecological zones: the high forests of the mountain tops and the low-lying grasslands of the Strickland. In the forests she was thought of as the owner of wild nut pandanus trees, which were a valuable food resource in season, and also of marsupials, which men hunted for their meat and decorative fur. She herself could take the form of a kind of marsupial, called *yukulini*, in whose stomach hunters could find *ipu rei* crystals, which were said to help give men "a good skin" and overall appearance when they traveled to other places. She also was said to inspire singers of epic cycles known as *pikono*, the plots of which were tied in with themes of the *palena anda*. Altogether this spirit takes on an aura of special significance in Duna thinking about the environment (compare Brutti 2003 on ideas regarding Yuan-Ku, a powerful female spirit figure among the neighboring Oksapmin people).

She was not thought of, however, as the sole powerful spirit of the wild. Her powers were held in conjuncton with those of a male spirit, the Tindi Auwene, "owner of the land." Each parish was said to have its own Tindi Auwene. Like the Payame Ima, his domain was the depths of the high forest. People had to respect his domain when they entered it. They needed to speak quietly. They also had to use a special vocabulary called "pandanus talk" to refer to things of the forest itself. If people respected him as they should, he would protect them from dangers in the forest, but if he did not like intruders he could make them lose their way. When a person or a hunting dog was lost in this way, their companions would call out a special invocation to the spirit, addressing him by his name. If they heard a noise in return, this meant that the lost ones were with the Tindi Auwene and he would release them.

The senior man of Haiyuwi parish, PK, once brought two stones to Hagu and declared that one was the petrified heart of the Tindi Auwene and the other was a stone axe of an ancient kind that came in through trading ties with Oksapmin from the west. Both stones were relics of the spirit. Like the *tsiri*, the Tindi Auwene could be thought of both as ancestral/dead and as contemporary/living. PK went on to say that the Tindi Auwene and the Payame Ima generally went together (Stewart and Strathern 2002a: 64). That is, they were seen as allied spirit forces, one male and the other female, who held sway over the arena of the wild forest and its valuable products. Only agnates of a given parish were permitted officially to know and to invoke the particular Tindi Auwene of their own parish's forest area. Clearly this prescription ritually marked out the idea of the precedence of agnates in guaranteeing the integrity and separate identity of the parish territory as such. And clearly, even though all overt rituals directed toward spirits ceased after the Duna were formally converted to Christianity, both the Tindi Auwene and Payame Ima are still much in the thoughts of at least the senior people in the parishes we know. Part of the reason for this is because the indigenous spirits were and are seen as inextricably bound up with the landscape itself. The landscape at large is imbued with innumerable cultural associations, communicated and reinforced in courting songs, mourning songs, stories of origins, and the *pikono* ballads. All of these genres are full of references to specific places and the doings of people in them. The places remain a part of people's lives, so the memories and traditions associated with them tend to be preserved vividly in this way.

This is not simply a matter of cultural continuity. Duna lifeways have been subjected to sharp ruptures and transformations over time, especially since the 1960s, with the beginnings of colonial administration and the advent of national Independence in 1975. The landscape has been cleared of the overt markings of previous sacred places and shrines. At Aluni, school buildings and playing ground, a health center and a marketplace, were all constructed over an area that previously held cult shrines. Following Christian practice, a collective cemetery for the dead was also established at one side of the area. And most recently a new compound of dwellings and a church for Seventh-Day Adventists was set up at the western end of the playing ground. Old ritual centers were replaced with new ones, and many of the older associations are probably not well known to younger generations of people, although they remain meaningful to their seniors. In a general sense, the old associations of the landscape remain in reserve, to be called upon and resuscitated if circumstances suggest this. Cultural forms are also malleable. After the deaths of two Aluni men in 1996, putatively from witchcraft attacks, special graves were made for them, following the pattern of covering the graves with a roof, within the Seventh-Day Adventist compound at Aluni. The graves were visible from a distance and marked the church's particular concern with the perceived problem of witchcraft in the community.

The Duna tend to associate places where mining companies have made surveys, or actually taken up operations, with their own notions of the sacred (see also Biersack 1999; Jacka 2001; Macintyre 2001). Resources such as oil, gold, and copper, which these companies look for and seek to exploit, are themselves seen as substances of sacred power. The thinking here parallels the Duna's general notion that particular places in the environment are sites where magical power originally flowed to people. We have seen how, according to one narrative, wealth items, such as cowries and pigs, were originally granted to people by a *tsiri* spirit, in return for the sacrificial death of a woman (in one version a man's sister, in another a man's wife and child who are taken by flood waters brought on by the *tsiri*'s magic). The parish origin story of Aluni also encodes this notion. In this an ancestor of the whole parish, called Bulireterete (a name of an "epic" kind, not an ordinary name of people today), mysteriously receives pigs from the Alu lake, which lies at the far western end of Aluni territory toward the Strickland River. A man from the neighboring parish, Haiyuwi, secretly spies on Bulireterete on one of these occasions when the lake spirit is releasing pigs to him, whereupon the pigs disappear. The sequence here recalls the motif in the narrative of the magical garden the Payame Ima makes for her ritual partner in the *palena* cult. When viewed by others not authorized to do so, the garden vanishes. The transmission of magical power depends on keeping it restricted to the proper channels: the same message that underlies the agnatic ideology of the *anoagaro* lines within each parish.

In the Aluni origin story the connection with the Payame Ima is explicitly made. It is she who grants the magical pigs to the ancestor Bulireterete. He hears the laughter of a woman and traces it to a fruit pandanus tree nearby (Stewart and Strathern 2002a: 98). He seizes the tree, which transforms itself into various shapes, including a snake, but then becomes a woman, who finally agrees to marry him. She lays down a condition that he must never refer to her wild origins as a pandanus tree or snake woman. Bulireterete's marriage parallels the idea that the Payame Ima chooses a senior bachelor to be her consort in running the *palena* cult, with the difference that in this case the human male chooses the female spirit, and actually coerces her into a marriage from which she bears a son. The story ends tragically, again implicating a Haiyuwi man as guilty of violating the spirit's wishes. Bulireterete kills a pig and the wife wants its backbone for herself. But the Haiyuwi man, who is distributing the meat, ignores her request and her husband tells her not to complain. In retribution she takes her boy up in to the hills. There she changes into a nut pandanus tree and the son into its fruits. In his grief and remorse the husband turns into an *umeli* bird, which can still be heard sorrowfully crying for her.

Both the *tsiri* and the Payame Ima, then, were seen as sources of wealth items, requiring sacrifices or proper respect in return for them. These notions are not restricted to the Aluni Valley. Similar ideas surround the large lake at the Kopiago Administrative Station, which the Australians set up in the 1960s. A former ritual expert from a group near the station, Sane-Noma, used to carry around with him in a pouch a highly unusual stone head figure, a representation of a *tsiri* of the lake itself, called Tsiri Harola (Stewart and Strathern 1999a: 83). The *tsiri*'s name, Harola, is probably cognate with Haroli, the name the Huli people, neighbors of the Duna, give to their bachelors' cult. Goldman (1983: 325–6) relates Haroli to "acorn" and suggests the term has phallic connotations. The same covert meaning might attach to Sane's stone. Sane declared that the stone brought him wealth, and he further linked this idea to prospecting activities by companies. He declared that at nighttime the stone had a light emerging from it, i.e., it glowed, and he conjectured that it itself might be made of gold or copper. Later, he went on, the spirit of the stone came to him while he dreamt and directly told him it would reveal to him places where minerals such as silver, copper, gold, and iron could be found, so that he could take these samples to white men working for mining companies and be rewarded by them. Sane eventually deflected his ambitions in this regard by selling the stone instead to the Papua New Guinea National Museum, for a respectable sum of money; so the stone did actually bring him wealth.

The tendency to link such ideas of wealth either with the *tsiri* spirit or with the Payame Ima is shown in another folktale, in which Papumi and Lukumi, two Payame Ima spirits, leave the Aluni Valley area and travel westward to a place called Oko Mamo. There they resettle themselves on top of Mt. Fubilan, where the huge gold and copper mine at Ok Tedi was later established. By implication, the story makes a connection between the spirit women and the presence of valuable minerals in the environment. It also suggests that the local Valley people have some claim to those resources via "their" spirits, who migrated to the place where gold was found. Taken together, all of these stories suggest that old and new forms of wealth in the environment equally belong to the domains of indigenous spirit beings.

From early colonial times the Aluni Valley Duna have witnessed the passage through their area of foreigners in search of mineral wealth. The very first explorers of their area, the Fox brothers, in the 1930s, came looking for gold, without success. Assistant District Officer Desmond Clancy led a large patrol into the Strickland area, with 13 indigenous police and 150 carriers, along with 3 Australasian Petroleum Company geologists. Such a large party, avowedly in search of oil after Huli men had brought mineral oil into the government station at Tari, must have made a huge impression on the people and have been the cause of a ramifying set of rumors about its purposes. At this time, in 1954, the Duna area was restricted to outsiders and the Strickland Valley area was scarcely explored. The expedition's discoveries of the population and their dramatic landscape prompted the Administration to set up a government station at Lake Kopiago (Sinclair 1966: 113–16).

From early times, then, the Duna's experience with the white outsiders linked these intruders to mining projects, and this continued with further explorations by the Kennecott company, which was initially involved with the Ok Tedi mine. ML, a leader of the Yangone group, asked in 1991 about an iron marker stake that Kennecott's surveyors had supposedly set up at Kambaiyareke in his parish territory. Were they going to come back? Why did they put the stake there? His questions were prompted at least in part by the coincidence that the stake was planted near the mythical dancing place of the *tsiri*, who gave people cowries (Stewart and Strathern 2002a: 142). Early in 1991 the Aluni community was buzzing with the idea that a company was about to come (on April 4) and set up a work-camp there in conjunction with a drilling rig for a mine.

Nothing came of these rumors and speculations. Over the years, however, the people's interest in mining and prospects of wealth from it were maintained by the news of the activities at Ok Tedi and by the establishment of a small monitoring station near the Strickland River, called SG3, in Yangone territory, maintained by the Porgera Joint Venture gold mining company to test the levels of mineral elements in the river. The company was required to do this by the government, since its mine tailings were discharged into a river system that feeds into the Strickland. In 1991 there was only a minor level of interest among the Valley people about this practice. During the 1990s the situation, however, dramatically changed.

The mine itself was set up in 1991, and it was some time before communities possibly affected by its operations began to express

5.1 View of Porgera gold mine showing the extensive areas of rock stripped away and the network of roads snaking through the site (1998). (Stewart/Strathern Archive)

5.2 The Porgera mine site showing access roads and some of the installations for refining the gold (1998). (Stewart/Strathern Archive)

disquiet about the tailings issue. During the 1990s also concern over the environmental impact of the Ok Tedi mine gradually built up, and as the Valley people visited Tabubil, the mine site, or returned from working there they picked up news of conflicts over its impact and brought ideas home. People's fears were greatly accelerated by an accident at the Porgera mine in which red oxide had been discharged along with the tailings and these had colored the Strickland red as far as the Duna area. The station manager at Kopiago wrote a report about this event, recording the people's view that the red color was a mark of "poison" that was killing fish, vegetation, and wild pigs that came down to drink at the river or in creeks near it. From this time onward people began to reinterpret deaths that they had previously attributed to witchcraft, declaring that now they understood these to have happened because of the river pollution. Valley people often have ties and traditional rights of fishing, hunting, or gathering in the environs of the Strickland, so they quite regularly eat the products of the area. Hence they could reasonably suppose that they might have ingested some of the new poison from the river via the food chain. People were also willing to combine explanations, for example saying that people had been weakened by the poison and were finished off by witches, or vice-versa.

The change in cosmological perspective was not absolute. With leadership drawn from Yokona parish, beside the river itself, and also from Aluni, a Landowners Association was formed in order to demand compensation from the company for the deaths and damage putatively caused. The accident was not repeated, and there were continuing disagreements about the scientific evidence supporting or negating the allegations of serious pollution. The company, in any case, was required in 1998 by the government to pay compensation to all the riverfront groups for their use of the river water to carry away tailings, separately from the question of levels of pollution that the tailings caused.

At this point, the mythology of the Yuro Ima reentered people's consciousness. When we were asking about the pollution issue in 1999, we were struck by the way that the senior men of different groups who talked to us had the name of this female spirit on their lips and in the forefront of their minds. They explained to us that the spirit, whose presence they used to detect regularly by the appearance of a light on the river, was now not in evidence. Either she had died, or she had gone away, because she was upset by the pollution of the river. Since the Yuro Ima was also said to have looked after all the wild game of the area, including its flora and fauna, her departure was a serious matter, a sign of cosmological imbalance and danger. People explicitly said that this was why they had been so insistent that the company pay compensation to them. They definitely interpreted the tailings payments as a form of compensation for pollution, even though technically they were not and the pollution issue remained to be tested in court, and they drew on their own mythic view of the world as their prime means of negotiation with the company.

This was not all. To the same Strickland River waterfront area there came in 1997–1998 an oil prospecting company seeking to make a preliminary drilling. They had chosen a spot on a ledge on the far side of the river, on the Oksapmin side away from the immediate areas of Duna habitation. Duna leaders staked their mythological claims to this area, citing narratives that linked their ancestors with the spot where the drilling was undertaken. In all probability the Oksapmin leaders did the same on their side. A few of the Valley's younger men found employment with the oil company, and others migrated down to the missionary airstrip at Ekali where planes landed bringing materials and supplies for the venture. There clearly had been tremendous excitement and anticipation of future benefits to flow from this operation among the Valley people as a whole. However, in the event, the elaborate and costly drilling exercise was unsuccessful. It appears that the drilling bits met a layer of impenetrably hard rock deep down and could not reach further to determine if oil lay beneath it. The camp had to be disbanded and in 1999, when we were staying again at

Hagu, we watched a string of helicopters carrying dismantled equipment back to various destinations in the Southern Highlands Province. People began to drift back to their upland home settlements from the Strickland, while some were still pursuing issues of the environmental impact of setting up the camp and the rig.

These events were accompanied by a remarkable further development of local narratives, designed in part to give a more than technical explanation of why the drilling failed. One thing people said was that the rig had been placed on the wrong side of the river. Originally, they said, the camp had been set up firmly on the Duna side, but a Papua New Guinean worker from a different ethnic area, Simbu Province, had persuaded the company, against the recommendations of its own expatriate geologists, to move it to the other side, on the grounds that the Oksapmin people would be easier to deal with than the Duna. This narrative, then, placed the blame for failure on a wrong decision made by an ethnic outsider. The idea here was that there was actually "a lake of oil" to be found, but the oil rig had wrongly been set up above the rock ledge.

A further, and more wide-ranging, narrative was created by an activist leader of the Yangone group. It spread and was picked up by interested persons of all the groups that claimed a stake in the oil site.

5.3 Ekali airstrip seen from the lawn of the Evangelical Church of PNG mission area. The oil-rig site is in front of the steep escarpment behind it. New temporary homes built by Duna people from the Aluni Valley are visible in the foreground (1999). (Stewart/Strathern Archive)

The essential elements of the story were that a boy of the Yangone group was walking down from the work camp area to the actual oil rig, when he was stung by a bee and fell down a deep hole. There he encountered two young spirit women, who looked like white women. They took hold of him and they all walked on until they came to a large underground city with tall buildings and cars, and everything in this city was made of money. Then the boy saw a giant man, and the giant pointed to a pipe coming into the city that was aimed at his chest. "Do you see that?" he said. "Here, take this iron bar and hit the pipe with it." For four days the boy worked at battering the pipe until it was bent back and broken. The giant man gave him a number of presents in return, including money, and told him to close his eyes, after which he found himself back on the pathway to the oil rig. He told his story to everyone. The story also noted that there were two white men living underground in the magic city, who said that later they would work with the Duna people.

In this narrative the two spirit women are versions of the Payame Ima, interpreted as belonging to the Yangone group and therefore as reappearances of the Hoyape Ima and her sister from the earlier mythology. The huge giant is the Tindi Auwene, representing all the indigenous powers of ownership of the land and its secrets, penetrated and threatened by the intrusive drill from the oil rig. The vision of the underground city corresponds to a cargoistic image of all the wealth that flows from capitalist enterprise, here, however, attributed to the domain of the Tindi Auwene. The commodifying power of capitalist enterprise is reflected in the idea that everything in the city is literally made of money—even the toilet houses, as one narrator put it (Stewart and Strathern 2002a: 155). The spirit women and the giant are portrayed as working together. The women appear in the form of a bee that stings the boy and sends him to them underground, so that they can conduct him to the giant and enlist his help to prevent the drill from piercing the giant's heart and killing him. In another detail, the giant is said already to have holes in different parts of his body, corresponding to mines in other parts of Papua New Guinea. The Duna Tindi Auwene thus comes to stand for the land of the nation of Papua New Guinea as a whole. The two white men in the city are *tama* spirits, whether local or otherwise, signs that the spirit forces are able to stand on either side of the divide between the locals and the outside world. Altogether the narrative is an astonishingly condensed version of the contradictions, desire, strategies, and value judgements that surrounded the whole presence of the rig in the landscape. It is a testimony to the power of the mythical mode of expression to give meanings to events that press in on people from the outside world.

What the future held for this project and others like it was unclear in 1999. Some people said the company men had declared they would be back in a year or two to try again, but whether this was a firm intention or a vague suggestion, and what its basis was, we were not able to establish.

Conclusion

This chapter has explored how the Aluni Valley Duna people's basic ways of interpreting their environment and the sources of their prosperity within it have fed into their responses to mining developments in their area. We have shown how, by historical contingency, the Strickland River is both an important focus of Duna mythology and ritual and a site of contentious mining and mining-related activities and events. The result of this conjuncture was a remarkable set of narratives in which the prominent spirit figures of the Payame Ima and the Tindi Auwene were drawn upon in order to construct sets of claims and explanations of events such as the extent of river pollution and the abortive drilling exercise by outside companies. Nothing in the earlier narratives about these spirits exactly prefigured their dramatic roles in the new stories of the 1990s; yet everything in these new stories fits well with the underlying orientations of the older mythology. Indigenous knowledge of myth is like a fertile substratum of soil

5.4 The authors at Ekali; airstrip and oil rig in background (1999). (Stewart/Strathern Archive)

from which under certain conditions new plants may spring forth. It was striking to us that until 1999 no one had foregrounded to us ideas about the Yuro Ima, the spirit woman who swims in the Strickland. When the issue of compensation for water-use came up, her name was on the lips of every senior person with whom we worked.

This page intentionally left blank

Chapter 6

The Duna in Regional Context

The Highlands Provinces of Papua New Guinea became a focus for intensive ethnographic research from the 1950s onward through to the 1990s, when conditions in many parts of them have become too disturbed to allow field projects to be safely pursued. This ethnographic interest stemmed in the 1950s from the very recent "discovery" of the region as a whole by the outside world and the realization that the Highlanders possessed vigorous and colorful ways of life, based on intensive horticultural regimens, elaborate exchanges, intensive religious rituals, and a flair for personal self-decoration with shell ornaments, bird of paradise plumes, and marsupial furs worn on occasions of feasting, peace-making, and gift-giving between rival groups and individuals (see, e.g., O'Hanlon 1989).

These indigenous social patterns were rapidly influenced by the same outside world from which came anthropologists interested in documenting the Highlanders' indigenous lifeways. After the conclusion of World War II the Australian Administrations in what were then the two separate entities of Papua and New Guinea moved quickly to introduce the people to forms of cash cropping, the development of expatriate-owned plantations and their demands for local labor, political education, and the development of Local Government Councils followed by elections for Legislative Assembly positions leading up to Papua New Guinea's national Independence in September 1975. These were all developments that occurred at relatively breakneck speed. Christian missionaries from many different churches had also been at work, in some places from the times of "first contact" in the 1930s or 1940s, altering people's religious practices either sharply or gradually. For the younger generations, both the Administration and the missions set up schools in which the English language was taught as the first step toward the acquisition of the new knowledge needed to become "modern." The narrative of "progress" away from a "primitive" past was introduced as a part of the ideology underpinning all of this introduced change.

How do the Aluni Valley Duna fit in with this overall picture? They are essentially a people whose lives are peripheral to the centers of development. Geographically they live in an area extensively canvassed by mining prospectors, as we have seen, in between two huge mines, Ok Tedi to their west set up in 1984, and Porgera in Enga province to their east begun in 1991. Their imaginations have been filled with information about these projects and their lives changed by them, but no such project had up to 1999 been established among them. This circumstance goes a long way to contextualizing the events we have reviewed that took place in the 1990s in the Valley area. It is important to realize further that Ok Tedi and Porgera are not the only big mining areas in the region. The Southern Highlands as a whole has seen an explosion of these: gas fields in the area of the Huli people, and further to the south around Lake Kutubu extensive finds of oil, bringing in millions of kina of royalties to local groups and an intractable host of social problems and reactions involving escalating conflicts between local groups demanding compensation for all kinds of impacts and both the companies and the provincial and national government bodies. A huge scheme was set underway to build a gas pipeline from the gas fields themselves down to the southern coast of Papua and thence all the way to Townsville in northern Queensland, Australia. Closer to the Duna area there was a frenetic gold rush by indigenous small-scale miners at Mount Kare in Enga Province between 1988 and 1990 (Ryan 1991). Aluni Valley Duna have lived with fragmentary news from all these places in the hinterlands of their own existence since the 1980s.

There is a sharp contrast here with some other parts of the Highlands. One of the first areas to be subjected to intensive change in the Central Highlands was Mount Hagen. Here Catholic and Lutheran missionaries moved in soon after gold prospectors and Administration officers in the 1930s. Apart from some early gold mining at Kuta south of Mount Hagen by Danny Leahy, one of the first explorers from outside, mining did not become significant. Instead Hagen became a center for the production and sale of coffee and tea, both from large plantations and small holdings, and for general commerce, banking, and trading. While the people are dependent on the vagaries of world prices for coffee and on the vicissitudes of disease and weather that affect the crop generally, coffee does provide a fairly regular monetary income to most families within the Province. A necessity for this is the existence and maintenance of vehicular roads on which coffee-buyers can travel regularly. The colonial Administration oversaw the construction of these roads, supplemented later by the efforts of local politicians on behalf of their own people; so that, by and large, the road network has in the past been adequate, although serious problems have arisen in more recent years over funds for road maintenance. Roads are also quite often unsafe because of the depredations of criminals (*raskol* in Tok Pisin) and the dangers of intergroup fighting. Hageners refer to coffee as their "green gold," meaning they rely on it as Southern Highlands areas have tended to do on mining royalties.

In the Aluni Valley no regularly viable vehicular road has penetrated into the area, although the road out from Kopiago station via Horaile and the Tumbudu River was intermittently passable early in the 1990s. Subsequently, up to 1999, for lack of maintenance funds, the section of the road from Horaile to Aluni became overgrown and waterlogged, in places choked by grasses, in others blocked by slippages of mud. At no time, it seems, had it been regularly maintained. In earlier years the road had been used by government officers, but in this regard Kopiago like other outlying areas fell victim to the transition to Independence in 1975 and the sharp reduction in patrolling activities that accompanied this transition, along with the switch to Papua New Guinean nationals as public servants, replacing the mostly Australian expatriates of colonial times. Fewer funds seem to have been allocated for patrolling work and basic road construction in remote rural areas, especially after government income from royalties was adversely impacted by the loss of revenue from the giant Bougainville Copper Mine following disturbances there in 1988. Public servants themselves tend to prefer station-based or urban jobs. The agricultural officer for the Kopiago area was absent most, if not all, of 1991. It was said that he did not care to work on a remote out-station, and no extension work was carried out. Coffee trees, planted many years earlier, grew huge for lack of pruning, and there was little point in harvesting the coffee berries because there was no marketing outlet. This lack of a marketable crop grown on their own land tended to focus people's ideas even more on the mirage of mining wealth.

There were "cargoistic" ideas about roads, too. A rumor swept through Aluni in 1991 that money was coming to forge a brand new road not just from Kopiago to Aluni but from Aluni down the Valley all the way to the Strickland River. Men declared themselves eager to take up the work and they expected loads of shovels and bush-knives to be delivered soon. But nothing eventuated.

So far the picture we have portrayed is one of government neglect of a remote area and a consequential lack of economic development of the kind that could bring the people some sustainable monetary income. In these circumstances many of the men in the Valley had spent periods of time on contract labor elsewhere, either on coastal plantations owned by expatriate companies or more recently in Highlands towns, including Mount Hagen. C. N. Modjeska, an early ethnographic fieldworker whose main work has been carried out at Horaile, found a colony of Duna people established in a squatter settlement in the capital city of Port Moresby. Cities remain a collage of historical memories in the minds of Valley men who have spent time or been based there. Earlier images of carefree times drinking Cokes or beers and listening to popular music are colored by later experiences of violence and danger as cities such as Port Moresby became centers of crime in their squatter areas, largely beyond police control. Given these mixed experiences, it is not surprising that most men return home and settle down to gardening, pig-rearing, hunting, and participating in local exchanges. They bring with them a certain amount of money, which is injected into local economic circuits. Some men do seem to stay away permanently. At Hagu the brother of the resident *anoagaro* leader had been permanently in Moresby since before 1991. A half-brother had often been away at Ok Tedi working as a cook, but by the mid-1990s appeared to be settling in again.

Roads are at best a mixed blessing in rural Papua New Guinea communities. Universally desired by the people and promoted by politicians as the means of progress, they quickly bring to the countryside the vices, as well as the benefits, of the towns. They are essential for the efficient deployment of tradestore goods, health patrols and medicines to stock local Aid Posts, the transport of teachers and pupils into and out of rural schools, and the like. But they also bring criminals, drugs, alcohol, and risky sexual practices that lead to diseases such as AIDS. Incursions of these elements have become the bane of Lake Kopiago station.

At Aluni, even though the road was barely usable, sets of young men frequented it in 1991, walking out from Horaile to take part in night discos that were put on by local people to raise money for projects by charging a gate (entrance) fee. The discos were held in the abandoned buildings of a former primary school where some of the younger adults had in previous years learnt a modicum of English until the teachers, mostly from the Huli area, all left, some said in fear of the local witches. As an experiment in fund-raising the discos were not repeated, because they caused so much trouble. For days before and after them outsiders, male and female, came into the area, playing cards, drinking alcohol, and disturbing local patterns of decorum. It was evident that if the road were improved these categories of people from nearer to the Kopiago station would be regular, and unwelcome, visitors.

The lack of economic development sets problems for the Duna in terms of their desires for wealth. But the same set of circumstances means that their subsistence practices and daily patterns of life have been relatively undisturbed. In the Valley there is a shortage of people rather than a shortage of land. There is no significant population pressure on gardening land overall, and most families have access to adequate amounts of land, whether bush fallow or intensively gardened sweet-potato mounds, to meet their needs. Since only a minor amount of food is marketed at Aluni, and is purchased among the locals themselves, there is no pressure to alienate resources. Large tracts of forest are available at both high and low altitudes for gathering nut pandanus, planting and harvesting fruit pandanus, and collecting mushrooms and other wild fruits, as well as hunting for cassowaries, marsupials, and wild pigs. The people are vulnerable overall to floods, droughts, and epidemics of pneumonia, malaria, and encephalitis/ meningitis, and at these times they suffer for being remote from centers of aid or health services, as happened to them in 1997–98. But on a daily basis they are better off than many people in overpopulated parts who have dedicated their best land to permanent tree crops such as coffee and hitched themselves to an economy in which the relative cost of imported store foods is very high in comparison with crops they can grow themselves. In other words, the Valley people's lack of economic development has to some extent safeguarded their subsistence base and their commitment to maintaining it.

So far we have reviewed largely the economic aspects of change. We turn now first to politics and then to religion. We have seen earlier (chapter 4) how important at local level the role of the *kango* has been and how during the 1990s in each parish in the Valley a few senior men, all endowed with much knowledge from the past, were at the forefront of settling local disputes, handling compensations, negotiating brideprice payments, and the like. In the past, they would also have been prominent in organizing periodic rituals for the *rindi kiniya* complex (chapter 5). Since colonial times, their roles had been placed alongside a whole range of introduced ones: health orderlies, teachers, government officers, local government councillors, and politicians at provincial and national levels. In the Valley, however, these various new roles did not impinge much on a daily basis, and *kango* themselves were eligible to become councillors and politicians. The Kopiago council did not collect poll taxes and hence lacked its own means of raising money, so it was less powerful or effective than it might otherwise have been. In 1991 an elected provincial government was in operation at the Southern Highlands Province headquarters in Mendi, and a local Aluni man held a position within the government structure as well as being an elected member.

Previously an Aid Post orderly at Aluni itself, this politician had been able to use his position to get K20,000 allocated for the Horaile to Aluni road, and this explains why the road was at that time occasionally viable. By 1995 provincial governments, often suspended for misuse of funds, had been abolished, and the national Member of Parliament did not belong to the Aluni side of the electorate. Funds therefore for Aluni dried up, since MPs tend to look after their immediate support bases rather than their electoral constituents as a whole. By 1999 the Valley people were inclined to think that the national government no longer cared about them. They pinned some of their hopes on the establishment of a new Health Centre at Aluni, the installation of which was just beginning when we left the field. Health issues were much on their minds as a result of droughts and forest fires of the preceding years and epidemics of sickness that had followed. The Papua New Guinea Health Department was chronically short of funds to provide even standard medicines to its rural Aid Posts, and the Porgera Joint Venture Company, as a part of its community outreach and attempts to gain acceptance of its activities, had undertaken, through a tax credit scheme, to provide the building for the new Health Centre and to arrange for some personnel to staff it. But the longer term prognostication for this project also would depend on future Company policies and decisions, not on what local leaders or politicians might say (see Banks 1993 for an assessment of such projects).

The major change from the immediate past that the colonial power brought with it was "pacification," the quelling of fights between local sets of people and the encouragement to settle disputes by compensation ceremonies or by recourse to the courts. The Valley had, by all accounts, remained a relatively peaceful place since the 1960s, when administration began, up to the 1990s. Government ability to enforce control was, however, notably weak. The police station at Kopiago was understaffed, and lacked transport and a working radio in 1991. Its situation can hardly have improved in subsequent years, although the Australian army undertook to repair some broken-down station houses as a part of Australian aid. There was no magistrate regularly in residence. Cases referred by the police had to go to Tari or Mendi, both far away. In 1991 people had been expecting that Village Courts, long in place elsewhere in the Highlands, would soon be introduced and would empower their elected magistrates to work with police to control their areas more effectively. These courts did not materialize, and the *kango* were left to their own devices to handle the accusations of theft, sexual wrongdoing, assault, and misappropriation of garden land that formed part of the flow of events (see chapter 4).

As with the absence of a road and the lack of cash-cropping, it is possible to argue that the failure of Village Courts to materialize was not necessarily a bad thing, since the *kango* relied on their own knowledge and networks and their techniques of persuasion and shaming to bring disputes gradually to a conclusion. Often they would hear aspects of, or developments in, the same case, over succeeding Saturdays during a number of weeks or even months before resolving an issue. This was the way of handling matters they had evolved since the 1960s, and if it was cumbersome and imprecise it was also flexible and generally without severe repercussions on themselves or others.

Elsewhere in the Highlands, for example in Hagen, Village Courts since the later 1970s rapidly established themselves as the regular way of handling minor disputes and bringing them to a close. Their major defect was that they could not handle matters of collective violence, and as the problems associated with violence reemerged and became serious in these areas the Village Courts were revealed as impotent. The courts could also be very partial and biased or corrupt, without adequate supervision on a regular basis to check these tendencies. Proceedings themselves became disorderly and rowdy at times. Police were not always on hand to help. Hence the Duna may not be so bad off after all without the Village Courts, at least as these exist in other Highlands areas. What they do need is regular access to a magistrate's court for serious cases they cannot settle themselves and some police backup in sending cases to court; neither of which they had up to 1999.

By 1999 it was evident to us that other influences were spreading at an increasing pace into the Valley. Already in 1991 there had been stories of how certain men were secretly obtaining guns and holding them ready in case they were needed in any renewed kinds of fighting. Beyond Kopiago station to the southeast lay the Duna parishes that stretched to Koroba and the interchange between the Huli and the Duna areas. There were stories of large-scale fights involving guns that had broken out, or were even becoming prevalent in this part of the Duna land. Because of the ramifications of cognatic networks of kinship and the obligations associated with these, some Valley men were linked into these fight areas and might be called on to participate. They would need guns to do so, and they said that they had begun to stockpile these, but without any plans or sense of a need to keep them for conflicts within the Valley itself. Knowing that it was illegal to possess guns without a license from the police, they kept their weapons and their knowledge of each other's weapons secret from outsiders.

By 1999 the situation had changed further. The Valley people must have been aware of the deteriorating conditions of order in places such as Porgera, Enga Province as a whole, Tari and Mendi townships, and Mount Hagen. They must have learned ways of making home-made guns from metal barrels and wooden stocks that had been adopted since the 1980s in Hagen and elsewhere. In addition they would have heard stories of the sophisticated weapons possessed by criminals and by tribal fighters and politicians' militias in Mendi. Further, some troublesome cases had occasioned the gathering of large moots on an interparish basis. Two cases that came up in 1999 while we were in the field both involved suicides under questionable circumstances. Relatives of many parishes gathered to discuss issues of accountability and compensation, and high rates of compensation were set (Strathern and Stewart 2000d). Feelings also ran high, and men began appearing openly not with bows and arrows but with a variety of guns—purchased shotguns but also home-made rifles and home-made pistols. On one occasion we attended a wealth transfer at a marriage near where the other discussions were taking place. We were surprised to see a conspicuous display of guns at this event also. Many of them were decorated with strips of colored plastic, red being a favorite. Young men sat listening to debates about the brideprice, fingering their weapons on their laps. Some men stood at the side with rifles upended in their hands as though they were sentinels. We were told they were on their way to the compensation discussions and had their weapons always by them in case of need. In 2001 we learned from correspondence that actual fighting had broken out in some areas and that one of our main collaborators had been seriously hurt or beaten up in a fracas.

Violence prior to and after elections has for many years been a problem in the Highlands (for an overview on this see Dinnen 2001; Stewart and Strathern 2002d). From newspaper reports prior to and after the national elections in 2002 we learned that the problem had escalated to new levels, with an epicenter of violent activities precisely in Mendi, the administrative headquarters of the Southern Highlands Province. The roots of this situation appear to have lain in a case of severe conflict that had already divided the Mendi area and caused severe disruption in it, following the previous elections in 1997. An electoral dispute between two powerful politicians, Dick Mune and Anderson Agiru, as to which of them had properly won the provincial governor's seat for the Province was followed by Mune's accidental death on the day when he was setting out to hear the verdict of the Supreme Court in Port Moresby on the dispute. His car's brakes failed and he was thrown out of the vehicle and died. His supporters claimed that sorcery by Agiru's supporters, who were afraid the court would rule against Agiru, had caused the event and that it was no accident but a violent political act. Large-scale fighting and numerous acts of vengeance killings followed these suspicions. At a later stage it seems that whole groups became embroiled in fighting and the press reported that two groups in particular were waging a bitter war and finally were going on rampages in Mendi town itself, terrorizing townsfolk, raping women, shooting up and looting shops, and driving through town in vehicles reinforced with home-made armor plating. The police were unable to stop all of this. Prominent politicians lay low. Public institutions ceased to function. The provincial hospital and local high school had to be shut down. Eventually a peace and good order committee was set up to try to end the fighting and negotiate a settlement.

The conflict was not fully over by the time the elections were scheduled to take place. The press reported a roster of electoral abuses, including intimidation of voters, highjacking of electoral boxes, and the insertion of false votes into boxes. Before the election was held in Kopiago, the station manager was reported as saying that he would not allow any planes to land at the Kopiago airstrip, for fear that these would bring violent gangs of supporters, perhaps with weapons and alcohol, into the area. His efforts to control things do not seem to have worked. One candidate, a lawyer, had earlier been kidnapped and held prisoner as a part of the general disturbances around Mendi, until Anderson Agiru apparently arranged his release. When it came to the counting of votes, the manager announced that only three out of about thirty ballot boxes had been turned in and every one of the votes in these had been cast for the sitting Member, Herowa-Agiwa. Not surprisingly, there was skepticism and conflict about whether on such a basis the Member could be declared rightfully reelected. Steps were taken in this case and a number of others to ask for an election writ for a new election to take place. How this affected in detail the Valley people we do not know; but it must have been deeply disturbing and accompanied by intensified factional conflict, making a return of violence the more likely. Since it was widely reported that candidates were surrounding themselves with armed henchmen recruited from youths in their areas, some of the younger Valley men who had in 1999 taken to carrying their guns more openly than before, may have been drawn into the potentially violent processes of electoral competition. By late 2002 the Southern Highlands Province was still in administrative chaos and there was a continuing struggle between the Minister for Inter-Governmental Relations, Sir Peter Barter, who had been appointed as interim Governor of the troubled Province, and other M.P.s for the Province's electorates over who should control funds and policies for the future.

In analytical terms the most important point to keep in mind here is that these episodes of violence do not stem from any overwhelming predisposition on the part of people, nor are they welcomed by the people as a whole. They are rather the result of the specific intertwining of national parliamentary and local politics, interpreted in contexts where contemporary ideas of sorcery and suspicions of trickery between people have become rife. Such processes are beyond the capacity of the *kango*, creative and knowledgeable as they are, to control or even modify. They constitute one of the most urgent problems facing successive governments, such as that headed in 2001 by the veteran politician Sir Michael Somare, who was Papua New Guinea's first Prime Minister in 1975. Solutions to chronic and large-scale bouts of violence have to be developed if the country is to remain a viable nation-state.

Problems on this scale have probably overshadowed other local problems that the Valley people have experienced in the sphere of religion and ritual. As we have seen, indigenous rituals concerned with "repairing the earth" largely ceased with the arrival of the Christian churches, but concern with the issues they dealt with did not. Duna leaders have displayed considerable creativity, as we have argued in chapter 5, by adapting mythological themes to pursue new economic ends in dealing with multinational mining companies. They have been able to do so because Christianity never destroyed the ideology of *malu*, the principle that each group has its own sacred origins that guarantee its rights to land and resources. Either missionaries were unaware of *malu* or they decided not to meddle with this arena of life.

With regard to *rindi kiniya* (the rituals for the earth), the introduced dogma has been that the world is entirely in the hands of God, but for a while there was considerable consternation and confusion about the possibility that the world was in any case about to end at the millennium, in accordance with esoteric teachings of the Book of Revelation in the Bible. Could world's end be prevented by rituals, and if so, what was the right Christian practice to follow? Throughout Papua New Guinea as a whole these same questions were being asked, and the growing political and economic disorder that we have remarked on made them more intense. Nevertheless, the teachings of specific churches differed on this issue. The Baptists, who were predominant in Hagu, held to the view that the day for the world to end was known only to God, and those who preached otherwise were mistaken or deceived. The Seventh-Day Adventists, who had grown in numbers in Aluni in 1997 and 1998, took the line that since we did not know the day or the time, we must always be ready and act *as if* the world were about to end. The Apostolics, influenced by the evangelical and charismatic movements, were inclined to think the end was near, but they were without much influence in Aluni other than with some Kunai parish people resident there. Elsewhere in the Highlands, for example in Hagen, the influence of the Pentecostal Assemblies of God church was widespread and for several years there was a great apprehension and concern that the world was already in the years just before the end, during which only those properly saved would be taken up to Heaven in the Rapture. This idea acted as a very effective recruiting device and rallying cry for the charismatic churches, enabling them to eclipse the more conservative Catholic and Lutheran churches that had been dominant in the Western Highlands since their first entry into the area in the 1930s. Around the time of the millennium itself, the message of world's end began to be transmuted into ideas of a "new world" that was about to emerge. Since that time it is likely that millennial enthusiasms and fears have generally slackened. The crest of this wave of concern missed the Valley Duna, since no Assemblies of God church had been set up there.

One issue in the religious sphere did deeply concern the Valley people. This was the issue of witchcraft. In Duna thought witchcraft (*tsuwake kono*) is power possessed by some people that leads them to desire the consumption of human life-powers (*tini*). Witches are said to kill people in order to eat them in this sense. Serious sicknesses are occasionally attributed to witchcraft. For example, in 1991, when two apparently robust adult women fell sick and died, witchcraft was blamed. Since the establishment of the Baptist church in the 1960s, the church authorities had prohibited people from using the traditional remedy against witchcraft: to hire a ritual expert as a diviner to hold a special stick, the *ndele rowa*, which could lead him to the house of the witch responsible. The witch could then be asked to confess her wrongdoing and remove her witchcraft powers. If this was done, the sick person might survive. If the divination was done after a death, and the witch did not confess, she might be made to climb a tree and hang herself. No doubt concerned about this retributive violence that the *ndele rowa* might bring in its wake, the church had banned its use.

Unfortunately, the church could itself offer no firm remedy against witchcraft. Christian prayers in themselves were not thought effective either to protect or to cure people. Nor did the churches dismiss the idea of witchcraft as nonsense or claim that witchcraft powers were spurious. The problem therefore remained at a deep level, particularly because it was thought that the daughter of a known witch was likely herself to grow up and become one when she had married and experienced sexual relations and gave birth to a child. Witchcraft, people thought, was being reproduced in the world without any means of checking it. The church pastors had difficulty stopping people from seeking out diviners. There was suspicion against some of the prominent *kango* in the Valley, who were all staunch churchgoers and supported the pastors in this stand, since people said that these *kango* were sometimes polygynous (i.e., had two or more wives by customary marriage), and often had one wife who was herself said to be a witch.

Matters came to a head in late 1996 (Strathern and Stewart 2000b: 104–10). Two men out with others on a hunting expedition from Aluni in the grasslands of the Strickland were unexpectedly burnt to death in a fire that swept through a gully where they were trapped. They had hurried on before the rest of the hunting party. People thought that perhaps witches, in the form of wild pigs, were impelling them to rush on in this way to their death. Their grieving relatives took the matter into their own hands and sent for a divination expert from the Strickland area. This man arrived and duly identified four local women as the witches involved. Then these women, under duress, proceeded to confess to the deed. They were threatened and grass fires lit around one of them to burn her body and intimidate her. The witches were required to pay compensation to the kin of the dead, but because of their confessions their lives were spared.

In April of 1998 another witchcraft episode took place. The resident *anoagaro* leader in Hagu and his wife lost two young children, a boy and a girl, in an epidemic of sickness that swept the settlement. The family got little help from the Health Centre at Lake Kopiago, where they had in desperation taken the children, and they were deeply upset. First, the daughter had died with her neck bent back in a way that is supposed to indicate a witch attack. Then on their return home, the little boy died in the same way, in spite of the father killing a pig as a sacrifice and warning any witches not to use their powers against him. Again, after these deaths, one local woman, in-married into Hagu, confessed to being involved with others whom she named as the witches that killed the children, out of jealousy, she said, of the relative wealth of the family and because of a land dispute with them. In the ensuing confusion this woman was accidentally killed by one of her own relatives. The trauma of these events disrupted the settlement enormously. A complicated series of expensive compensation payments had to be made for the death of the woman before the issues surrounding the living women accused of being witches themselves could be settled. Intimidated, these accused women left Hagu.

The churches were involved because they forbid their members to take part in compensation payments relating to witchcraft; yet such payments were obligatory in this context. Seventh-Day Adventists were permitted to contribute to but not to receive from such compensations. The Hagu people who were Baptists and embroiled in the affair were all cut off from communion in the church while events continued. Later, they would be allowed back in. But the situation was difficult, because the leading family in the settlement was involved and it had lost the only successor at the time to its *anoagaro* line. Yet the old pastor of the church was himself the father of the man whose son had died.

The departure of the witches seemed to signal a possibility the situation would quiet down. However, in 2001 we learned that the family had left Hagu and gone down to Aluni, because some of the supposed witches had returned to Hagu. In the meantime another son had been born to this family. They had given to him the name of the one who had died earlier and, in the desire to keep him safe from the vengeful attentions of the returned witches, they had abandoned their houses and resettled far enough away for the witches' powers not to extend. (Witchcraft powers tend to operate locally, on neighbors.)

This case history shows the deep and unresolved quandaries that the fear of witchcraft produces among people. A further, cosmic dimension entered into these fears around the time of the millennium. People said that the resurgent actions of witches were due to the increased energy of Satan in the world, owing to the fight between the powers of "good" and "evil" in the "last days" before world's end. From an analytical viewpoint, we can note that this theological doctrine itself could increase people's suspicions that witches were active and color their interpretations of sicknesses and deaths accordingly. Fear of witches would then increase, much as it did in Europe in the sixteenth and seventeenth centuries when the theological doctrine of the Witches' Sabbat and their putative pact with the Devil was attached to village-level popular ideas of the specific malevolent acts of witches and sorcerers against their neighbors, often in pursuit of some sense of their own resentments for wrongdoings against them.

The supposed complaints against their neighbors of the Hagu women identified as witches are reminiscent of the historical context in Europe, in which those slightly better off than others tended to be the accusers, assuming themselves to be the object of jealousy and therefore likely to be attacked. The complaints are diagnostic also of the context we outlined at the beginning of this chapter: the relative lack of access to money or to goods obtainable by money among the Aluni Valley people. That, and their vulnerability to sickness because of the deficiencies of health care and the demise of their indigenous rituals of sacrifice, has provided a fertile arena for the recrudescence of witchcraft ideas and accusations. While we cannot document an exactly similar circumstance from elsewhere in the Highlands, it is quite possible that the picture we have given here applies not just to these Duna people but more generally wherever a similar conjuncture of historical factors is at work.

Certainly it is clear from a multiplicity of studies, many based on contemporary materials from Africa, that witchcraft and sorcery ideas, long seen as historically transcended phenomena in Europe, are very much a part of contemporary processes of conflict in these contexts (see also Stasch 2001). The basic circumstances involved often include: the presence of uneven development, with increased disparities of wealth between people and between areas; the rise of Charismatic and Pentecostal-style churches in which witchcraft and the ideas of Satan and sin are closely interwoven; and the inevitable conflicts, jealousies, resentments, and projections of ill will that accompany such economic and religious changes (Comaroff and Comaroff, eds., 1993; Comaroff and Comaroff 1999; Moore and Sanders, eds., 2001; Stewart and Strathern 2003b).

Chapter 7

Concepts of Tradition and Change

Ideas of social evolution from "primitive" to "civilized" stages informed the early beginnings of anthropology in the nineteenth century. When these ideas were abandoned with the advent of synchronic studies of how societies functioned at a given time, a different set of problems was created. If the former theories pressed societies into an evolutionary model of change, synchronic theories offered no model of change at all, concentrating rather on continuity and social reproduction. In turn synchronic theories and approaches have given way to the realization to which we referred in our Introduction, that the ordinary state of society is one of change and that all societies have their complex histories, encoded in their own narratives and practices and, in principle, being accessible in archaeological records. Along with this realization goes another, that static and mechanical views of what constitutes a people's "culture" fail to represent this reality of historical change (see Lambek 2003).

At the level of individual actions and interactions between people, the idea that cultural ideas and practices are variable and subject to negotiation brings to the foreground the notions of agency and choice, creativity, strategizing, and manipulation in the pursuit of interest. At the collective level the same idea leads into the study of changing forms of historical consciousness and expressions of identity in political and economic contexts, especially those of colonial and postcolonial experience.

Our Duna case study has been intended to contribute to these trends of analysis and theory. Stressing that ideas are variable and shift over time does not commit us to abandoning entirely the concepts of social structure and customary behavior that informed earlier theoretical orientations in anthropology. It does make it easier to understand how change comes about. The same domain of agency that can lead to change can also lead to a rejection of, or resistance to, changes that are disadvantageous, unwelcome, externally imposed, or greatly out of accordance with local values. An open-ended approach to culture therefore leaves us in a good position to understand either change or resistance to it. We do not assume, by this approach, that the people are fully cognizant of the ramifying effects of all changes on their lives. We do assume that people are on the whole quite conscious of their overall positions in life and attempt to come to terms with and modify or ameliorate these as best they can.

One of the first collections of studies to bring many of these points to the fore in Pacific anthropology was James Carrier's edited collection *History and Tradition in Melanesian Anthropology* (1992). As Carrier notes, the points were not in themselves new, and he offered the volume as a "reminder," but one that was needed at the time (Carrier 1992a: viii). In his Introduction, Carrier first questioned the categorical distinction between Us and Them that tended to underlie earlier representations of people and interpreted their societies "as if they were alien entities that are pure beings isolated from Western influence" (1992b: 3). This criticism clearly harks back to Edward Said's charge of "orientalism," based on a putative contrast between the West (Europe) and the Orient (the Middle East), in which the West is seen as dynamic and changing and the Orient as unchanging, bound in tradition (Said 1978). The result is an exotic representation of the Other. Said's critique was a powerful influence in creating what Marcus and Fischer (1986, second ed. 1999) called the crisis of representation in anthropology, a crisis centering both on problems of change in the societies studied and on the standpoints that anthropologists brought to these questions.

The kind of ethnography that was the focus of critique in Carrier's volume was characterized, he maintained, by a number of features. These include the following:

1. A search for the "authentic," i.e., the representation of the "other" outside of or prior to contexts of change (1992b: 12–13).
2. Essentialization, i.e., the tendency to see societies as states of being rather than in processes of change, as a result of which colonization is seen "as a kind of ontic rupture that ends the village's old, authentic, static state" (p. 14), and custom is seen as a product of a long continuous past rather than recent innovations.
3. Isolationism and passivism, i.e., attempting to clearly mark the village society off from others around it and assuming that when people change they passively accept the ways of Western modernization.

4. Linked to isolationism is unidimensionality, in which observers look at the historical effects of outside influence on a society and misrecognize these as elements of an unchanging traditional life.
5. Finally, mirroring, which consists of setting up an ideal picture of the observer's own culture, as when a Papua New Guinean society is represented as being based purely on a "gift" ideology and Western society on "commodity" ideology. An oversimplification at best, this contrast, which has been used as a rhetorical model by a number of anthropologists, has contributed, Carrier argues, to the idea of complete difference and separation between the people studied and the anthropologist's own world (p. 17).

Carrier does not overstress these points. He recognizes (p. 30) that areas differ in terms of the degree to which they have changed or been exposed to the outside world, and that there are some that have been relatively isolated and others that have experienced more than a century of intensive changes. He concludes that "there is no reason to assume that there is a uniform Western impact on Melanesia" (ibid.). In our study in this volume we have been concerned to delineate processes of change among the Aluni Valley Duna that are comparable to those that have taken place elsewhere but together make up an experience that is at least in part distinctive, even within the wider language area of the Duna population as a whole.

Of the contributors to Carrier's volume, two in particular followed up his valuable remark about unidimensionality and the tendency to see things that are in fact the product of change as evidence of a "traditional" structure. These two were Margaret Jolly and Nicolas Thomas. Jolly in her paper criticized the work of Annette Weiner on the Trobriand people of Milne Bay Province in Papua New Guinea. Weiner had argued that women in Trobriand society represent the timeless cosmic cyclicity of life, symbolized among other ways by their manufacture and distribution of banana-leaf bundles and grass skirts at funerals. Women told Weiner that their bundles were "just like your money" (Jolly 1992: 46) and the bundles could be exchanged for introduced trade goods as well as indigenous foods. One young man criticized the use of these bundles and the amount of money it could take to produce them, a view that Weiner attributed to the notion that he had been away and had begun to think "in Western capitalist terms" (Jolly 1992: 47, quoting Weiner 1980: 274). (Here we see the influence of a gift versus commodity model of society.) Jolly observes in response that it is commonly men who have entered directly into the new commodity economy in Papua New Guinea, and historical conflicts between men and women do often arise out of this situation. This circumstance, she argues, a thoroughly historical one, is what lies behind women's insistence on the importance of the bundles and skirts, rather than any expression of their timeless, cosmic status in the society. Here we may comment that in the process of historical contact, local people themselves often come to make stereotyped statements of difference between themselves and outsiders; and in the Melanesian context, such statements tend to center on the issue of money. Nicholas Thomas quotes the anthropologist Miriam Kahn's work among the Wamirans (also of Milne Bay Province) and the importance they accord to food sharing, which they expressed to her in the contrastive aphorism "We are taro people, but where you come from, people are money people" (Thomas 1992a: 75, quoting Kahn 1986: 14). Thomas argues that such self-characterizations arise out of the contrastive experience of contact itself and would not be expressed in the same way outside of that experience. In other words, the claim to identity being expressed is a claim to difference. By implication also it may be seen as a statement of resistance to the outside world and its ways of life. The claim by Trobriand women that their bundles and skirts are "just like money" can also be seen in the same way, but more as a kind of "separate but equal" ideology, where "just like" means "just as good as, for our purposes—which are different from yours."

The whole question of how money has been received into Papua New Guinea societies marked by gift exchange has been extensively canvassed (see Akin and Robbins 1999 and the individual studies in it including Strathern and Stewart 1999c on Hagen, and a later collection by Breton 2002 and the contribution to it by Stewart and Strathern 2002c). Attitudes to money are much more complex than can be encompassed by stereotypical characterizations, and they change over time also among the same people. One feature that we have picked for emphasis is the well-known tendency in Highlands societies to incorporate state money into the people's own ceremonial transactions. As we have argued for the Hagen area, this creative historical choice, which was neither enjoined nor forbidden by the colonial power, simultaneously domesticated money, making it a part of the local culture, and alienated the people's own control over their social reproduction, since it made this dependent on the means of earning money through wage labor and cash-cropping. This act of incorporation makes it impossible for people simply to contrast themselves as the Wamirans did to Kahn. Their own perceived identity doubly locks them in with the outside world (through their embracing money in their exchanges) and continues to differentiate them from outsiders (who do not have bridewealth, compensation, *moka* exchanges [see Strathern and Stewart 2000a on *moka* exchanges], or the like). Perhaps this complicated and ambivalent situation is closer to the social realities in most parts of Papua New Guinea than the stereotyped contrast made by either anthropologists or local people in certain reified contexts.

It is a different question to ask, Why do people make these statements about themselves? Here the arguments of Thomas and Jolly come directly into play. What people are seeking to do is to make some strategic statements about their identity. Contrasts will serve them in this regard, and so it is to contrasts that they go when they can. In the process, what they do is to reify their own culture, making it a conscious symbol of their overall identity. Culture here becomes something other than a set of practices that people follow on a day-to-day basis. Indeed it may not correspond to daily practice at all. Instead it becomes rather a discursive object, imbued with ideology. Thomas argues this point for Fiji during British colonial control. Focusing on the category of *kerekere*, the practice of asking for assistance from kin and neighbors, he suggests that the salience of this notion for Fijians themselves arose from their self-definitions in colonial and postcolonial times. In colonial times *kerekere* came to be a part of the ethnographic ways in which the colonial power sought to define the Fijians as "others," with a strictly communalistic social order, one that held them in a relatively "primitive" state. Later Fijians themselves had to come to terms with the category as it had been created in colonial ethnography. As Thomas notes, "the meaning of *kerekere* as substantivized practice derived largely from the fact that it was the target of policies that sought to foster individualism and dismantle the communal social order" (1992a: 72). Ironically "the communal social order" was itself partly an artifact of both colonial ethnography and colonial influence on indigenous Fijian society. Though Thomas does not bring this point to the fore, it is important to realize that the Pacific Islander Fijians are also at pains to distinguish themselves from the Indo-Fijians whom the British first brought to Fiji as plantation laborers and who subsequently have become prominent in capitalist commerce and politics.

Thomas's concept of substantivization corresponds closely to the themes found today in literature on "the politics of tradition" and also in the literature on "the invention of tradition." These themes go together since in both instances they refer to the conscious use of statements about tradition for the purpose of forging an identity that can operate in a particular new political and economic context. Roger Keesing (1992: 227–8) points out how categories and ideas introduced and given a pejorative sense in colonial times may subsequently be given a counterhegemonic twist by the people themselves. This argument applies well to *kerekere* as a category: "substantivized" by the colonial authorities as an example of an "undesirable" custom blocking the way to individual development, it was later taken on by the people as an example of their "Fijian way" in opposition to the capitalist world.

This brings us to the question of "resistance" generally (see also here Scaglion and Norman 2000 on this topic; on Fiji see Kaplan and Kelly 1994). Roger Keesing was very interested in the notion of resistance, both because of his own involvement with Marxist forms of analysis and because the pagan Kwaio people of the Solomon Islands, whom he studied for over 30 years, had maintained a long drawn out battle with British colonial authorities and subsequently their own indigenous government. In other words the Kwaio with whom he worked were preeminent resisters against the outside world. As Keesing's study makes clear, this by no means indicates that they simply persisted in their traditional ways and turned their backs on the outside world, even if their own discourse might suggest so. For one thing, they were enmeshed with the outside world as laborers and settlers in the capital city of Honiara. For another, their disastrous engagement with the British colonial authority led to a ramifying set of events that defined much of their subsequent history. In 1927 Basiana, a Kwaio warrior and strongman, who had felt himself insulted by a colonial officer, William Bell, assassinated Bell by smashing his skull with the butt of his rifle at the time of tax collection in his area (Keesing 1992: 65). The choice of the tax collection time for this act indicates Kwaio opposition to the imposition of the head tax. But the more immediate motivation was that a blood bounty had been placed on Bell's head and Basiana intended to claim it.

The colonial government's reaction was extreme. They mounted a punitive expedition, staffed with islanders of groups not friendly with the Kwaio, and the expedition caused great destruction, killing people and livestock, and desecrating ancestral shrines. For years afterward, and to this day, the Kwaio have continued to claim compensation, first from the British and later from their own government, for this colonial depredation. A people embittered in this way might be expected to exhibit continuing resistance to government control. Keesing argues that the situation was exacerbated by the fact that "the colonial officialdom...was organized in a racially constructed 'caste' system in which whites did virtually no physical labor, interacted with 'natives' in limited situations requiring extreme deference, and expressed contempt for the supposed primitivism, dirtiness, savagery, and ignorance of indigenous Solomon Islanders" (1992: 228). Early colonial regimes were certainly more extreme than the latter-day ones that operated in the New Guinea Highlands effectively from the 1950s onward, and this historical difference must be borne in mind here, although definite traces of the practices Keesing describes entered into the world of the Highlanders also. What is striking, however, is the relative *lack* of resistance to colonial control that held in the Highlands in the years leading up to Independence.

Before leaving the Kwaio case, and returning to this point for the Highlands and for the Duna in particular, we should note another factor at work in the Kwaio case: a considerable proportion of the Kwaio themselves had left the pagan heartlands and gone to live in coastal settlements as followers of the Christian missions. Keesing himself recognizes this (e.g., 1992: 138–44). He tends to present the picture, however, from the viewpoint of the pagans with whom he worked, noting for example disputes about the land used by the Seventh-Day Adventist mission for a hospital, which "extended up the hill close to several shrines, some of which were still used by the pagans for sacrifice" (p. 139). One of the missionaries staffing the hospital, Mr. Dunn, was shot as a result of resentment over this issue (ibid.). This act cannot have endeared the non-Christian Kwaio to the outside authorities, any more than the assassination of another missionary in 1911 and the killing of Bell in 1927. Subsequently "many Christians have now become well educated, a good many of them overseas" (p. 141), while "traditionalists in the bush have for the last twenty years remained diehard and defiant" (p. 142). Yet Christians and pagans are in some way locked together in opposition over a shared world of meanings. The pagans know what Christian customs are and vice-versa. Pagans think that the Christians can flout traditional taboos because their Christian God gives them the power to do so. Christians in turn do not disbelieve in the ancestors. They think the powers of the spirits are real enough, but they regard them in some ways as manifestations of Satan. Pagans and Christians in a sense therefore require each other to maintain their own solidarity in opposition to the other (Keesing, p. 142). They share a common heritage yet take "strikingly different stances towards it" (p. 144).

This intense oppositional context, in which the pagan Kwaio feel themselves to be historical victims and beleaguered opponents of change in the name of the ancestors, undoubtedly has led the Kwaio male elders to develop their project of encoding their "Kastomu" as a firm set of rules derived from the past and to be followed in the future. They have thus been engaged in the processes of substantivization and reification that Margaret Jolly and Nicholas Thomas have identified.

This process is a political one, because it is generated out of political oppositions that have grown up historically. It is not so much that traditions are "invented" here, but rather that they are made more rigid and codified in an attempt to preserve them against change. As Keesing recognized, such a codification goes against the spirit of customary practices from the past, which far from being rigid were flexible and open to change. The paradox, and the irony, involved here, then, lies in the fact that people themselves come to recreate their culture in an image that anthropologists who study them have come to reject on theoretical grounds. The historical fact is that changes do happen and cycles of such reification may be followed later by more flexible definitions and approaches, depending on circumstances and who remains in power. In the case of the Kwaio, "Kastomu" was very much a concept of the older traditional leaders, though it could be used as a general rallying cry to oppose Christians and outsiders. Another generation of leaders might decide to take a different line. The local leaders in Keesing's time, however, seem to have been locked in their concern for the past and determined to get a settlement for their historical wrongs as a basis for their existence in the future.

No issues on such a catastrophic scale have concerned the Duna, or indeed other Highlands peoples. Their encounter with colonialism came later, when as we have noted colonialism's own culture had somewhat changed. Like the Kwaio they have been a small, peripheral population on the edge of bigger economic developments. Unlike the mountain Kwaio, but like most other Highlanders in the same situation, they have consistently tried to reach out to any opportunities offered to them.

They appeared, on the face of it, rapidly to accept administrative control in the 1960s and just as rapidly to abandon their own complex rituals in order to adopt those of Christianity. Such actions can be understood only as a result of a desire to obtain the benefits they thought would flow from their acquiescence to colonial hegemony. By the same token, if the benefits are not obtained, we would expect disgruntlement to set in. Change has also neither been so wholesale nor so voluntaristic as this description might suggest. With regard to initial pacification, the superior firepower of the government's own forces would be enough to encourage the Duna to stop fighting, although not necessarily to accept that they would do so permanently. They would continue to accept new institutions and ways of handling disputes as long as these worked well for them. It is interesting that along with abandoning organized interparish fighting they ceased their practices of aggressive *ndekao* sorcery between enemies, carried out by professionals on behalf of their groups. It was as though this kind of sorcery was another kind of weapon that could now be abandoned—or placed in storage. Most recently, as we have seen in chapter 6, the further stages of this history are being "written." As life becomes more "lawless" and government control weaker and more uncertain, so the weapons have come back and with them the propensity to fight and the modes of organization to support this. Guns make this process the more potentially lethal and terrifying to the mass of people. Pacification begins to appear as a historical mirage or interlude rather than a permanent institutional change. This was not historically inevitable. More effective government and a greater spread of benefits could perhaps have forestalled it.

The case of Christianity is different from that of pacification. Many observers have noted how deeply rooted the idea of Christianity has become for many populations, urban and rural, in Papua New Guinea and throughout the Pacific. The studies, for example, in Barker's edited collection of 1990, Robbins, Stewart and Strathern, eds. (2001), and Stewart and Strathern, eds. (1997, 2000) all point in this direction, and ethnographies such as those by Gewertz and Errington (1991), Errington and Gewertz (1991), LiPuma (2001), Knauft (2002), Robbins (n.d.), and Strathern and Stewart (2000a) attest to this also from a number of areas. Equally, such observers have noted that the kind of Christianity that tends to have the greatest appeal has been Pentecostalist and Charismatic. Aspects of this lend themselves to blending with local forms of custom, even though on the surface of things Pentecostalists declare that they make a complete break with "pagan" culture and see all aspects of it as connected with Satan. Dreams, prophecies, omens, figures of speech with concealed meaning, and marvelous happenings all form a lively part of Pentecostalist activities, and all of these have their close analogs in indigenous cultural patterns. But whether the specific form of Christianity is Pentecostal and Charismatic or not, in all cases there tends to be a strong local stamp placed on Christian ideas and practices. While in many places, as a result of early missionary rhetorical teachings, people have learned to declare that in their pre-Christian past they lived in darkness and that now their lives are completely different (see., e.g., Errington and Gewertz 1991: 71–96), such statements are usually made in formal contexts for outsiders to hear. Internally, as Dalton (2001: 122) points out, people may express more complicated and nuanced views. For instance, in the Rawa area of Madang Province where Dalton worked many young men "expressed dismay when they learned of some of the 'good' customs associated with the men's spirit house—particularly the expressive playing of a pair of male and female flutes—had been given up for the sake of modern village unity...some of the old men of the village told me they felt the white man had 'taken their power away' and for that reason would not divulge their knowledge about the old religious institutions" (Dalton, pp. 122–23). It was in the same spirit that in 1967 a young man in Pangia in the Southern Highlands inveighed privately against the Lutheran Mission in his area for taking away all their old spirit cults and wondered if they would ever revive them. Counterhegemonic remarks of this kind abound in the records, along with formal statements about progress and betterment that find expression on public occasions. And Christian concepts over time can alter people's basic concepts, for example regarding "body" and "mind" (Bamford n.d.).

The kinds of attitudes people express depend on the length of time a mission has operated in the area, how its personnel have dealt with the people or integrated with them, what its own church doctrines are, and many factors of this sort. The memories that are constructed out of these experiences also differ.

Jeanette Mageo (2001) has pointed this out, indicating as do contributors to her volume that memory is also selective and may leave out things that no longer suit with people's ways of thinking in the present. For instance, early experience of missionary activities may be quite traumatic. In the Duna area, as in Pangia also (see Stewart and Strathern 2001b), this early contact period in the 1960s involved the missionaries and/or the indigenous evangelists deliberately flouting local taboos, challenging the powers of spirits in the name of God, and urging people to destroy their sacred objects such as spirit stones on grounds that they were not just "evil" but dangerous and must be destroyed. In Pangia in the 1960s these memories were fresh and still recounted with a sense of trauma and puzzlement (Stewart and Strathern n.d.b). Among the Duna in the 1990s who had experienced these same sorts of processes, the memories were muted, and the people also progressively revealed that they had quite a few of these old spirit stones around and a great deal of the rosters of mental knowledge that went with them.

Over time people may edit out episodes of violence in their own history. This may go along with their construction of Christianity as their own popular religion, voluntaristically accepted from the beginning. Barker, in reporting on the long established Anglican church among the Maisin people of Collingwood Bay in Oro Province, Papua New Guinea, stresses the consensual and gradual way in which this church established itself from 1891 onward, with a relatively tolerant philosophy, no extensive or overt economic agenda or resources, and a predominant use of Melanesians from elsewhere as the immediate evangelists (Barker 1990: 176–7). He contrasts this benign gradualism with the traumas of the early pacification process in which the government police came and shot three men and forcefully coopted leading men as village constables. Nevertheless, he points out that mission and government needed each other and were generally mutually supportive. This history seems accurate enough; but perhaps the Maisin themselves have edited out over time early phases of mission activity with more conflictual aspects to them, simply because the Anglican church became over time identified with their whole way of life, until the more recent arrival of Pentecostalist believers among them and the factional conflicts that ensued as a result.

The Duna tend to maintain incorporative and supportive narratives of both early administration and early mission activities among them. Government officers stopped fights, built roads, jailed people, and brought supplies of valuable shells and later money. Missionaries gave authoritative directions on which customs should be given up and which could be maintained. The Duna's complaint is rather that the people who came in these projects left and have not returned, leaving the locals only partly in control of the new knowledge and resources they need to achieve the kind of changed existence the outsiders had advocated. They do not entirely condemn their own past way of life, and just beneath the surface they are much concerned about the loss of the *rindi kiniya* rituals to keep the earth and the cosmos in good repair. This concern with the loss of *rindi kiniya* defines the dominant mode of counterhegemonic thinking about the world among thoughtful Duna people. It is relatively muted and not used openly to challenge the influence of pastors and church officials. But it is there, and has the potential to develop further in any situation of crisis, as did the discourse about witchcraft and the need to combat it in the late 1990s. At that time, as we have seen, the authority of the pastors and the *kango* was successfully challenged, leading to a renewed recourse to older divination practices.

The "politics of tradition" has to be understood, then, as always related to a moving present, the time at which tradition is invoked rather than the past that it evokes. As Laurence M. Carucci notes, "Recollections look outward to link interpretations of the past with occurrences of the present" (2001: 82). This is demonstrated very clearly by the new narrative of the Tindi Auwene spirit that emerged among the Aluni Valley Duna in 1999, as we have discussed in chapter 5. In this light, statements about "tradition" have to be understood as statements about the present, turning the diachronic dimension back into the synchronic. Perhaps this is one of the main reasons that since the early 1990s anthropologists have focused much critical attention on the concept of tradition, starting from the "invention of tradition" approach of Hobsbawm and Ranger (1983), and moving to the more nuanced and complex debates initiated in the work of Jocelyn Linnekin (1983, 1991), Linnekin and Poyer (1990), Margaret Jolly (1992), Nicholas Thomas (1992a, 1992b), and Jolly and Thomas (1992), among others (e.g., Guo 2003; Hoskins 1998; Keesing and Tonkinson 1982; Schiller 1997). As Jolly and Thomas (1992: 241) point out, already by the time of their guest-edited collection for the journal *Oceania*, there was a burgeoning literature on the politics of tradition, in Asian as well as Pacific studies, mostly dealing with the kind of conscious objectification of custom that exercised Keesing in his Kwaio studies. Thomas (1992b: 223) observes that this objectification usually involves a celebration of tradition but it also allows its inversion, i.e., "a rejection of what was customary in favor of its antithesis." As a result, "the dichotomized structure of neo-traditional culture consistently generated ambivalence toward, and occasionally outright rejection of tradition" (ibid.).

This is a significant observation. Making a conscious object out of tradition facilitates either its promotion or its rejection (see Rohatynskyj 2001 for an interesting application of this point). Here we can see the same mechanisms at work on either side of a divide. Missionaries and latter-day indigenous church officials tended to dichotomize the old, pagan ways of life as bad and the new, Christian ways as good. Revivalists promoting indigenous culture may simply invert these propositions, accepting the dichotomy between old and new but labeling the old good and the new bad. The same relationship held between the pagan and Christian Kwaio whom Keesing studied. This point gives us a key to understanding many of the ongoing debates about change that take place among Pacific islanders themselves. As anthropologists standing back from these debates, it is important for us to question the terms of the dichotomy itself. First, dichotomies between the old and the new reify both rather than seeing them as fluid, historical practices. Second, the dichotomy implies an absolute opposition, which again does not correspond to the complexities of real life. And third, it follows from this that the problem of change is presented as a hard choice to embrace either the new or the old. As Thomas argues, modified forms of subsistence and exchange-based economies are not necessarily incompatible with farming for cash or taxes, but they may tend to be represented as such in arguments between classes in a new state, colonial or postcolonial (Thomas 1992b: 223).

Dichotomizations of this kind, introduced from the outside, have been a part of the historical experience of the Duna since the 1960s.

Pacification was the antithesis of warfare, and Christianity the antithesis of indigenous religion in the rhetorical narratives of the government officers and missionaries who came to work among the Duna. Such forms of classification allow little room for nuanced perceptions of what may be compatible or advantageous in "custom" by comparison with "modernity." And the negative evaluation of the past is likely to generate over time its dialectical opposite, a return to a positive evaluation of traditions previously denigrated, especially if "modernity" does not bring with it material results promised or imagined.

In practice the Highlanders have had available to them more than this model of exclusive choice between "tradition" and "modernity" in reflecting on their experiences of change since colonial times. In Hagen one dominant mode of thought in the 1970s and 1980s was what we may call the "two-handed model." The Kawelka leader, Ongka-Kaepa, expressed this model when he spoke of "law and custom together, we hold onto both of them, law with the right hand and custom with the left, we will not give up either of them, the two will stay in a competitive relationship with each other." Here "law" stands for introduced development, change, "modernity"; "custom" for indigenous ways, continuity with the past, "tradition." Ongka expresses his belief, or his wish, that both should remain a part of people's lives, existing in a kind of productive dialectic. Hageners today still seek to achieve this end.[1]

The contributors to Jolly and Thomas's collection bring up two further points. Robert Foster has concentrated on the concept of commoditization, the idea that societies and nation-states influenced by capitalism come increasingly to reproduce themselves through the production and exchange of commodities. Foster (1992: 285) argues that in Tanga, New Ireland, where he worked, the category of *kastom* ("custom") "acquired its current contours as the result of a struggle over the control of cash-cropping. This struggle pitted a small number of "big-men" who promoted and directed local copra societies against a large number of men who increasingly favored individualized (household) rather than 'cooperative' methods of cash-cropping" (loc. cit.). In this conflict, people tried to define cash-cropping as a domain of *bisnis* ("business") antithetical to *kastom*, which was seen as the proper domain of the "big-men." In this model of change we see a similar contrast to Ongka's distinction between law and custom, and an attempt to confine big-men (such as Ongka himself in his society) to the realms of tradition, with its rules of reciprocity outside of the sphere of money. In particular Tanga big-men dealt with mortuary rituals, just as Hagen big-men dealt with *moka* exchanges. Ongka, in his formulation, attempted to see the two sides of life as symbiotic, if competitive. The Tanga formulation suggests instead a struggle between generations or sections of the community. Since mortuary rituals were crucial for reproducing the Tanga matrilineages over time (by reordering and reasserting ties to productive land), some Tanga men accordingly saw cash-cropping as a threat to the principle of matrilineal descent on which their society had been based. Foster recognizes that this struggle is itself a product of change, and that the Tanga people's concept of an opposition between their traditional society and the forces of capitalist change is very similar to, if not identical with, the models of Melanesian society that some theorists, using the distinction between gifts and commodities as a classificatory device, have propounded (Foster 1992: 287, referring to Thomas 1992a, at that time still in press).

By implication, Foster is arguing, as we do, that the dichotomies themselves, rather than being historically accurate representations, are the motivated products of the experience of change and are rhetorical devices that people appeal to in the course of political and economic conflicts. As anthropologists, it is worth reemphasizing, what we have to do is to recognize that past and present, custom and development, do not actually exist in a simple dichotomous way. Not all things of the past are given up even if people say they are. The present always incorporates aspects of the past, whether people are conscious of this or not. Further, when people do attempt to revive past customs they do so in changed contexts, which change the meanings and value of the customs involved. Those who reject and those who promote "tradition" may be equally involved in the processes of change that surround them. One thing that is certain is that change is always occurring in societies.

Ton Otto adds a further note of complexity to these discussions. From the study of the people of Baluan Island in Manus Province, he notes that the people's discourse revolves around different institutional domains, which the Baluanese themselves refer to as "government," "custom," and "Christianity" (Otto 1992: 270). Here we see an indigenous classification of spheres that appears intended to keep evaluations in the different spheres separate, and in another sense to keep all the spheres going without them entering into disruptive conflict. And Otto notes that "when social practices move across domain boundaries, the different idioms may come into open conflict" (p. 276). For example, he cites the case where a local "big-man" or *lapan* attempted to use a customary ritual to coerce people into supporting a particular candidate in a parliamentary election: an attempt that raised protest and disagreement. Those who disagreed told the *lapan* that *kastam*, based on obligation, could not enter into elections, which must be based on freedom of choice.

In practice, of course, because of the overall involvement of the people with the world, these spheres or domains do interact and influence one another. But it is interesting to see people's attempts to keep them separate as a way of controlling the disruptive effects that change may bring. It is interesting also that people do sometimes bring domains creatively together without conflict occurring, or even as a way of handling conflict. A prominent way of dealing with conflict in Hagen has become the use of Christian prayers before meetings at which issues are to be discussed. The message of Christianity to avoid violence in conflict is brought to bear on the situation, thus bringing together "church" and "government."

People's ideas about "custom" may, then, differ according to the domain under discussion. Custom may be good for certain village contexts, but not for national politics. Alternatively, themes drawn from custom may precisely be drawn on in order to bolster identities in the regional or national sphere (Otto and Thomas 1997; Foster, ed. 1995; Borofsky, ed. 2000). Christianity, as a new form of custom, is also often drawn into the national sphere in this way, bolstered by the idea that Papua New Guinea as a whole is a "Christian country." Or figures from indigenous mythology are adduced in order to occupy a new semantic space. Jeffrey Clark (1997: 85) suggests that for the Huli people of the Southern Highlands (neighbors of the Duna and culturally related to them), one particular figure, the water-spirit or Iba Tiri, had come to represent the "unsatisfactory nature of Huli experience with the state." The Iba Tiri in Huli thought is a trickster figure mediating between the good and the bad, so he is a suitable enough figure for an ambivalent relationship of this kind. The comparable figure of the Ipa Tsiri (*tsiri*) in Duna folk-perception shows some of the same characteristics (he is the giver of wealth in cowries, as we have seen, but he also can cause floods, possess people, and demand heavy sacrifices on pain of throwing ashes at people and making them sick). So far, the Valley Duna have not brought the Tsiri figure into the domain of the state, as Clark speculates the Huli have done. This may be largely because they have not been greatly concerned with the state other than to criticize its *lack* of presence in their lives. They have, however, explicitly brought their Tindi Auwene figure into the domain of public relations with big businesses, as we have seen.

Throughout this running set of observations we have continually sought both to explore the main dimensions of the "politics of tradition" focus in recent anthropological studies and to explain how these are or are not applicable to our Duna case study. We have had in our minds the search for illuminating comparisons, whether based on similarities or differences, ascertainable patterns capable of understanding and explanation. We have characterized the Valley people's geopolitical situation as peripheral to the major effects of capitalist change, and pointed out that this is not entirely to their disadvantage even if it runs counter to some of their desires. They also have made historical choices comparable, that is, similar, to those of many Highlands people, first embracing pacification then questioning it as forces of violence have emerged on their own geographical horizons; and abandoning many of their rituals and customs as a part of the process of taking up Christianity, but shaping the new religion to some of their own ends and recreating their own stories of origins in contexts of negotiations with mining companies (Stewart and Strathern 2002a). Our materials here bear comparison with a handful of other recent studies on historical change in the Highlands and "mountain Papuan" areas. We take four such studies for a brief consideration in our next chapter. In each example we will use the study in order to make further observations about the Duna case.

Conclusion

"The politics of tradition" theme in contemporary anthropology has proved a fruitful way in which to examine the ironies and complexities of change in the lives of people. Tradition may be invoked either as the source of good or as the source of evil in the past. The rhetorics

7.1 *Anoagaro* man of Hagu with decorations for Independence Day, showing the scenery at his back and the bow and arrows in his left hand. He has a necklace of cowrie shells (1991). (Stewart/Strathern Archive)

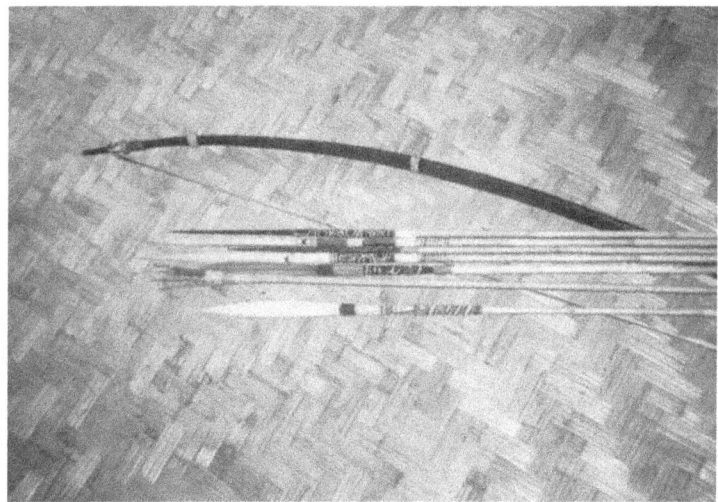

7.2 A black-palm bow and a set of arrows with varied points for spearing pigs or shooting birds. The arrow hafts are decorated in black, white, and red. One design conventionally represents "bird's entrails" (1998). (Stewart/Strathern Archive)

of government and missions have tended to cast these rhetorics in a dichotomous way, which the people themselves have taken up as models of and for their own senses of identity. The Duna whom we know have participated in these processes. They early on accepted pacification and embraced the new religion of Christianity, abandoning many of their own rituals. They never, however, completely accepted a notion of their past as "bad" or the present as "good." They have refashioned many ideas from the past, such as *malu* narratives of origins, giving them a use in their contemporary world of dealings with the outside. And they have tentatively put together elements of Christianity and indigenous custom. The greatest threat to the stability of their existence comes from the kinds of disturbed political conditions of their province that emerged during the national parliamentary elections of 2002.

In their own creative efforts to deal with questions of change in their lives, the directions they have followed correspond well to those concisely articulated for the Pacific region in general by Richard Feinberg in his collection of studies on the politics of culture in the Pacific Islands (co-edited with Laura Zimmer-Takakoshi): "Islanders...draw on their experience to fashion and refashion concepts of tradition, transforming and revalorizing vital concepts and practices in the process" (1995: 94).

This page intentionally left blank

Chapter 8

Empowering the Past?

Constructions of the past have emerged as a crucial theme in the study of change in Pacific societies. As we have seen, the past is construed and reconstrued in accordance with people's shifting interests and concerns. People empower their past when they want to invoke it as a means of legitimizing or achieving their current aspirations. In this case the past becomes a resource for them to tap into and in so doing they reshape it. Different periods of the past may come into play in this way at different times, or the same periods may be given very different evaluations. In the opposite scenario, people reject their past, or a portion of it, in order to praise or reinforce their ties with powerful forces in their contemporary world. In these contexts the past is seen as bad and the narrative invoked is one of rupture with the past and of progress away from it, often seen as "modernization." When disillusionment sets in, people may shift again into the other modality, in which the past is again empowered as an inspiration or model for the future. Neither schema need unequivocally hold. In practice both may be employed at the same time in relation to different domains of life. The people may see some aspects of the past as good and others as more questionable or to be rejected. A particular area, because of its history, may be more inclined to one view than the other. Whether this amounts to "plural modernities" or different responses to common forces of "modernization" is difficult to determine (compare the studies in Knauft 2003 on this point).

In this chapter we look at four historical ethnographies, recently published, in relation to this general scheme, and use them to make some further observations about the Duna and the process of change in general.

The Simbu: A Mountain Valley and Beyond

The first of the studies we choose is Paula Brown's 1995 monograph, *Beyond a Mountain Valley*, based on her long-term fieldwork since 1958. Paula Brown's work is of interest here because she herself observed many changes over time and because from the start she was concerned with problems of change as well as with ecological adaptation and the impact of cash-cropping, based on the population of the Naregu tribal group around Mintima in Simbu Province. As Brown points out, although she had from the first intended her study to be "a running chronicle of Simbu life," she did not in the 1950s and 1960s anticipate the changes of the 1970s and 1980s: "a new phase of tribal warfare, incipient stratification, accusations of witchcraft, Papua New Guinea Independence, and the electoral practice of candidates for office" (1995: xiii). She notes also that her later work was increasingly concerned with the people's interactions with outsiders (ibid.). These same vicissitudes and changes of focus have followed every long-term fieldworker in the region.

The Simbu are a relatively large and prosperous language group in the central highlands of Papua New Guinea. Intensive horticulturalists with in many places high population densities, they also in the past held elaborate ritual cycles and ceremonies celebrating their production and slaughter of pigs for visitors, at which they decorated themselves elaborately with wealth goods, shells, plumes, and furs, and made complex speeches about local politics. Their main ceremony was the *bugla yungu* pig festival, held at intervals of years. The Kuman language speakers, the predominant group, numbered some 50,000 people, divided into 55 tribes, already in the 1930s (Brown 1995: 13).

Brown gives us a detailed history, based on both archives and oral testimonies, of contact between the Simbu and the Australians, beginning with the first explorations and patrols of the 1930s. Like many others, she notes the apparently rapid response the Simbu gave to the imposition of pacification. Leaders who spoke of themselves as warriors in the past reported to her proudly that they had become workers for the government because "good things have come from the white man" (p. 139). In this narrative the time of the warriors is given a heroic status, but the time of the colonial government is seen as good because of the material wealth it brought. The narrative is typical of the Central Highlands, including Mount Hagen west of the Simbu, in the 1960s. In Simbu a small cloud was visible on the horizon: disputes over land had emerged, precipitated by the Administration's policy of freezing land boundaries between groups at the point in time of establishing administrative control (surely a case of misplaced synchrony, since these boundaries were merely artifacts of the history of fighting and exchanges between clans and tribes that would shift over time). The competition over land was much increased both by population growth and by the widespread introduction of coffee growing for cash.

When Independence came, the Simbu leaders heavily invested in political competitions for office, using lavish expenditures at parties that mimicked the pig festivals as occasion for soliciting and garnering support and shaming rivals. Cartons of beer became units of gift-giving on these occasions. The Simbu politics of wealth and prestige was imported into parliamentary contests and helped to form the general culture of wealth that has subsequently shaped a good part of Papua New Guinea politics. The attractions of politics led many people to contest elections, and voters also rapidly became dissatisfied with those they elected, for failing to keep their (unrealistic) promises. Brown notes that by 1987, "twelve years after independence, most of the elders and the middle-aged colonial cohort found fault with postcolonial life. They praised the kiap order, the leaders of the past, and distrusted the new leaders" (p. 231). These views are exactly mirrored by those of leaders in Hagen at the time (see Strathern and Stewart 1999b, the life story of Ongka-Kaepa). Younger leaders at the time were better educated and highly competitive.

Brown ends her study on an upbeat note, but with a warning inside it. She suggests that with education and further economic development "the Simbu capacity for competition may make the highlands a center for advanced technology" (p. 257). She speculates that "the heroes of such a transformation" may emerge from a newly educated generation. But "the dark side of the future involves existing warfare, robbery, gangs, and political venality" (ibid.). She expresses confidence that the new heroes "will deal with these issues just as the old ones confronted the problems of their times" (p. 257).

This narrative of the Simbu is in many ways typical for the great central sweep of the Highlands language groups from the Gahuku-Gama near Goroka in the east to the Enga and the Huli in the west; in other words, for the bulk of the Highlands region. These central areas have experienced the greatest economic development and prosperity by comparison with more peripheral groups. They have also been beset by the most severe problems of disorder, violence, and crime. If the Aluni Valley Duna had not in 1999 been outside of the ambit of cash-cropping, roads, urbanization, and direct involvement in national political competition, they also would more quickly have experienced these same problems. As it was, the signs of future trouble were already there, though muted by comparison with the Simbu.

"Modernity" Among the Gebusi

Bruce M. Knauft studied the Gebusi people in 1980–1982 and again in 1998. His experience of the Gebusi world is unlike that of Paula Brown and some others who made regular if shorter visits to their field areas over a span of years. Knauft's long-term interest in the people he studied has been punctuated by two intensive periods of work during his own professional lifetime. He presents the results of this restudy in the form of "before" and "after," 1980 in contrast with 1998, exploring what he has identified as a form of "vernacular" modernity that characterized Gebusi life in 1998. Vernacular here refers to the variations in ways that people aspire to be "modern," although central to this aspiration in many parts of the Highlands is often the desire for economic development and money that can be spent on particular lifestyles.

The Gebusi are a small population living in rainforest conditions on the Strickland Plain in the Western Province of Papua New Guinea. In 1980 they numbered only about 450 persons, no more than a single large clan group in terms of the Simbu, yet they were a relatively distinct cultural and linguistic group. They lived in scattered long-houses, from which they ventured to forage, hunt, process sago, and make gardens in wide areas of forest to which they had access. They kept few pigs. Population density was low. Their lives focused on obtaining food and sharing it and on a complex of ideas centered on suspicions of killings by sorcery or witchcraft that surrounded every death, seances that were held in order to contact the spirit world and identify witches, and raiding parties to take vengeance on those identified. Ritual feasts held between groups were marked by elaborate and distinctive forms of decoration, dancing, and singing. Gebusi life alternated between an emphasis on conviviality or "good company" and the "violence" that accompanied vengeance parties. Vengeance killings meant that the Gebusi had a comparatively high homicide rate, though they had none of the large-scale warfare that took place in the Central Highlands.

They first came under administrative control in the 1960s, and were relatively amenable to influence, probably because prior to contact they had been vulnerable to incursions by the more powerful Bedamini people, whom the Australians spent much effort in "pacifying" (Knauft 1985: 13). After a short period of time in which they had some access to earning money, after 1975 these opportunities decreased (p. 14). Warfare and raiding had been stopped, and the people had considerable desires for trade goods (p. 15). They had some experience working for companies drilling for oil or looking for gold, but little development in their own area.

By 1998 the people with whom Knauft had worked had relocated to a site near the Nomad station airstrip, calling this by the name of their old village settlement, Gasumi, and adding "Corners" to it, indicating that it now conceptually occupied a corner of the station area (actually a 30-minute walk south of the station itself). This process of relocation is quite typical for some remote areas where a new facility such as a government or mission airstrip is established. In the Central Highlands also, when the Highlands Highway was first built many people shifted from the hills to live closer to it, in order to sell and buy produce and claim land near it. Over time these areas can become overcrowded and violent. Such has apparently not yet happened at Nomad. The Gasumi people relocated quite willingly, in order to experience "a life with an airstrip, churches, a school, markets, sports teams, an aid post (health clinic) and a government office" (Knauft 2002: 23). They still have the forest and the river in which to forage, hunt, and fish, so their life must participate to some extent both in new and in old activities. Proximity to the station, however, brings with it a continuous desire for Western goods, foods, and opportunities (Knauft, p. 43).

Homicides among the Gebusi had fallen by six-fold between 1980 and 1998, and Knauft reports that there had been no killings in the community he studied for a decade up to 1998. But the shift to Gasumi Corners had come about because of an outbreak of sorcery accusations and a number of related events that Knauft describes in detail (pp. 68–79). Somewhat ironically, the national government officers who had replaced the Australians at Independence had come to be involved in these sorcery trials because, unlike the Australians, they took sorcery seriously and believed in it. But they could not countenance the traditional vengeance killings of reputed sorcerers. Instead they placed them in jail. Another man who did take revenge for the supposed death of his wife by assault sorcery was sent to jail in Port Moresby, from which he came back as a strong convert to Christianity. He and others became advocates for a "new way," in which vengeance killings were to be given up by the people's own choice (not just by police coercion) as a part of their aim of achieving "modernity."

Social changes were thus a result of a desire for the advantages of a new world, not simply a product of control or fear. Knauft also suggests early on (p. 8) that the Gebusi see these changes "as a process of direct exchange (*sesum degra*) in which customs or spirits that are 'backward' or 'backsliding' are replaced by those that are 'new' and 'come up on top' " (compare also pp. 38–9). This terminology comes from the new Christian context. The jailed killer who came back from

Port Moresby declared, "my old spirit has been exchanged in direct reciprocity for Jesus" (p. 78). The historical process involved entails what Knauft calls a kind of passivity and submissiveness to authority, but in counterpoint to this is the very active desire for tangible benefits, as we have argued for the Duna case. As with the Duna, it is not that people no longer believe in the old spirits. They have just put them to one side. And they use a rhetoric of progress that again must be derived primarily from Christian teachings in which aspects of their old "culture" such as sorcery and vengeance killings are seen as shameful and retrograde: the inversion of tradition, in Nicholas Thomas's terms. Gebusi passivity is marked by the attribution of all knowledge, responsibility, and vengeance-taking to God, and justice is deferred until the afterlife. The Duna certainly learned this same rhetoric; but, as we have seen, for them it did not quite deal with the problem of witchcraft, since Christian prayers were not thought strong enough to combat this. Some ambivalence over such issues perhaps also remains with the Gebusi people of Gasumi Corners, especially since their new community was formed out of the breakup through sorcery trials of their former place. The doctrine of sin has been drawn on by Gebusi in order to insulate themselves from the dangerous aspects of their past. Sorcery and killings of sorcerers were both labeled as sin. Sin must be, in this rhetorical voice, avoided and it will be judged by God, not by the courts or the police. Knauft has an illustration of this point of dogma in a reproduction of a church poster in which "God takes retribution against sorcerer-like individuals" (opposite p. 119). The picture shows the sorcerer's whitish-colored spirit stretching down into Hell while his kin mourn and demons greet him with spears while other sinners burn in fire. It is in a sense the Devil himself, then, who punishes the sorcerer.

At Nomad station Evangelical, Seventh-Day Adventist, and Catholic denominations of the Christian churches were all present, but 60 percent of the Gasumi community were Catholics, and most of the preaching was done by local evangelists, some from the Ok area (which lies west of the Duna, quite far away from Nomad) (Knauft, p. 141). The evangelists' sermons are the prime means of ideological teaching that seeks to form and reform Gebusi ideas of the past and the future. They also are a means, Knauft argues, by which "Christian" cosmology at Nomad "links adherence to God's work with the moral progress and beneficial goodness of a modern world" (p. 149). In this, "sinister forces of tradition and divisiveness are pitted against Christian devotion, obedience and the goodness of self-discipline" (ibid.). The Papua New Guinean nationals who are public servants at the station reinforce this viewpoint, apparently, since they are all churchgoers and church supporters. As Knauft comments, these outsiders "are imbued with the authority of modern agency while villages carry the onus of failure and individual inadequacy" (ibid.). Most people, Knauft adds, go to church regularly "and accept the authority of the pastors" (p. 152). Young men seem to be a little ambivalent about it all, torn between a desire to be good church members and equally strong tendencies to talk about drinking beer, which Knauft tells us is not available at Nomad, and attending dances and feasts (p. 156). The Seventh-Day Adventists were stricter than the Catholics about modes of behavior and their pastors stressed the idea that the Second Coming of Christ would soon occur, so that "the importance of hurrying one's conversion to beat the passage of time emerges centrally in SDA doctrine" (p. 163). The Evangelical Church of Papua New Guinea used personal testimonies in which the congregation themselves in a sense were the givers of sermons about morality. They too use "the Manichaean opposition between tradition and Christianity," employing the rainforest, the original home of the people and the animals in it, as a symbol for all that is pagan and "bad" (p. 167). In spite of all this, Knauft found that most people were not too concerned about the end of the world. "We go to sing [in church] and we've given up smoking tobacco," some men said (p. 169). Knauft suggests that "dedication and lack of dedication are linked in a continuing cycle" (p. 171). Nevertheless, overall, Christianity and modernity are seen as inextricably linked (p. 172).

One of Knauft's aims in the book is to reveal the local variability that can exist beneath the general rubric of modernity (p. 247). Given the indigenous diversity within Melanesia, he notes, it would be surprising if there were not local versions of modernity there. One local feature among the Gebusi is that modernity has produced a recessive form of agency that actually increases "social subordination to outsiders" (p. 248). It is doubtful whether this new cultural form owes much, however, to Gebusi culture of the past. It does correspond to Thomas's "inversion of tradition," as we have seen. With Gebusi, instead of the past being empowered, it is explicitly disempowered. And this is because it has been altered by the agency of government and church authorities, who in this instance seem to have worked together in producing this result. The major reason why this has happened appears to be the extreme isolation of Nomad station and the small size of the Gebusi population, although perhaps other Gebusi are not so influenced as those in Gasumi Corners have been. Nor is it only isolation as such that has been at work. The station itself has functioned as an insulated microcosm of the aspects of "modernity" that is the focus of Knauft's book. Church services involve the locals in a subordinate position to the station elite and the predominant use of *Tok Pisin* reinforces this pattern. To some extent, we may suggest that the local development of a vernacular practice of Christianity has actually been inhibited rather than realized in this locally modern context, because much of Christianity has been understood through English-based rather than Gebusi-based concepts.

In its sociopolitical aspects, then, the Gebusi experience may be typical of some other outstation places, but it is not typical of circumstances in the Central Highlands. On the other hand, the themes that appear in the Highlands are highlighted in the Gebusi case very starkly, because of the great dominance of the churches (but we should note the absence of a Pentecostal church; the ECPNG is decidedly not Pentecostal in its emphases). The idea of "exchanging the past" is also one that probably has much applicability beyond the Gebusi case. It applies to people like the Duna who gave up their indigenous rituals in order to obtain a new life, as a kind of expected quid pro quo. And the underlying sacrificial implications do link with deep themes in other Highlands cultures, where sacrifice is also a quid pro quo activity. The problems for the people arise when the expected second round of the exchange does not eventuate.

Also, the process of "exchanging the past" is not one that has arisen only in this day and age. The Duna have narratives of exchanging old practices (religious and otherwise) with ones introduced by neighboring New Guinean groups. This process went on before Australian government influence or mission activity ever entered into the area. What is significant to explore in looking at situations of change is what motivates it and what are the forces that produce it.

Pangia: "Steel to Stone"

Pangia is an administrative district in the Southern Highlands Province of Papua New Guinea, inhabited by speakers of the Wiru language, who number some 20,000 people today. Jeffrey Clark's ethnography about these people, published after his death, concentrates on the narrative of colonialism in the area up to 1975, the year of Papua New Guinea's Independence. His main interests in the book lie in telling the narrative from the viewpoint of the Takuru villagers, followers of a revivalist Wesleyan church; and in reflecting further in the creation of the "docile" colonial subject, the "subaltern" of Bruce Knauft's work. Clark's work is tied in with the Politics of Tradition approach, since he was a research associate in a project under this rubric, headed by Nicholas Thomas, whose work we have cited earlier.

The Pangia people are horticulturalists and pig rearers who held periodic festivals at which they slaughtered large numbers of pigs and distributed the meat to a wide variety of kin and affines, notably matrilateral kin. They came under effective administrative control only in the late 1950s and early 1960s. As we commonly learn in relation to the Highlands, they appeared rapidly to accept pacification and Christianity. We have seen this pattern already for the Duna, and have noted its connection with a metaphor or trope of exchange. Clark adds to this the argument that "it was the resonances created between whites, spirits, God, wealth, and cults, which amplified the perceived power and prestige of Europeans, and accounted for Wiru fears and expectations of their presence" (Clark 2000: 64; see also Bashkow 2000 on attitudes to whites in Oro Province). Here Clark is drawing both on Wiru ethnohistory (the people's own accounts) and on a large corpus of earlier writings about the theme of "first contact" in the Highlands (see, e.g., the film "First Contact" by Bob Connolly and Robin Anderson and the book by the same authors 1987; Schieffelin and Crittenden 1990). Everywhere, the newcomers were greeted as spirit categories. Clark reports the Wiru saw the whites as *kapona* spirits, connected with steel, aeroplanes, flying axes, and forms of sorcery. In some places they were perceived as "red cannibals" (Clark 2000: 43). Wiru women were said to expose their genitals to aeroplanes to make them go away, as they would also do if sorcerers were thought to be lurking around (p. 45). In a further association, some of the early explorers were thought of as "sons of the Female Spirit" because they came from the same direction as had recently the new cult of this spirit. The predominant theme here is power, with more than a touch of malevolence.

The Australian Administration in Pangia sought the rapid incorporation of the area into its scheme of development. Local government councils were set up. Coffee-growing and cattle schemes were introduced. "Voluntary" labor (enforced by the sanction of jail) built roads under guidance from the government patrol officers (A. J. Strathern 1984). The Administration at first also welcomed a number of missions to help them with their overall project. Catholics, the Evangelical Bible Mission, Wesleyans, and Lutherans all came and established stations and spheres of influence. The people themselves suffered a severe influenza attack and a period of collective "madness" around 1960, after which they turned more to the missions, in order to obtain protection from sickness and the perceived increasing encroachments of assault sorcerers (Clark, p. 98). People destroyed their cult houses and sacred stones in order to encourage missions to come and settle with them, in a kind of fervor to create a new age (Clark, p. 99; compare Lattas 1998). Clark points out (ibid.) that fear was also involved. This can be corroborated from the remark made by the Councillor for Lawe, a remote village in the southeast corner of the Wiru area, at a pig festival in 1967: "we are very much afraid of God here (*Gote-ne piri tumbea toko*)." Fear should not be ignored as a factor in early colonial history, and it was amplified by the perception of whites as spirits. Fear along with desire: the missions gave out valuable blankets, steel axes, and shells to settlements in order to keep their loyalty (Clark, p. 100).

In fairly short order the Wiru became disappointed that their hard work for the government and their acceptance of the missions by sacrificing their own culture (or at least their previous cult objects) did not lead to more economic gain. They became known to outsiders as "mercenary." They themselves turned to new churches in the hope of getting benefits from them, for example to the Pentecostal Full Gospel Movement, which came in the early 1970s and stressed a theology of miraculous powers (p. 105). As Clark points out, the missions were often assisted by indigenous evangelists from the Hagen and Ialibu areas who went to great "lengths to denigrate cult houses and the power of the spirits, including smearing excrement on cult stones" (p. 110, referring to A. J. Strathern 1984: 35). The confusion of the Wiru in response contributed to their outbreak of collective "madness" and also to the forms of ecstatic possession encouraged by the Evangelical Bible Mission (p. 128): both "madness" and possession can be seen as extreme ritualized responses to change. The missionaries themselves appear to have seen it as a way of casting out Satan and accepting the Holy Spirit (p. 133), a sort of cleansing or expurgation of evil followed by the advent of spontaneous singing and praying.

Wiru men also, however, Clark argues, experienced the colonial process as one in which their gardens lost fertility and they themselves somehow "shrank" in size, a perception of their subjection to colonial power, the creation of the "docile" subject to which Knauft also refers. Perhaps this feeling is related to the missing second round of the exchange that people think of colonialism as instigating, the round in which they would receive benefits. Clark suggests that Europeans may have been seen as unjustly holding on to secrets they should have revealed as the pathways to wealth (p. 150), thus producing a cargoistic undertow of resentful feelings in response. The Wiru gave up their old cult stones in order to get the new cult "stone" of money (see also Stewart and Strathern 2001b). (Throughout the Highlands the term for money incorporates the idea of "stone," because shilling coins were the first form of money introduced; and Clark speculates that this means that money is seen as a kind of cult object.) Speaking presumably of Wiru perceptions, he notes that "Christianity is based on obtaining control of money, *kue*, which is in European hands" (p. 165). This reads very like Knauft's point that for the Gebusi, Christianity and modernity are tightly linked, except that the association with whites had disappeared among Gebusi by 1998. In both of these case histories we see a narrative of mission domination. But the Pangia narrative also shows the turn of resentment, disappointment, and the development of pejorative stereotyping on both sides. History in the 1970s in Pangia had proceeded further along that line than apparently it had among the Gebusi in 1998. As for the Aluni Valley Duna, their situation in the 1990s resembled a moderate version of the Pangia case, probably influenced by the fact that they had no road and no cash-cropping to speak of. But because of the intervention of the mines in their area and their rediscovery of their own origin stories or *malu* as a resource for gaining benefits, they had at least one aspect of their former culture that was no longer "recessive." Another similarity between the Gebusi at Nomad station and the Duna of the Aluni Valley was that they both were said to be receiving some resource benefits from the Community Outreach section of the Porgera Joint Venture mining company (personal communication from officers in that section of the PJV company, 1999).

The Magic of Modernity? The Maring Case

Our final comparative case is the Maring people of the Bismarck Range and the Jimi Valley north of the Melpa of Mount Hagen, numbering some 7,000 people in the 1970s and extensively studied by Roy Rappaport and others (Rappaport 1968, 1999) and by Edward LiPuma (1988, 2001). LiPuma's second book deals with the Maring's perception of modernity, using a theory of "encompassment" to explain this perception. Encompassment here refers to the pervasive effects of European influence on the Maring, with all the familiar ingredients of pacification, missionization, introduced economic enterprise, education, political change, and overall cultural transformation. LiPuma speaks of events as "waves of encompassment" washing over the Maring (p. 67). He captures well the sense of generational change the Maring, like many other Highlanders, feel: "I am like my father, but my sons resemble me less each day...because their bodies have been nurtured by your [Western] food, your medicine, your language, your schools, your religion, your laws" (2001: 67). Encompassment has thus for the Maring "created a permanent divide between the time of custom and the time of law, the epoch of the ancestors and that of Jesus, the era of great shamans, and the modernity of biomedicine. It was *the* historical event that founds and contextualizes all other events" (ibid.).

LiPuma is here appealing to the epochal idea of history in Papua New Guinea cultures, i.e., people's tendency to see things in terms of a before and after effect. Of course, this particular view is also itself in part a Western artifact, created by the imperative we have seen in the case of many missions to make people reject their past in order to achieve a Christian future. But LiPuma is using the concept in a broader and more existential way: the creation of a historical consciousness that feels a sharp separation from the past, whether that past is an object of nostalgic praise or of rejection.

The magical part of modernity is much like the aura of spirit power that Clark writes about in relation to perceptions of Europeans in early colonial Pangia. As Knauft does, LiPuma stresses the local character of the values that emerge from the hybridization of Western and Maring ideas and practices, so that even as money, for example, "advances the commodification of the local world, it is infused with a complex of culturally specific meanings" (2001: 187; see also Strathern and Stewart 1999c, 2000a). Nevertheless, the Maring have according to LiPuma adopted a dichotomous view of the past and the present in which their previous pearl shell and pig economy is seen as more limiting and narrow, and their present access to money as giving them wider horizons and opportunities. The past thus becomes divided from the present, as it has been for the Gebusi of Gasumi Corners. One of LiPuma's collaborators, Moses, "a high school graduate, a devout Anglican and a successful businessman" (p. 200) put it this way in an interview: "Believing in Jesus and learning to use money to make *bisnis* (business) are what will allow us to develop ourselves" (p. 201). This statement again echoes the Gebusi sentiments Knauft reports on. The Maring, however, have had more access to business development than the Gebusi, so there is more ideological emphasis specifically on becoming wealthy through enterprise in Moses' statement. This combination of "Jesus" and "business" cannot fail to remind us, in a general way, of the association between Protestantism and capitalism proposed by the sociologist Max Weber (Weber 1992). Perhaps the fact that the Gebusi studied by Knauft were largely Catholics is significant in this regard. (It is extremely important to recognize the difference in the practices and ethos of the various churches that have established themselves in different areas— they cannot all be clumped together simply because they are all Christian religions.) Also relevant here is that Gasumi Corners offers very few opportunities for business activity beyond the business of the church itself.

LiPuma devotes a chapter to "the magic of the evangelical," explaining in some detail the ideology and practices of the Anglican Mission. Despite the Mission's claim to be sensitive to Maring customs, when custom conflicted with Christian rules, such as the rule of monogamy, the Anglican conception was "that Maring culture stood between and corrupted God's natural order because the Maring had not been exposed to His gospel" (p. 222). Thus "big-men" were "all but excluded" from Christianity (ibid.). In other ways the Maring themselves tried to assimilate the figure of Jesus into their cultural world, saying that they had learned from the Church "that Jesus Christ sits at the apex of their ancestral genealogy" (p. 226). This is certainly a "local" view. The Aluni Valley Duna, for example, would not share it. Their *malu* origin stories keep their own indigenous ancestors in focus. The example indicates, however, a basic syncretistic tendency among Maring. For them, the adoption of Christianity "did not preclude their involvement in other forms of belief, such as people's continuing faith in traditional curing rites, sorcery, and other forms of magic" (p. 238). Here LiPuma also notes, as others have done before, that Highlands peoples have long traditions of importing "foreign" rituals, on the basis that these are seen as bringing new powers with them. The introduction of the Female Spirit cult to many areas in both Hagen and Pangia was facilitated by this idea (see Strathern and Stewart 1999d). The missionaries, of course, saw things in a more exclusivist way. Their dichotomous view was imposed on their local evangelists and underpinned by new consumption patterns. LiPuma gives us a snapshot of young trainees waiting on the airstrip at Koinambe mission station "dressed in pleated shorts, sunglasses, wristwatches, broad beamed hats, and leather shoes, waiting for a plane that will take them to the seminary in Popondetta [an old Anglican stronghold] where, in their own words, they will become priests and return "to teach these bush kanakas [natives] to know God and become civilized" (p. 245). This image underlines LiPuma's own general position that "while local agency is alive and vibrant...it is still the West that is imposing, itself, not the other way round" (p. 297). He recognizes that the processes involved are patchy and contradictory, for example because (if not in Maring perceptions) "the intentions of Christianity are not those of capitalism" (p. 304). But the overall encompassing effect of modernity is to shift local cultures "into the common flow of the capitalist nation-state" (p. 307). Such an overall effect, if it does indeed hold, precludes the possibility of simply empowering the past. The Maring, like the Gebusi, have largely inverted tradition and disempowered their past in order to reach out for an imagined future.

The Duna: Past and Present

In terms of their development of historical consciousness, there are clear parallels between the Duna and our last two cases, Pangia and the Maring. Each of these two areas has experienced a moderate degree of development, probably followed by a decline in government and mission presence over time. In both areas the dominant influence seems to remain that of the church, though to a lesser degree than with the Gebusi. In the case of the Duna, which we have examined in this book, a similar dominance by the missions appears, strengthened by a clear decline in administrative activity. But the Aluni Valley Duna have been left much more to their own devices, it seems, owing to the lack of regular outside mission influence on them that was so intense in the 1960s. The lack of cash-cropping and of a road in the Valley has also increased their isolation. While from some viewpoints, including from time to time their own, this isolation is a source of frustration, from another perspective it has gradually given them a breathing space. If they are encompassed, they are at least not regularly squeezed by the forces of change. It was in this context that they were able to redevelop their own *malu* to cope with the opportunities and constraints introduced by mining companies. They were thus able to create their own politics of tradition, which entailed a selective process of giving back value to the past as a means of pursuing their interests in the present.

After 1999 and up to 2002 the major threat to this new germ of interest in, and use of, tradition among the Duna has been posed by the kinds of violence that Paula Brown and others (e.g., Standish 2002) have identified as linked with electoral violence among the Simbu. Such violence was so extreme in the Southern Highlands Province, to which the Duna belong, that in the 2002 elections the various seats in Parliament for the different constituencies could not be declared and supplementary elections had to be planned. The biggest immediate danger for the Duna, then, as for the majority of ordinary people in their province and country who do not want this kind of violence to be a regular part of their lives, is that their own tentative politics of tradition will be overwhelmed by a form of neotraditional politics that all too clearly is connected with capitalist encompassment, but is equally clearly connected with desires for wealth and power that also were a part of the activities of people in the past. The conjuncture of past and present is as problematic here as it is in many parts of the world today.

Chapter 9

Change Among the Duna: A Synopsis and Some Wider Implications

Models of Local Change in Papua New Guinea

Models of recent historical change among local populations in Papua New Guinea have themselves been changing over the last decade. Some earlier studies tended to suggest that these societies were preadapted to capitalist-style economic development (Finney 1973). Later, when economic and political instabilities brought with them bouts of renewed intergroup fighting, analysts discussed the emergence of class-based inequalities and their intersection with the resurgence of tribal animosities (Amarshi, Good and Mortimer 1979). Finally, when most of the societies had been subjected to radical changes, some ethnographers retreated to the level of reconstructed models of "Melanesian sociality," seen as the opposite of "Western individualism," and then proceeded to trace the emergence of individualism as a product of capitalist hegemony or domination. This historical progression can be seen as involving a complete volte face with regard to the supposed basic characteristics of the societies in question: from being seen as "pre-adapted" to capitalism to being constructed as antithetical to it.

The broader truth is that these societies themselves encapsulated a number of trends that could lead in different directions according to modes of historical articulation with the world. Individualism and communalism ran together in the mingling streams of social relations among them. James Carrier (1992c) has applied the concept of articulation effectively to the analysis of change in Papua New Guinea. Articulation refers to the ways in which local populations are affected by outside forces and at the same time respond to them. How, then, would we in general characterize the articulation of the Aluni Valley people with the outside world? First, their basic mode of subsistence has not been altered and they are only peripherally involved in smallholder cash-cropping. Therefore, no class-based local system of relations has emerged. In this they contrast with, for example, the Simbu and the Hagen peoples. Second, cash is earned through out-migrant labor, so that the Valley people are enmeshed in industrial and agricultural plantation enterprises that are a part of transnational capitalist organizations. Returning workers bring back money, which enters the circuits of exchange via brideprice and compensation payments, causing a rise in the scale of these payments. Historically, cash also replaced the cowries used in local transactions previously, linking the Duna as both workers and consumers to a new world of desires and perceived necessities. From that time their local society was hitched, clearly and unequally, to a wide set of forces outside of the Valley. The institutions of brideprice and compensation remained but they came under the variable influence of external pressures. Third, the Administration stopped intergroup fighting and encouraged people to settle disputes with payments of wealth, reinforcing but also altering patterns of compensation and leading to a proliferation of minor and major compensation payments in people's lives. Fourth, and finally, Christian missions practically made a complete sweep of overt indigenous ritual practices, encouraging evangelists and pastors to burn sacred stones, profane sacred pools, and set up churches everywhere to replace local cult houses, emptying the landscape of its visible markers of indigenous religiosity.

By the same token, the people became in principle dependent not only on the Christian God but on the representatives of that God who came to them from the outside world. More recently, they were also, and rather confusingly, incorporated into a new nation and state that proclaimed its independence and sovereignty and pursued both a "modernizing" and a "traditionalizing" policy: urging economic development but praising the retention of selected aspects of traditional culture. Most recently of all, the Aluni people came to realize that they were neglected by their own government because of a chronic shortage of funds. They identified patterns of corruption and incompetence among public servants, and they began to re-arm themselves, with new weapons, as problems of social control emerged among them.

This brief narrative itself reveals the mixed character of changes: apparently minor in some regards, extreme in others. What it does not reveal is the dimension of what Carrier called the internal effects of articulation. Nor can it encompass the ingenuities with which Duna people negotiated with or transformed certain impositions of change laid upon them. And finally, it does not allow us to follow through the ramifications of historical processes that have resulted from an initial set of changes.

The first internal effect of economic articulation was the switch from shells to state money and the entry of cash into exchanges. This change set up a potential for conflict between junior men, who earned the money, and seniors, who were in charge of all public social events involving the use of wealth items. This conflict is largely resolved through the percolation of cash into the exchanges themselves. Once in a circuit of exchange, cash becomes available to everyone, although not equally. But we can see an incipient pattern whereby young men who have worked elsewhere are expected to pay greatly increased cash portions of their brideprice, a pattern that could either bring them power or could act as a continuing economic leveling device. In any case, the rise in brideprice has led to difficulties in adjusting past to present because of the generational rule that the daughter's brideprice repays that of the mother and the problem of "index-linking" this to inflation over time. These are the kinds of intricate problems that outsiders to a society rarely see, but can lead to severe management problems for local mediators. They are also the kind of problems that are ignored or not often taken into consideration by planners for economic development.

These economic changes have not led, as they did among the Ponam Island people studied by Carrier (1992c), to the loss of control by the local *kango* or male leaders. It is remarkable that this category of men had retained such prominent positions in community affairs since the 1960s, and in spite of the complete loss of a roster of rituals by which their power had been underpinned in the past. This is one of the most paradoxical aspects of change. However, the paradox is quite explicable if we consider a number of factors at work. First, although the first Baptist missionary in the 1960s made a number of ritual pronouncements that have subsequently been treated as "canonical," and all the senior leaders are involved one way or another with Christian churches, the area has been left to itself to a remarkable degree since then. This circumstance has allowed contradictory patterns to quietly coexist without acute surveillance from outside and to be mediated by senior leaders working in concert with long-standing pastors in the area. At Hagu, the pastor himself in the 1990s had been appointed in the 1960s, and was an agnate of the leading descent line who would have become a ritual leader in the old system if he had not converted to Christianity. Second, the abandonment of overt ritual practices by no means indicates a comparable abandonment of notions regarding the dead and spirits of the environment. As is common in such circumstances, the previously honored spirits are thought of as still existing and as having some potential influence. The old religion is not declared to be false, but rather erroneous in the sense of sinful. Mixed ideas emerge, along with debates and uncertainty. Where, for example, do the spirits of the dead really go? Christian dogma states that those who died unbaptized go to "the place of fire," but people think that sometimes the spirit hovers near the place of its grave, and women in their funeral songs enjoin the spirit to fly up to the local rock shelter in the hills where the dead are congregated.

While the powers of magic are said in some instances to be broken through the non-observance of proper taboos, some taboos, especially on behavior in the high forest, are still carefully observed. The ancestral stones, or *auwi*, are said by some people to be unwilling to emerge to the surface of the land as they used to, because of the presence of the church, but they remain there in waiting, to see how things will turn out in the longer run. Rationalizations of this sort project a picture of a world in abeyance rather than abolition. Particularly in the spheres of witchcraft and in stories of first origins, indigenous ideas hold sway. As in other places around the world, witchcraft ideas are as much a reflection of contemporary stresses and problems as they are a carry-over from the past (Moore and Sanders 2001). And origin stories, as we have seen, have been reshaped to form a major tool in dealing with mining companies. Christian ideas of world's end and the millennium, finally, blend, if uneasily and partially, with indigenous ideas of cyclicity in generational time (Stewart and Strathern 2002a). In sum, religious articulation has led to a very complex set of ingenious internal adjustments as well as to a number of unresolved issues and anxieties. This pattern is a product of strong early influence, followed by later isolation and institutional neglect.

A similar pattern is found when we look at the overall history of government influence. We can discern three periods: initial explorations and patrols up to c. 1960; the establishment of administrative influence, 1960–1975; and the decline of that influence since national Independence, 1975–present. In the initial period, the local people viewed the incomers as spirits or like spirits and felt that their emergence could herald another ash fall from the sky or some other cataclysmic events. The explorers were folded into the encompassing local mythology and sense of history. In the second period, the colonial power set about its project of encompassing the people with a battery of changes: pacification, introduction of first shell wealth and then state currency, road-building, primary schools, health services and baby clinics, the distribution of new types of seeds, local government councils, and the beginnings of parliamentary democracy. All this was in line with policy throughout the Highlands, and had the clear aim of homogenizing change processes and enfolding them in the colonial mantle while preparing the people for later Independence. In the third period the mantle has become frayed and torn apart in places. The locals do not encompass the outside world, nor yet does the outside world entirely encompass them.[1] People fit into the new order in some ways and not in others, and this may be the result of their own choices or simply a result of historical events that have impinged on them. The lack of a viable road, for example, has greatly inhibited cash-cropping, while allowing the people to manage their own affairs without much interference. Leaders feel the strain of dealing with local issues without either administrative backup or the possibility of open recourse to force, as used to occur in the past. This circumstance explains the constant refrain of the leaders during the 1990s, that they needed to have the long-awaited Village Court system instituted in their area. In this system magistrates are elected or chosen by the people and serve for a specified period, operating in accordance with national regulations but able to apply local custom to a range of cases. The Village Courts are supposed to be assisted by police, and magistrates are to use Peace Officers to arrest and bring in persons accused of criminal offences. They issue summonses for civil offenses and can jail persons who fail to appear after three summonses have been served. Elsewhere, these courts have worked well for a while, later tending to break down with deteriorating situations of both social control in general and lack of funding from government. They are supposed to collect fines and to be partially self-sufficient, but corruption in the use of funds has in places led to disillusionment and abandonment. Nevertheless, for the Valley leaders these courts offered their only hope for strengthening their own hands. Their powers diminished by other changes, they looked to the government to strengthen them. But no courts had been set up by 1999, and it is unlikely they have since been set up.

By 1999, as we have noted, men had begun to openly carry guns to public meetings, reverting to precolonial patterns of appearing armed and ready to fight over disputes, but with a more lethal form of technology. In 2002 the situation worsened all over the Southern Highlands, the province in which the Duna live, largely owing to competitive violence both before and after national elections. Bands of youths armed with guns intimidated voters and one another, acting as bodyguards to candidates. In some instances they hijacked ballot boxes, ensuring that only votes for their chosen candidates were cast; or they filled out false ballots and stuffed these into the boxes. After the elections, there was so much disorder that in many electorates, including that for Koroba-Kopiago, to which the Duna belong, no election result could be declared. The areas immediately around the provincial headquarters, Mendi, lapsed into violent disarray, and the national government had grave difficulty in attempting to reestablish order. Backbiting and accusations of corruption among government ministers and officials made the situation worse. In the Huli area, south of the Duna, electrical pylons bearing power supplies to the Porgera mine were cut down by landowners demanding payments in royalties and services for their areas. The mine is important for government revenue as a whole, and riot police were dispatched to safeguard the repair of the pylons. A massive fire burned down many government department buildings in Mendi itself, leaving a large new building, named after a deposed governor of the province, Anderson Agiru, intact. We do not know how much the Aluni Valley people were affected by these events, but it is certain that they could only have exacerbated existing chronic problems of lack of government services, notably in relation to supplies of medicines for health centers and aid posts.

It is not enough to see these processes as "resistance to modernization." The people all want development. What they protest against is their perceived share in development, which they consider too small. Politicians vie for resources they can obtain if they win elections, and they resort to violent means to do so. Democracy, by this process, undoes itself, and articulation with the outside world results in a kind of self-strangling through excessive and unregulated competition. Areas such as the Aluni Valley may in some ways, as we have argued earlier, be more fortunate than those at the epicenter of conflicts such as Mendi, Tari, and Mount Hagen. But their isolation also means that they continue to slip further away from their own hopes and expectations for the future. In these circumstances they are likely to continue to look for the next arrival of mining prospectors as their best hope for obtaining new wealth.

Seen in theoretical terms, this synopsis reinforces the point that modernity is not single and whole, but multiple and partial. Reviewing economic, political, and religious changes, we can see their complex interrelations. But we can also see that they do not add up to an overall picture of consistent change. Instead there are currents and countercurrents, and the unforeseen repercussions of different processes react upon one another in ways that are often highly unpredictable and unfavorable for the people. The contemporary scene is not "modern" in any simple sense. It is mixed and shot through with many strands from the past and from the outside. Moreover, we cannot say which elements are "traditional" and which are "modern" since many elements partake in a complex way of both characters. Elements may also be evaluated differently by different people (see Dambrowski 2002 on change among Inuit people in East Alaska, USA, for parallels). This confluence of elements shows most clearly in the sphere of ritual. For example, the position of Christian pastor, we have noted, is sometimes held by an agnate who would be, and still to some extent is, the holder of important knowledge in the sphere of origins (*malu*). The pastor is thus in structural terms "traditional," but in functional terms "modern," if we wished to put it this way. Funeral customs show an analogous conflation of concepts. In accordance with Christian custom, bodies are buried below ground rather than being exposed on platforms as before; but the coffin is laid on a support in the cavity of the grave and a hole is left for bodily fluids to drip into the earth. A roof is raised over the grave and after some time the bones may be discreetly removed and given secondary burial in rock caves where the spirits of the dead are supposed to dwell. Quiet adjustments of this kind enable the Duna, in small arenas, to incorporate their past into their contemporary life, thus giving them a sense of identity in the midst of change. Such small adjustments, however, are vulnerable to the larger and noisier processes of history that surround them.[2]

Ethnography, History, and Theory

Debates regarding the relationship between ethnography as an account of localized relationships and situations, history as the flow of processes and events through time, and theory as a means of generalizing and explaining social phenomena, have recently been raised within anthropology in new ways. Over time in the history of anthropology itself, different "grand theories" or "metanarratives" have been employed as touchstones of effective analysis. So we have a progression through approaches stressing diffusion of customs, the integrative functions of practices, the mental models that underpin social relations, the material relations of production, or the processes by which social realities are reproduced and alter over time and space. Here we have paraphrased terms such as diffusionism, functionalism, structuralism, Marxism, and processualism that are the stock in trade of histories of anthropology. These theories in turn came under skeptical scrutiny from a congeries of viewpoints loosely characterized as postmodernism, in which all practices of knowledge-production, including theory-building, were placed in question. In turn, anthropology, and the social sciences in general, have entered into a phase of reconstructing approaches to explanations of social life, in dialogue with an emergent new metanarrative of globalization and modernity. This narrative leads us to see different local histories as all part of one big, larger process in which the directions are roughly the same everywhere and reflect primarily the influence of forms of capitalism.

Our work with the Aluni Valley Duna both belongs broadly to this way of seeing the world and offers some cautions and criticisms in relation to it. To begin with, as we and many others have stressed (see, e.g. Hirsch 2001), modernity is not a single phenomenon nor does it belong exclusively to any one epoch of time. In its most neutral sense it simply refers to "now" time in contrast to "then" time, where there is a sense of historical change or difference between the two. This sense of difference is at its strongest when it corresponds to an idea of rupture with the past, producing a feeling of discontinuity. More broadly we ourselves have described modernity as a moving horizon of change, in which the future continues to look different as a result of past changes. The basic concept here is the overall feeling of change itself, which neither necessarily implies rupture nor excludes aspects of continuity. Of course, people's experience of historical flows is not even: some times are clearly experienced as more marked by ruptures than others. But the overall problem of using the idea of modernity as an explanatory concept is that it tends to transpose processes of change that have occurred in the societies of Western Europe over time directly onto "Third World" contexts. There is some justification for this transposition, if only because colonial and postcolonial agents of change have themselves attempted to impose their chosen models of society on others around the world. But these attempts, and the response to them, have not been uniform. Hence anthropologists have tried to take such a lack of uniformity into account by referring to multiple "modernities," in succession to the idea of multiple cultures that informed earlier work in the field.

As Englund and Leach (2000) discuss in some detail, this concept of multiple modernities still tends to preserve within itself a model of overall change in the direction of ideas such as commodification, individualism, and globalization. In doing so, the idea tends also to attribute the causes of change to these abstract processes rather than to the choices of conscious human beings trying to solve their problems and achieve their aims. Again, it is not that the concepts have no applicability or heuristic value, but that they tend to dehumanize processes of change and to preempt their explanations, standing in, as Englund and Leach argue, where there is insufficient ethnography to provide a more nuanced set of accounts (Englund and Leach 2000: 236–7).

One of the most fundamental constituents of a localized, embedded account of change, then, is to convey throughout the sense of human agency at work, albeit against the odds in many instances, seeking to find ingenious pathways of life for itself. Our aim in writing this ethnography of change among the Duna has been to contribute to such an enterprise. In the first place, we have eschewed overgeneralizations about the areas of our primary knowledge. Although we speak of "the Duna" in general, we have dealt largely with the networks of relationship among fewer than a thousand people in a single valley and river complex, the Aluni Valley Duna. But these people have relationships that extend far beyond the Valley itself in many directions, to other areas in Papua New Guinea and to missionaries, government, and mining personnel who are variously linked into the massive structures of power that globalization theory dwells on. The relationships are as much a part of the Valley itself, seen in social terms, as are the immediate kin and locality ties that criss-cross the valley landscape. Our microethnography therefore intrinsically relates to macroprocesses. Second, these macroprocesses are all mediated locally. Nothing happens without its corresponding reactions and attempts to understand it by the local people. A valuable point Englund and Leach make is that local people are also social scientists studying their world and attempting to interpret it. This is certainly true of the Duna. In making their interpretive schemes they have tended to draw on the background of their own mythology, since this is concerned with the bases, origins, or foundations of things (encapsulated in the term *tse*). Hence their development of a special myth to interpret and handle the activities of miners drilling for oil near the Strickland River (see chapter 5). By a chance convergence the oil company set up its drilling operation close to the sacred sites of origin of a number of groups spread throughout the Valley. This geographical convergence helped to stimulate the local response and to engage persons of different groups in a vigorous debate and participation in the shaping of the new myth cycle. We have also to attend to individual elements: ambitions and struggles between groups and between emergent leading figures are a catalyst for the shaping of narratives. It is for this reason that we stress the point that local statements about custom and tradition are as much statements about the present and the desired future as about the past. Indeed, representations of "tradition" are always to be seen as themselves aspects of, and pointers to, change rather than neutral reports about a static past.

Finally, in the context of comparative regional studies of change, of the kind we have given in chapters 6 and 8, it is important to stress that the Aluni Duna had not, up until the year 2000 at least, experienced the degree of thoroughgoing economic changes that characterize the central cordillera of the Highlands from Goroka to Mount Hagen. Accordingly, some of the evidences of change in their area are subtle and patchy by comparison with these Central Highlands parts. But that does not mean that the changes are less significant or are not pervasive. Indeed, the people have been considerably affected, both mentally and socially, by the effects of mining developments in particular, as we have seen. While their subsistence base has not been markedly altered, their own economic horizons of expectation have been greatly shifted, so that they see their own subsistence mode of life in a different way: as sustaining them, but not affording them a pathway to wealth, as it did before through ritual and the production of pigs for slaughter. Pigs are still wealth, but are themselves seen in terms of monetary value. And Christian rituals do not accord pig sacrifices a central place in their system of values.

A final word here on the issue of violence. We do not know how deeply the Aluni Valley people were enmeshed in the complexes of violence that were unleashed in the process of governmental elections in 2002. They were certainly affected by this political turbulence, however. The elections were rescheduled and were held again in the first half of 2003, and after a close contest between two candidates from a single village beside the Kopiago government station, Aeyaguni, the winner was announced as someone who was a popular sportsman and had offered himself as a "people's candidate" without elaborate party support or monetary backing. This event represents again a capacity for self-reinvention, for turning history at least partly around, and for reversing a recent trend and reclaiming ground for a localized discourse that is a critique of politics on the one hand and a bid to elude the cycles of violence associated with the trends of the 1990s on the other. The test of this bid will be played out by everyday and dramatic performances in the next several years, enacted on the local stage with the wider forces of the world framing its horizons.

Notes

Chapter 1

1. For further readings about the Duna people that we discuss in this book see Stewart 1998; Stewart and Strathern 2000a, b, c, 2001a, 2002a; Strathern and Stewart 1999a, 2000b. Other works on the Duna include Haley 1996, 2002; Marecek 1979; Modjeska 1977, 1982, 1991, 1995, as noted above. This list is not exhaustive.
2. We use the term "parish" to refer to a territorially bounded area predominantly associated with the people of a major named social category defined in terms of descent. See chapter 2 for further exposition on this.
3. Further descriptions of gardening practices in the area can be found in Sillitoe, Stewart, and Strathern 2002, in Modjeska 1977, and Steensberg 1980. For more extensive comparative materials on gardening in the Highlands, see Sillitoe, Stewart, and Strathern 2002, Sillitoe 1996.

Chapter 2

1. For instance, ML, a prominent man (*kango*) of Yangone parish, listed eight such locality names in Aluni parish near the government station and another six further away, including Hagu itself. These lists are clearly flexible. ML's list omitted one place near the station, Mundukaraku, where people were living in the early 1990s. PK, a *kango* of Haiyuwi parish, listed 14 small place names within it, including one major cult site.
2. The kind of ambiguity or flexibility involved here is by no means peculiar to the Duna case or to the much vexed issue of cognatic descent as an analytical construct (on which see, e.g., Scheffler 1965; Glasse 1968; Keesing 1970; Jackson 1971; as well as Stewart and Strathern 2002a on the same data we have discussed here). A moment's reflection indicates that the same ambiguity or flexibility operates when we speak of a "New Yorker" or a "Londoner," or "a Scot" as opposed to an "English" person. Similar issues have also underlain the extensive controversies on New Guinea Highlands social groups in general, beginning with Barnes (1962). A. Strathern (1972) considered these issues

for the Melpa people of Mount Hagen. Such controversies in turn stemmed from debates regarding the nature of social groupings among African peoples characterized as having segmentary lineage systems, notably the Nuer people of the Sudan, as described by Evans-Pritchard (1940). The Nuer in Evans-Pritchard's account show the same distinctions between politico-jural/ritual, moral, and generally social definitions of what constitutes a "group" as we have identified here for the Duna. It is better to think one's way through the semantic problems in this way than to give up entirely on the concept of "group" as such and replace it with a set of analytically stated indigenous symbolic constructs as some observers (e.g., Wagner 1967) have attempted to do. While these constructs help to underpin group processes, they do not, in and of themselves, explain how such groups are constituted and function. The same constructs are often employed by the people to cover different domains of activity. Meyer Fortes's distinctions between the politico-jural and what he called the domestic or moral domain remain useful here (Fortes 1969). Equally, we need to distinguish between operational, representational, and explanatory models of society (Caws 1974). In cases where affiliations are in practice flexible or fluid, people's operational models may be "fractal" in character, allowing room for ambiguity, while their representational models are more clear-cut. At the level of practice, rather than ideology, it is clear that individuals and their actions are an important relevant variable for understanding patterns of affiliation and residence, as Paul Sillitoe has frequently and forcefully argued (e.g., Sillitoe 1979).

3. We follow here conventions established in Stewart and Strathern 2002a.
4. On these details compare Modjeska 1980: 307–8. PK's account resembles Modjeska's presentation quite closely, except that PK applies the term *ima-auwa* (*imaaua* in Modjeska's transcription) to agnatically defined subgroups in the parish, not to all the cognatic descendants of the parish founder, who for PK are called *tsene*. (This category is divided into *imagaro* and *anoagaro* categories.) Incidentally, our Aluni Valley collaborators did not invariably reject etymological exegesis of terms as Modjeska reports for Horaile (1980: 307). For PK, also, the term *ima-sana* (*imatsana*) is relative, not absolute. It is not a term for "parish group" as such but for wife-takers in relation to one's own parish, and is correlative to the term *imanggu*, which we have noted in table 2.2, note 2, above. A term that is used for parish is *rindi* , "land" or "ground," which is also used polysemously in wider contexts of reference for the ground in general. Modjeska usefully computes from his investigations that the 600 square miles of Duna land are divided into some 60 parishes (p. 307). Elsewhere (1977: 37) he estimates the total Duna population (in c. 1970) as 13,000 persons, with an overall population density of 10–40 persons per square kilometer. These are very moderate densities by comparison with Central Highlands peoples. See also Modjeska 1977: 95–100 on the concept of *rindi* (*dindi*) as parish. The term "parish" for these territories among the Duna is modeled on the

usage of Glasse (1968: 23) for the neighboring Huli people. (Glasse drew this term in turn from Hogbin and Wedgwood 1953: 243; Glasse ibid.) The Aluni Valley parishes have relatively small populations. If in about 1970 the total population was 13,000 and there were 60 parishes, average parish size was about 217 persons; while, as we have seen, the combined figures for Aluni (including Hagu), Haiyuwi, and Yangone in 1991 amounted to only 118 people.

5. *Pikono* are narrative performances carried out by expert singers at night and attended by an appreciative audience. They tell the exploits of youths emerging into manhood, often assisted by a version of the Female Spirit, the Payame Ima. They are often set in a world inhabited both by humans and by cannibal giants known as *auwape*, and they deal with the ambiguous interactions between *auwape*, male and female, and humans, personified in the figure of the *pikono nane*, the balladic or heroic youth who is the protagonist in the story. During the 1990s in the Aluni Valley such *pikono* performances were very popular, and might last all night. Recited in the dark, with skillful aesthetic repetitions encompassed in the use of arcane vocabulary, they endowed their performers with prestige and enhanced their community influence. While the men who were recognized for their skills in *pikono* chanting were usually those who also had a good knowledge of *malu*, the group origin stories validating rights over land, *pikono* and *malu* must be seen as very different genres of expression, even though some elements of narratives can appear in either of these genres. Aesthetically, a special feature of *pikono* is their blending of local and mythical landscapes, so that the familiar and ordinary is juxtaposed with or transformed into the strange and extraordinary. The same effect is achieved widely in folklore around the world when humans in their local areas suddenly stumble on the world of spirits, for example in Scottish folk tales in which Thomas of Ercildoune meets the Queen of the Fairies riding on her horse through the woods, and is taken away by her to her world hidden beneath the ground.

The formulaic character of line-building in *pikono* clearly parallels the modes of construction and creation apparent in oral epics around the world (see Stewart and Strathern n.d.a for detailed discussions on this point). Characteristically, when aesthetic repetition is employed in lines, a verbal phrase is repeated along with variant and evocative terms for a particular element such as the sun. The same technique appears in courting songs (*laingwa*) in which, e.g., many different terms for women's netbags may successively appear (see Stewart and Strathern 2002b for a further discussion of these courting songs).

Chapter 4

1. Women do not make this sort of speech, but women specialize in other types of oral presentation that are equally important to the continued

harmonious existence of the group at large. For example, women are the ones who specialize in mourning songs. These are sung as women form troupes to travel on foot to the parish where a funeral is to be held. They take turns singing during the funeral period, which can last for several days. Their songs entreat the spirits (*tini*) of the dead to go peacefully up to the high forest and not to linger among the living, where they might produce sickness or death (Stewart and Strathern 2000a, 2003a).
2. Further materials on these speeches appear in Stewart and Strathern 2000c: 21–27 (*tambaka* 1, 2, 3) and 33–37 (*tambaka* 5).
3. In *Yekeanda*, unmarried girls and youths met in specially built houses in which they sat together and played music to each other. The girls played on their mouth bows, while the youths played jaws harps. The youths who took part had to be those who had completed their time in the *palena anda* and were held to be fully grown and ready for courting. *Yekeanda* events were forbidden by the Christian missions and seem to have been discontinued well before the 1990s; but they were vividly remembered. In the 1990s "disco nights" were held in a brief attempt to raise money for communal activities. They were quickly discontinued after numerous sexual disputes ensued.
4. The number 14 for the Duna represents a cycle of generations from the beginning of a group up to an expected moment of dissolution for the group and the land on which it is settled. Sets of items used in ceremonial payments of wealth are also counted in 14s. One set = 1×14, two sets = 2×14, and so on. This applies to marriage prestations as well as to compensation for injuries. However, marriage payments are not explicitly likened to payments of compensation for injury in terms of any healing capacities or functions. The general expressions for these two categories of payments are different. Bridewealth is called *ima roupa*, which we gloss as "obtaining a woman in exchange for wealth," compensation is *tamba*, cognate with Huli *ndamba*, glossed by Goldman (1983: 62) as "closing," as we have noted in our text. See also Modjeska 1977: 194–209.
5. Women's ritual knowledge was a separate corpus of power that men did not necessarily know or share in.

Chapter 7

1. Ongka died on April 28 or 29, 2003. We received the news of his passing from a number of people in his community. He had expressed a wish to be buried back in his old place at Mbukl beside the grave of his son Namba. However, it was decided to place his grave prominently at Wayake, near to the entranceway to the former agricultural station at Kuk, probably as a marker of the claims of his wider group, the Kawelka, to this area and its potential resources. This act itself shows the blending of "traditional" and "modern" concerns that characterizes

contemporary life and death in Hagen. We were later informed that Ongka himself had changed his wish before his death and had asked that his grave be placed at Wayake. This placement gives him a continuing representative role for the Kawelka after his death.

Chapter 9

1. This ambivalent process of awkward and uneven articulation between government and people is also a product of the whole historical sequence that began with international pressures for the unification of Papua and New Guinea as a single independent state following separate earlier acts of colonization by Britain, Germany, and Australia. Political independence has been followed by stepped-up inroads made by global economic interests, in negotiation with Papua New Guinea's own economic policymakers, and by the consolidation and expansion of Christian churches, dedicated to making Papua New Guinea a "Christian country." The Aluni Valley Duna have had to devise their own responses to all of these influences. For an excellent comparable discussion of change, well grounded in local ethnography, see also Smith 2002.
2. The Duna people we have studied live in a remote rural area relatively far removed from the contexts of mass commoditization and consumption ably discussed by Robert Foster in his book *Materializing the Nation* (Foster 2002). One Duna man who had previously spent time in Port Moresby at one stage waxed eloquent and nostalgic about the times he had spent drinking Coca-Cola there. After his next visit he changed his mind about the "big-city." He had been in the thick of a gunfight between criminals and police in the Morata squatter settlement area in Waigani, and returned home shaken and less enamored of the city life. New consumption patterns are attractive to many rural people, and they do represent a kind of modernity; less attractive, however, is the rapidly rising price of imported store goods with the sharp decline in the value of the kina, Papua New Guinea's currency, since the late 1990s—a decline that is also a result of "modern" factors such as corruption in politics generally, the embezzlement of funds, the growth of violence, and the lack of investor confidence in the Papua New Guinea economy. It is these factors that impact very heavily on the rural populations by way of loss of services and a feeling of powerlessness, unmitigated by effective access to the goods by which the nation is "materialized" in the cities. Consequently, these material symbols cannot become the incorporative marks of the nation for the ordinary village people. Instead they mark the disjunction between themselves and city people with good access to money. For these rural people, the way to "the nation" could only be found through the effective restoration of government services to their area (see Strathern and Stewart 2000e).

This page intentionally left blank

References

Akin, David and Joel Robbins eds. 1999. *Money and Modernity. State and Local Currencies in Melanesia*. ASAO Monograph Series 17. Pittsburgh: University of Pittsburgh Press.

Amarshi, Azeem, Kenneth Good, and Rex Mortimer 1979. *Development and Dependency. The Political Economy of Papua New Guinea*. Melbourne: Oxford University Press.

Bamford, Sandra ed. n.d. *Embodying Modernity and Postmodernity in Melanesia*. Durham, N.C.: Carolina Academic Press.

Banks, Glenn 1993. Mining multinationals and developing countries: theory and practice in Papua New Guinea. *Applied Geography* 13: 312–27.

Barker, John ed. 1990. *Christianity in Oceania: Ethnographic Perspectives*. ASAO Monograph Series 12. Lanham: University Press of America.

Barker, John 1990. Mission station and village: religious practice and representations in Maisin society. In J. Barker ed. *Christianity in Oceania*, pp. 173–96. Lanham: University Press of America.

Barnes, John A. 1962. African models in the New Guinea Highlands. *Man* (o.s.) 62: 5–9.

Bashkow, Ira 2000. Confusion, native skepticism, and recurring questions about the Year 2000: "Soft" beliefs and preparations for the Millennium in the Arapesh region, Papua New Guinea. In P. J. Stewart and A. Strathern eds. *Millennial Countdown in New Guinea*, special issue of *Ethnohistory* 47(1), pp. 133–69. Durham, N.C.: Duke University Press.

Biersack, Aletta 1999. The Mount Kare python and his gold: totemism and ecology in the Papua New Guinea highlands. *American Anthropologist* 101: 68–87.

Billings, Dorothy 1998. New Guinea at corporate headquarters: Amungme versus the Freeport mining company. In *Ecology and Folklore* iii: 13–21, Prague.

Blong, Russell J. 1982. *The Time of Darkness*. Seattle: University of Washington Press.

Borofsky, Robert ed. 2000. *Remembrance of Pacific Pasts: An Invitation to Remake History*. Honolulu: University of Hawai'i Press.

Breton, Stéphane ed. 2002 *Questions de Monnaie*, special issue of *L'Homme 162*.

Brown, Paula 1995. *Beyond a Mountain Valley. The Simbu of Papua New Guinea*. Honolulu: University of Hawai'i Press.

Brutti, Lorenzo 2003. Qui A Tué Afek? Transformations Socio-Economiques et Continuité Culturelle chez les Oksapmin de Papouasie Nouvelle Guinée. Ph.D. dissertation, Paris.
Carrier, James G. ed. 1992. *History and Tradition in Melanesian Anthropology*. Berkeley: University of California Press.
Carrier, James G. 1992a. Preface. In J. G. Carrier ed. *History and Tradition in Melanesian Anthropology*, pp. vii–ix. Berkeley: University of California Press.
Carrier, James G. 1992b. Introduction. In J. G. Carrier ed. *History and Tradition in Melanesian Anthropology*, pp. 1–37. Berkeley: University of California Press.
Carrier, James G. 1992c. Approaches to articulation. In J. G. Carrier ed. *History and Tradition in Melanesian Anthropology*, pp. 116–43. Berkeley: University of California Press.
Carucci, Laurence Marshall 2001. Elison or decision: lived history and the contextual grounding of the constructed past. In J. Mageo ed. *Cultural Memory*, pp. 81–104. Honolulu: University of Hawai'i Press.
Caws, Peter 1974. Operational, representational, and explanatory models. *American Anthropologist* 76: 1–10.
Clark, Jeffrey 1997. Imagining the state, or tribalism and the arts of memory in the Highlands of Papua New Guinea. In T. Otto and N. Thomas eds. *Narratives of Nation in the South Pacific*, pp. 65–90. Amsterdam: Harwood.
Clark, Jeffrey 2000. *Steel to Stone: A Chronicle of Colonialism in the Southern Highlands of Papua New Guinea*, Chris Ballard and Michael Nihill eds. Oxford: Oxford University Press.
Comaroff, Jean and John L. Comaroff eds. 1993. *Modernity and its Malcontents. Ritual and Power in Postcolonial Africa*. Chicago: University of Chicago Press.
Comaroff, Jean and John L. Comaroff 1999. Occult economies and the violence of abstraction: notes from the Southern African postcolony. *American Ethnologist* 26(2): 279–303.
Connolly, Robert and Robin Anderson 1983. *First Contact* (film). Sydney: Australian Broadcasting Commission.
Connolly, Robert and Robin Anderson 1987. *First Contact*. New York: Viking.
Dalton, Doug 2001. Memory, power, and loss in Rawa discourse. In J. Mageo ed. *Cultural Memory*, pp. 105–29. Honolulu: University of Hawai'i Press.
Dambrowski, Kirk 2002. The praxis of indigenism and Alaska Native timber politics. *American Anthropologist* 104(4): 1062–1073, special issue, Guest Editor Dorothy L. Hodgson.
Dinnen, Sinclair 2001. *Law and Order in a Weak State. Crime and Politics in Papua New Guinea*. Honolulu: University of Hawai'i Press.
Englund, Harri and James Leach 2000. Ethnography and the meta-narratives of modernity. *Current Anthropology* 41(2): 225–48.
Errington, Frederick K. and Deborah B. Gewertz 1991. *Articulating Change in the "Last Unknown."* Boulder: Westview Press.
Evans-Pritchard, Edward E. 1940. *The Nuer*. Oxford: Clarendon Press.

Fairhall, R. J. 1958–1959. Territory of Papua and New Guinea, Patrol Report, Koroba no. 7. National Archives of Papua New Guinea.

Feinberg, Richard 1995. Introduction. In R. Feinberg and L. Zimmer-Takakoshi, guest editors, "Politics of Culture in the Pacific Islands," special issue of *Ethnology* 34(2): 95–98.

Finney, Ben 1973. *Big-Men and Business: Entrepreneurship and Economic Growth in the New Guinea Highlands*. Honolulu: University of Hawai'i Press.

Foley, William A. 2000. The languages of New Guinea. *Annual Review of Anthropology* 29: 357–404.

Fortes, Meyer 1969. *Kinship and the Social Order*. Chicago: Aldine Publishing.

Foster, Robert J. 1992. Commoditiztation and the emergence of Kastom as a cultural category: a New Ireland case in comparative perspective. In M. Jolly and N. Thomas eds. "The Politics of Tradition in the Pacific," *Oceania* 62(4): 284–94.

Foster, Robert J. ed. 1995. *Nation Making. Emergent Identities in Postcolonial Melanesia*. Ann Arbor: University of Michigan Press.

Foster, Robert J. 2002. *Materializing the Nation. Commodities, Consumption and Media in Papua New Guinea*. Bloomington: Indiana University Press.

Gammage, Bill 1998. *The Sky Travellers: Journeys in New Guinea, 1938–1939*. Melbourne: The Miegunyah Press (Melbourne University Press).

Gewertz, Deborah B. and Frederick K. Errington 1991. *Twisted Histories, Altered Contexts. Representing the Chambri in a World System*. Cambridge: Cambridge University Press.

Glasse, Robert M. 1968. *Huli of Papua: A Cognatic Descent System*. The Hague: Mouton.

Goldman, Laurence R. 1983. *Talk Never Dies: The Language of Huli Disputes*. London: Tavistock.

Grant, Neil J. 1956. Territory of Papua and New Guinea, Koroba Patrol Report no. 7. National Archives of Papua New Guinea.

Guo, Pei-Yi 2003. "Island Builders": Landscape and Historicity Among the Langalanga, Solomon Islands. In Pamela J. Stewart and Andrew Strathern eds. *Landscape, Memory, and History: Anthropological Perspectives*, pp. 189–209. London and New York: Pluto Press.

Haley, Nicole 1996. Revisioning the past, remembering the future: Duna accounts of the world's end. *Oceania* 66: 278–85.

Haley, Nicole Clair 2002. *Ipakana Yakaiya*: Mapping Landscapes, Mapping Lives. Contemporary Land Politics among the Duna. Ph.D., Australian National University, Canberra.

Hides, Jack G. 1935. *Through Wildest Papua*. London: Blackie and Son.

Hirsch, Eric 2001. When was modernity in Melanesia? *Social Anthropology* 9(2): 131–46.

Hobsbawm, Eric and Terence Ranger eds. 1983. *The Invention of Tradition*. Cambridge: Cambridge University Press.

Hogbin, H. Ian and Camilla Wedgewood 1953. Local groupings in Melanesia. *Oceania* 24: 58–76.

Hoskins, Janet 1998. *Biographical Objects: How Things Tell the Stories of People's Lives.* London and New York: Routledge.

Jacka, Jerry 2001. Coca-Cola and *kolo*: land, ancestors and development. *Anthropology Today* 17(4): 3–8.

Jackson, Graham 1971. Review article. Glasse, the Huli, and descent. *The Journal of the Polynesian Society* 80: 119–32.

Jolly, Margaret 1992. Banana leaf bundles and skirts: a Pacific Penelope's web? In J. G. Carrier ed. *History and Tradition in Melanesian Anthropology*, pp. 38–63. Berkeley: University of California Press.

Jolly, Margaret and Nicolas Thomas eds. 1992. *The Politics of Tradition in the Pacific*, special issue of *Oceania* 62(4).

Kahn, Miriam 1986. *Always Hungry, Never Greedy. Food and the Expression of Gender in a Melanesian Society.* Cambridge: Cambridge University Press.

Kaplan, Martha and John D. Kelly 1994. Rethinking "resistance": dialogics of "disaffection" in colonial Fiji. *American Ethnologist* 21(1): 123–51.

Keesing, Roger M. 1970. Shrines, ancestors and cognatic descent: the Kwaio and Tallensi. *American Anthropologist* 72: 755–75.

Keesing, Roger M. and Robert Tonkinson eds. 1982. *Reinventing Traditional Culture: The Politics of Kastom in Island Melanesia*, special issue of *Mankind* 13(4).

Keesing, Roger M. 1992. *Custom and Confrontation. The Kwaio Struggle for Cultural Autonomy.* Chicago: University of Chicago Press.

Knauft, Bruce M. 1985. *Good Company and Violence.* Berkeley: University of California Press.

Knauft, Bruce M. 2002. *Exchanging the Past. A Rainforest World of Before and After.* Chicago: University of Chicago Press.

Knauft, Bruce M. ed. 2003. *Critically Modern: Alternatives, Alterities, Anthropologies.* Indianapolis: Indiana University Press.

Lambek, Michael 2003. *The Weight of the Past: Living with History in Mahajanga, Madagascar.* New York and London: Palgrave Macmillan.

Lattas, Andrew 1998. *Cultures of Secrecy: Reinventing Race in Bush Kaliai Cargo Cults.* Madison: University of Wisconsin Press.

Leahy, Michael and Maurice Crain 1937. *The Land that Time Forgot.* London: Hurst and Blackett.

Linnekin, Jocelyn 1983. Defining tradition: variations on the Hawaiian identity. *American Ethnologist* 10: 241–52.

Linnekin, Jocelyn 1991. Cultural invention and the dilemma of authenticity. *American Anthropologist* 93: 446–49.

Linnekin, Jocelyn and Lin Poyer eds. 1990. *Cultural Identity and Ethnicity in the Pacific.* Honolulu: University of Hawai'i Press.

LiPuma, Edward 1988. *The Gift of Kinship.* Cambridge: Cambridge University Press.

LiPuma, Edward 2001. *Encompassing Others. The Magic of Modernity in Melanesia.* Ann Arbor: University of Michigan Press.

McPherson, Naomi ed. 2001. *In Colonial New Guinea: Anthropological Perspectives.* ASAO Monograph no. 19. Pittsburgh, PA: University of Pittsburgh Press.

Macintyre, Martha 2001. Taking care of culture: consultancy, anthropology, and gender issues. In Pamela J. Stewart and Andrew Strathern eds. *Anthropology and Consultancy*, special issue of *Social Analysis* 45(2): 108–19.

Mageo, Jeannette Marie ed. 2001. *Cultural Memory. Reconfiguring History and Identity in the Postcolonial Pacific*. Honolulu: University of Hawai'i Press.

Mageo, Jeannette M. 2001. On memory genres: tendencies in cultural remembering. In J. Mageo ed. *Cultural Memory. Reconfiguring History and Identity in the Postcolonial Pacific*, pp. 11–36. Honolulu: University of Hawai'i Press.

Marcus, George E. and Michael M. J. Fischer 1986 (second ed. 1999). *Anthropology as Cultural Critique: An Experimental Moment in the Human Sciences*. Chicago: University of Chicago Press.

Marecek, Thomas M. 1979. Social relationships in a Papua New Guinea Community. Ph.D. dissertation, Arizona State University.

Modjeska, Charles Nicholas 1977. Production among the Duna. Ph.D. dissertation. Australian National University.

Modjeska, Charles Nicholas 1980. Duna kinship terminology: an atrophied Iroquois system. In E. A. Cook and D. O'Brien eds. *Blood and Semen: Kinship Systems of Highlands New Guinea*, pp. 305–27. Ann Arbor: University of Michigan Press.

Modjeska, Charles Nicholas 1982. Production and inequality. In A. Strathern ed. *Inequality in New Guinea Highlands Societies*, pp. 50–108. Cambridge: Cambridge University Press.

Modjeska, Charles Nicholas 1991. Post-Ipomoean modernism: the Duna example. In M. Godelier and M. Strathern eds. *Big-Men and Great Men: Personifications of Power in Melanesia*, pp. 234–55. Cambridge: Cambridge University Press.

Modjeska, Charles Nicholas 1995. Rethinking women's exploitation: the Duna case and the material basis of Big Man systems. In A. Biersack ed. *Papuan Borderlands*, pp. 256–86. Ann Arbor: University of Michigan Press.

Moore, Henrietta L. and Todd Sanders eds. 2001. *Magical Interpretations, Material Realities. Modernity, Witchcraft and the Occult in Postcolonial Africa*. London and New York: Routledge.

O'Hanlon, Michael 1989. *Reading the Skin*. London: British Museum Publications.

Otto, Ton 1992. The ways of Kastom: tradition as category and practice in a Manus village. In M. Jolly and N. Thomas eds. *The Politics of Tradition in the Pacific*, special issue of *Oceania* 62(4): 264–83.

Otto, Ton and Nicholas Thomas eds. 1997. *Narratives of Nation in the South Pacific*. Amsterdam: Harwood Academic Publishers.

Rappaport, Roy 1968. *Pigs for the Ancestors*. New Haven: Yale University Press.

Rappaport, Roy 1999. *Ritual and Religion in the Making of Humanity*. Cambridge: Cambridge University Press.

Robbins, Joel 2001. Whatever became of revival? From charismatic movement to charismatic church in a Papua New Guinean society. In J. Robbins,

P. J. Stewart, and A. Strathern eds. *Charismatic and Pentecostal Christianity in Oceania*, special issue of the *Journal of Ritual Studies* 15(2): 79–90.

Robbins, Joel n.d. *Sins Between Cultures. Christianity, Cultural Change and Moral Torment in a Papua New Guinea Society*. Berkeley: University of California Press.

Robbins, Joel, Pamela J. Stewart, and Andrew Strathern eds. 2001. *Charismatic and Pentecostal Christianity in Oceania*, special issue of the *Journal of Ritual Studies* 15(2).

Rohatynskyj, Marta 2001. On knowing the Baining and other minor ethnic groups of East New Britain. In Pamela J. Stewart and Andrew Strathern eds. *Anthropology and Consultancy*, special issue of *Social Analysis* 45(2): 23–40.

Ryan, D'Arcy J. 1961. Gift Exchange in the Mendi Valley. Ph.D. dissertation, University of Sydney.

Ryan, Peter 1991. *Black Bonanza: A Landslide of Gold*. South Yara, Victoria: Hyland House.

Said, Edward 1978. *Orientalism*. Harmondsworth: Penguin.

Scaglion, Richard and Marie Norman 2000. Where resistance falls short: rethinking agency through biography. In Pamela J. Stewart and Andrew Strathern eds. *Identity Work: Constructing Pacific Lives*, pp. 121–38. ASAO Monograph no. 18. Pittsburgh: University of Pittsburgh Press.

Scheffler, Harold W. 1965. *Choiseul Island Social Structure*. Berkeley: University of California Press.

Schieffelin, Edward L. and Robert Crittenden 1990. *Like People You See in a Dream. First Contact in Six Papuan Societies*. Stanford: Stanford University Press.

Schiller, Anne 1997. *Small Sacrifices: Religious Change and Cultural Identity Among the Ngaju of Indonesia*. Oxford: Oxford University Press.

Sillitoe, Paul 1979. *Give and Take. Exchange in Wola Society*. Canberra: Australian National University Press.

Sillitoe, Paul 1994. *The Bogaia of the Muller Range, Papua New Guinea: Land Use, Agriculture, and Society of a Vulnerable Population*. Oceania Monographs no. 44. Sydney: University of Sydney.

Sillitoe, Paul 1996. *A Place Against Time*. Amsterdam: Harwood Academic Publications.

Sillitoe, Paul, Pamela J. Stewart, and Andrew Strathern 2002. *Horticulture in Papua New Guinea. Case Studies from the Southern and Western Highlands*. Pittsburgh: Ethnology Monographs no. 18.

Sinclair, James P. 1955–1956/1 and 2. Territory of Papua and New Guinea, Koroba Patrol Reports nos. 1 and 2, 1955–1956. National Archives of Papua New Guinea.

Sinclair, James P. 1966. *Behind the Ranges. Patrolling in New Guinea*. Melbourne: Melbourne University Press.

Smith, Michael French 2002. *Village at the Edge*. Honolulu: University of Hawai'i Press.

Souter, Gavin 1963. *New Guinea: The Last Unknown*. New York: Taplinger Publishing Co. Inc.

Standish, Bill 2002. Electoral governance in Papua New Guinea: Chimbu poll diary, June 2002. URL: *http://rspas.anu.edu.au/melanesia/pngrsourcepage.htm*

Stasch, Rupert 2001. Giving up homicide: Korowai experiences of witches and police (West Papua). *Oceania* 71(1): 33–52.

Steensberg, Axel 1980. *New Guinea Gardens*. London: Academic Press.

Stewart, Pamela J. and Andrew Strathern eds. 1997. *Millennial Markers*. Townsville: James Cook University, Centre for Pacific Studies.

Stewart, Pamela J. 1998. Ritual trackways and sacred paths of fertility. In J. Miedema, C. Odé, and R. A. C. Dam eds. *Perspectives on the Bird's Head of Irian Jaya, Indonesia*, pp. 275–90. Amsterdam: Rodopi.

Stewart, Pamela J. and Andrew Strathern 1999a. Politics and poetics mirrored in indigenous stone objects from Papua New Guinea. *Journal of the Polynesian Society* 108(1): 69–90.

Stewart, Pamela J. and Andrew Strathern eds. 2000. *Millennial Countdown in New Guinea*, special issue of *Ethnohistory* 47(1). Durham, N.C.: Duke University Press.

Stewart, Pamela J. and Andrew Strathern 2000a. Naming places: Duna evocations of landscape in Papua New Guinea. *People and Culture in Oceania* 16: 87–107.

Stewart, Pamela J. and Andrew Strathern. 2000b. Religious change in the Highlands of Papua New Guinea. *Journal of Ritual Studies* 14(2): 28–33.

Stewart, Pamela J. and Andrew Strathern 2000c. *Speaking for Life and Death: Warfare and Compensation among the Duna of Papua New Guinea*. Senri Ethnological Reports 13: National Museum of Ethnology, Osaka, Japan.

Stewart, Pamela J. and A. Strathern 2001a. *Humors and Substances. Ideas of the Body in New Guinea*. Westport, Conn. and London: Bergin and Garvey (Greenwood Publications).

Stewart, Pamela J. and Andrew Strathern 2001b. *Timbu Wara* figures from Papua New Guinea. *Records of the South Australian Museum* 34(2): 65–77.

Stewart, Pamela J. and Andrew Strathern 2002a. *Remaking the World: Myth, Mining and Ritual Change among the Duna of Papua New Guinea*. Washington, D.C.: Smithsonian Institution Press.

Stewart, Pamela J. and Andrew Strathern 2002b. *Gender, Song, and Sensibility: Folktales and Folksongs in the Highlands of New Guinea*. Westport, Conn.: Praeger (Greenwood Publishing).

Stewart, Pamela J. and Andrew Strathern 2002c. Transformations of monetary symbols in the Highlands of Papua New Guinea. In S. Breton ed.special issue of *L'Homme* 162: 137–56.

Stewart, Pamela J. and Andrew Strathern 2002d. *Violence: Theory and Ethnography*. London: Continuum.

Stewart, Pamela J. and Andrew Strathern 2003a. The ultimate protest statement: suicide as a means of defining self-worth among the Duna of the Southern Highlands Province, PNG. *Journal of Ritual Studies* 17(1): 79–89.

Stewart, Pamela J. and Andrew Strathern 2003b. *Witchcraft, Sorcery,*

Rumors, and Gossip. Cambridge and New York: Cambridge University Press.
Stewart, Pamela J. and Andrew Strathern n.d.a., eds. *Expressive Genres and Historical Change.* [manuscript near completion]
Stewart, Pamela J. and Andrew Strathern n.d.b. *Colonial Compressions* [manuscript in preparation]
Strathern, Andrew 1972. *One Father, One Blood.* Canberra: Australian National University Press.
Strathern, Andrew ed. 1982. *Inequality in New Guinea Highlands Societies.* Cambridge: Cambridge University Press.
Strathern, Andrew 1984. *A Line of Power.* London: Tavistock.
Strathern, Andrew and Pamela J. Stewart 1999a. *Curing and Healing: Medical Anthropology in Global Perspective.* Durham, N.C.: Carolina Academic Press.
Strathern, Andrew and Pamela J. Stewart 1999b. *Collaborations and Conflicts. A Leader Through Time.* Fort Worth: Harcourt Brace College Publishers.
Strathern, Andrew and Pamela J. Stewart 1999c. Objects, relationships, and meanings: historical switches in currencies in Mount Hagen, Papua New Guinea. In *Money and Modernity: State and Local Currencies in Melanesia.* David Akin and Joel Robbins eds. ASAO (Association for Social Anthropology in Oceania) Monograph Series no. 17. Pittsburgh: University of Pittsburgh Press, pp. 164–91.
Strathern, Andrew and Pamela J. Stewart 1999d. *"The Spirit is Coming!" A Photographic-Textual Exposition of the Female Spirit Cult Performance in Mt. Hagen.* Ritual Studies Monograph Series, Monograph no. 1. Dept. of Anthropology, University of Pittsburgh.
Strathern, Andrew and Pamela J. Stewart 2000a. *Arrow Talk: Transaction, Transition, and Contradiction in New Guinea Highlands History.* Kent, Ohio and London: Kent State University Press.
Strathern, Andrew and Pamela J. Stewart 2000b. *The Python's Back: Pathways of Comparison between Indonesia and Melanesia.* Westport, Conn.: Bergin and Garvey (Greenwood Publications).
Strathern, Andrew and Pamela J. Stewart 2000c. *Stories, Strength and Self-Narration: Western Highlands, Papua New Guinea.* Adelaide, Australia: Crawford House Publishing.
Strathern, Andrew and Pamela J. Stewart 2000d. Accident, agency, and liability in New Guinea Highlands compensation practices. *Bijdragen* 156(2): 275–95.
Strathern, Andrew and Pamela J. Stewart 2000e. Custom, modernity and contradiction: local and national identities in Papua New Guinea. *The New Pacific Review* 1(1): 118–26.
Thomas, Nicolas 1992a. Substantivization and anthropological discourse: the transformation of practices into institutions in neotraditional Pacific societies. In J. G. Carrier ed. *History and Tradition in Melanesian Anthropology*, pp. 64–85. Berkeley: University of California Press.
Thomas, Nicholas 1992b. The inversion of tradition. *American Ethnologist* 19(2): 213–32.

Trompf, G. W. 1994. *Payback. The Logic of Retribution in Melanesian Religions.* Cambridge: Cambridge University Press.

Wagner, Roy 1967. *The Curse of Souw.* Chicago: University of Chicago Press.

Weber, Max 1992. *The Protestant Ethic and the Spirit of Capitalism*, trans. Talcott Parsons, introd. by Anthony Giddens. London and New York: Routledge.

Weiner, Annette 1980. Stability in banana leaves: colonization and women in Kiriwina, Trobriand Islands. In M. Etienne and E. Leacock eds. *Women and Colonization*, pp. 270–93. New York: Praeger.

Wurm, Stephen A. 1964. Australian New Guinea Highlands languages and the distribution of their typological features. *American Anthropologist* 66(4) no. 2: 77–97.

This page intentionally left blank

About the Authors

Professor Andrew Strathern and Dr. Pamela J. Stewart are a husband and wife research team. They have worked in the Highlands of Papua New Guinea (PNG) over a number of years, primarily with the Duna people of the Southern Highlands Province of PNG and the Hagen people of the Western Highlands Province as well as the Pangia people of the Southern Highlands Province. Some of their recent co-authored books on their research in these areas include: *Collaborations and Conflicts. A Leader Through Time* (2000, Fort Worth: Harcourt Brace College Publishers); *Arrow Talk: Transaction, Transition, and Contradiction in New Guinea Highlands History* (2000, Kent, Ohio and London: Kent State University Press); *The Python's Back: Pathways of Comparison between Indonesia and Melanesia* (2000, Westport, Conn. and London: Bergin and Garvey, Greenwood Publishing Group); *Stories, Strength and Self-Narration: Western Highlands, Papua New Guinea* (2000, Adelaide, Australia: Crawford House Publishing); *Oceania; An Introduction to the Cultures and Identities of Pacific Islands* (2002, Durham, N.C.: Carolina Academic Press, co-authored with Laurence M. Carucci, Lin Poyer, Richard Feinberg, and Cluny Macpherson); and *Horticulture in Papua New Guinea: Case Studies from the Southern and Western Highlands* (2002, Ethnology Monographs No. 18, Pittsburgh, PA., co-authored with Paul Sillitoe).

Strathern and Stewart have a broad range of interests within anthropology, including the presentation of life-history materials and other forms of oral narratives. *Collaborations and Conflicts* details historical change among a group of people (the Kawelka of Hagen) primarily through the narratives of one leading figure in the community with additional commentary from his grown daughter and analysis by Strathern and Stewart. The Hagen leader, narrating his life-history, is Ongka-Kaepa, the man whom many anthropology undergraduates know from the ethnographic film *Ongka's Big Moka* (directed by Charlie Nairn). Ongka's life-history supplements the film by explaining further the context in which the events depicted took place and the historical changes that occurred after the film was completed. Further materials on Ongka's life-history have been presented, along with a set of life-history materials from other places in Oceania, in *Identity Work: Constructing Pacific Lives* (Stewart and Strathern eds., 2000, Association for Social Anthropology in Oceania Monograph Series No. 18. Pittsburgh: University of Pittsburgh Press).

Other areas in which the authors have been interested include medical anthropology and ritual/religious studies. They are the co-editors of the Medical Anthropology Series and Ritual Studies Series published by Carolina Academic Press and of the *Journal of Ritual Studies*. They have also co-authored a number of books in these two areas: *Curing and Healing: Medical Anthropology in Global Perspective* (1999, Durham, N.C.: Carolina Academic Press); *Humors and Substances: Ideas of the Body in New Guinea* (2001, Westport, Conn. and London: Bergin and Garvey, Greenwood Publishing Group); and *Remaking the World: Myth, Mining, and Ritual Change* (2002, Washington, D.C. and London: Smithsonian Institution Press). They have co-edited three further volumes: *Millennial Countdown in New Guinea* (2000, Special Issue of *Ethnohistory* 47.1, Durham, N.C. Duke University Press); *Millennial Markers* (1997, Townsville, Australia: JCU, Centre for Pacific Studies); and *Charismatic and Pentecostal Christianity in Oceania* (2001, Special Issue of *Journal of Ritual Studies*, 15.2, co-edited with Joel Robbins).

The authors have explored gender relations, within the framework of interpretive anthropology, in their book, *Gender, Song, and Sensibility* (2002, Westport, Conn.: Praeger). The work opens up a perspective on gender relations at the point of courtship and marriage, taking readers into the world of courting songs, folktales, ballads, myths, and rituals that formed an important part of the way in which gender relations were imagined and performed in the Papua New Guinea Highlands. The book reveals the sensuous and emotional modalities of expressive genres and their aesthetic qualities. Both women and men are shown to have complex expressions of emotional dispositions in the spheres of courting and the choice of marital partners. By entering into these domains, the analysis modifies earlier ideas of Highlands societies that had been concentrated on antagonisms, behavioral taboos, separation, and domination as themes in gender relations in the Highlands region.

Stewart and Strathern are also concerned with contemporary global issues and the ways that anthropology and anthropologists participate in these. Their co-edited collection *Anthropology and Consultancy* (2001, Special Issue of *Social Analysis* 45. 2, Adelaide University), confronts the dilemmas inherent in anthropological practice nowadays. Their co-authored books *Violence: Theory and Ethnography* (2002, New York and London: Continuum Publishing) and *Witchcraft, Sorcery, Rumors, and Gossip* (2003, Cambridge: Cambridge University Press), both explore violence and "terror." In *Violence: Theory and Ethnography*, the authors examine several empirical studies and theories regarding violence, emphasizing contemporary cases in which ethnicity, nationalism, or religious conflict, enter the arena and challenge interpretation, such as in Sri Lanka, Rwanda-Urundi, or Northern Ireland. A significant argument of this book is that the motivation for revenge acts powerfully, and can be modified only through positive exchanges between groups. In the book on witchcraft, the authors combine two classic topics in social anthropology in a new synthesis: the study of witchcraft and sorcery and the study of rumors and gossip. They do this in two ways. First, they show how rumor and gossip are invariably important as catalysts for accusations of witchcraft and sorcery. Second, they demonstrate the role of rumor and gossip in the genesis of social and political violence, as in the case of both peasant rebellions and witch hunts. Examples supporting the argument are drawn from Africa, Europe, India, Papua New Guinea, Sri Lanka, and Indonesia. They include discussions of witchcraft trials in Essex, England, and in Scotland in the seventeenth century, witch hunts and vampire narratives in colonial and contemporary Africa, millenarian movements in New Guinea, the Indian Mutiny in nineteenth-century Uttar Pradesh, and rumors of "construction sacrifice" in Indonesia.

In addition to their work in Papua New Guinea, the authors have carried out fieldwork in Europe (primarily Scotland and Ireland) and Taiwan, and have also worked in Japan, Australia, and The Netherlands. *Minorities and Memories: Survivals and Extinctions in Scotland and Western Europe* (2001, Durham, N.C.: Carolina Academic Press) explores historical and contemporary expressions of identity in Scotland. The authors' current research project in the border area of the Republic of Ireland and Northern Ireland explores some of these same issues as seen from the point of view of Irish heritage.

Further information about the authors can be found at their webpage: *http://www.pitt.edu/~strather/*

This page intentionally left blank

Index

agency, creative, 162
Agiru, Anderson, 114–115
Aluni station/parish, 13, 14, 22, 25, 26
  Baptist pastor of, 25
  moots held at, 74
  changes in landscape of, 96
  discos at, 111
Aluni Valley, general descriptions, 10–11, 12–13, 14–16, 22
  parishes in, 25–26
  population of, 26
  churches in, 56–64
  administration in, 66–68
  leaders in, 70
  changes in, 108–120
  vulnerability to sickness in, 120
  peripheral to capitalist change, 136
  compared to Simbu, 141
  with Gebusi, 146
  with Pangia, 149
  compared with other case-studies, 152
  population in, 165
Amarshi, Azeem, 153
anda pirapea, 14
anoagaro, 28, 30, 110, 118
  see also descent, kinship, *kango*
Anthropology, theory in, ix–x
  Marxist, 23, 126
  historical anthropology, 23–24, 121–122
  and culture as discursive object, 125
  theories of tradition, 132
  on ethnography and history, 159–162
  resistance theory, 158
apa, 32
Appadurai, Arjun, 7
Arawe, Simon, 65, 112
ash fall, 18
assault sorcery, 80–81
"authenticity," 122
auwape, 165
auwi, 59–60, 62, 91

Baluan, 134
Bamford, Sandra, 130
Barker, John, 129, 130, 131
Barnes, J. A., 23
Barter, Sir Peter, 116
Bashkow, Ira, 147
Basiana, 126
Bell, William, 126
Biersack, Aletta, 96
big-men, 133
Billings, Dorothy, 5
birds, 10
Black, John, 16–17
Blong, Russell, 18
bodies, struggles over, 71
  and compensation, 81
Bogaiya, 10, 11, 80
Borofsky, Robert, 135
Bougainville, 68
brideprice/bridewealth, 32, 77
  specific examples of, 45–52
  and compensation, 166
Brown, Paula, 140–141
Bulireterete, 97

burial practices, 55, 58–59
  painting skulls in, 61
  and struggles over bodies, 71
  at Aluni, 96, 159

capitalism, 133–134, 150, 153
  and commoditization, 167
cargoistic ideas, 109
  in Pangia, 148–149
Carrier, James G., 122–123, 153, 154, 155
Carucci, Laurence M., 131
cash-cropping, 5, 69
  coffee, 108, 141
  see also Simbu, Pangia, Maring
cassowaries, 10, 20, 38, 42
Caws, Peter, 164
change, theories of, 121–123
  among Kwaio, 125–128
  among Duna, 128–137
  dichotomies of tradition and change, 132, 137
  see also "modernity," politics of tradition, tradition
Christianity, 6, 18, 38, 87, 96, 116, 129–30
  Anglican, 130–131, 151
  Apostolics, 56, 63, 117
  Assemblies of God, 117
  Baptists, 3–4, 14, 25, 47, 51, 56–57, 60, 63, 65, 88–89, 116–117, 119
  Catholics, 54, 60, 64–65, 144, 147
  Evangelical Church of Papua New Guinea, 63, 145
  Lutherans, 55, 130, 147
  Pentecostalists, 56, 120, 129, 131, 148
  Seventh-Day Adventists, 55, 64, 89, 96, 117, 119, 144–145
  sin, and Satan, concepts of, 119
  South Seas Evangelicals, 55
  studies of, 129–131
  sycretistic, 129
  Wesleyans (Methodists), 147

Christianity and change, 135, 137
  in Gebusi study, 142–146
  in Pangia study, 146–149
  and Evangelical Bible Mission, in Pangia, 148–149
  among Maring, 149–152
Clancy, Desmond, 19, 98
Clark, Jeffrey, 135, 146–149
colonial adminstration, 2, 14, 18–23
  patrol by Neil Grant, 54
  by CPO Fairhall, 55
  and road construction, 65
  and health, 67
  and wage labor, 67
  by Desmond Clancy, 98
  British, in Solomon Islands, 126–128
  in Pangia, 146–149
  among Duna, 156
  history of, 167
Comaroff, Jean, 120
Comaroff, John, 120
compensation payments, 19, 20, 21, 22, 51
  and speeches, 69–72
  and witchcraft, 69–70
  examples of, 77–83
  women's roles in, 83
  for tailings, 101
  claimed by Kwaio against governments, 126
conflicts, 70–83
  heard in moots, 74–77
  and compensation, 77–83
  over elections, 114, 115, 116
Connolly, Bob, and Robin Anderson, 147
cosmos, ideas of, 21, 76
  and Strickland River, 101
courting practices, 40–43
  contemporary problems over, 43–44, 51
Crittenden, R., 147
crops, 12, 14, 20
  peanuts, 22

Dalton, Douglas, 129–130
dances, 40
descent, 3, 23–24, 25
   and agnatic lines, 26–28
   example of Haiyuwi, 30–32, 36–37
   and generational cycles, 63
   effects of cognatic rules of, 71, 86
   anoagaro and Payame Ima, 94
   matrilineal, among Tanga, 134
"development," disappointment over, 74, 148
discos, 110, 166
divination, 38
   with *ndele rowa*, 93, 117
dogs, 27
Duna people, general descriptions, 10, 68
   changes among, 108
   synoptic analysis of changes among, 154–158, 161–162

earth-oven, 13
Ekali, 11, 13, 17, 19, 63, 101–102
elections, 114, 162
electoral violence, in 2002, 114–115, 137, 152, 157–158, 162
Enga, 5
Englund, Harri, 160
environmental issues, at Strickland, 100–104
Errington, Frederick, 129
ethnohistory, 25, 30–32
European Union, 9
Evans-Pritchard, E. E., 23, 164
explorations, 16
   by Fox brothers, 16
   by Taylor and Black, 16–17
   by Sinclair and others, 18–23
   by Clancy, 19

Feinberg, Richard, 137
Female Spirit, in Pangia, 147
Fiji, 125, 126
Finney, Ben, 153
Fischer, Michael, 122

forest, 13, 14, 26, 85, 95
forest fires, 85
Fortes, Meyer, 23, 164
Foster, Robert, 133–134, 167
Fox brothers, 16, 17, 18

Gammage, Bill, 17
gardening, 12, 20, 22, 163
Gasumi Corners, 143
Gebusi, 142–146
gender, 20, 23
   in moots, 74–75
   and women's speech/rituals, 165, 166
generational issues, 6, 43–44, 85, 149
Gewertz, Deborah, 129
gifts, and sacrifice, 92–93
Glasse, Robert M., ix, 23, 46, 51, 165
globalization, x, xi, 160–162
gold, 16, 96, 108
   see also Porgera gold mining company
Goldman, Laurence R., 64, 69, 97
Good, Kenneth, 153
group structure, ix
   flexibility in, 163
   see also descent, kinship, *kango*
guns, 6, 66
   build-up of, in Duna area, 113–114
   home-made, 114
   as sign of weak government, 129, 157
Guo, Pei-yi, 32

Hagu, 14, 25–26, 47, 51, 63, 68
Haiyuwi, 17, 25, 26
   genealogy of, 30–32
   descent patterns in, 36–37
   Itake group in, 36–37
   leader in, 70
   man of, in origin stories, 97
health officers, 67
   health issues in Aluni, 112, 120

Herowa-Agiwa, 115
Hewa, 11
Hides, Jack, 19
Highlands region, research in, 107–108
   changes in, 107–108
Hirsch, Eric, 160
historical consciousness, 19, 52, 63–64
   and constructions of the past, 139
homicide, 143
Honiara, 126
Horaile, 11, 36
   origins of Mone group in, 36
   Catholics at, 55, 64
   road through, 109–110
Huli, ix, 11, 19, 20, 23, 30, 48, 51
   lawini among, 51
   and *ndamba pi*, 69
   as place of imprisonment, 72
   and bachelor's cult, 97
hunting, 27

Ialibu, 18
Iba Tiri, 135
imagaro, 28, 30
initiation, 40, 94
   see also *palena*

Jacka, Jerry, 96
Jolly, Margaret, 123, 125, 132, 133

Kahn, Miriam, 124
kango (leaders), 4, 31, 32, 33, 38, 40, 48–49
   role of in bridewealth, 50–52
   as 'men of speech', 69–73
   and *tambaka*, 69–72
   in compensation cases, 77–83
   and *malu*, 85
   and knowledge of stones, 92
   and Payame Ima, 94
   in each parish, 111
   as dispute mediators, 113
   and relationship to witchcraft, 118
   in change, 155, 157–158

kastom, 133
Kawelka, 133, 167
Keesing, Roger M., 125–128
Kelapo (Kerabo), 21
Kennecott, 98–99
kerekere, 125
kinship, 3, 24, 26–28, 29, 30
   in Haiyuwi, 30–32
   kinship terms, consanguineal, 34
   affinal, 35
   and descent in Haiyuwi, 36–37
   cognatic emphasis in, 37–38, 45, 73
   and distribution of wages, 68
   and compensation, 70–83
   mother's kin, 72
   and fighting obligations, 113
   see also marriage, descent
Knauft, Bruce M., 129, 139, 142–146
Koroba, 11, 18, 22, 48, 64, 113
Kunai parish, 25, 37
Kwaio, 125–128
   and resistance to Christianity among pagans, 127
   acceptance of, by others, 127

Lake Kopiago, 10, 13, 18, 20, 21
   stone figure from, 22
   plane landed on, 54
   administration at, 55–67
   health centre at, 67
   officer in charge at, 73
   District office at, 81
   condition of station at, 112
Lake Kutubu, 20, 108
Lambek, Michael, 121
landscape, 16, 96
language use, 11
Lavani Valley, 20
Leach, James, 160
Leahy, Michael, 19
limestone, 20
liminality, 40
Linnekin, Jocelyn, 132
LiPuma, Edward, 149–152
liquor, 66, 110

local government councils, 74, 87, 111
Lora, Owen, 65–66, 100

Macintyre, Martha, 96
McPherson, Naomi, 56
madness, 147
magic, 20
  hunting, 27–28
  forest as domain of, 28
  for growth, 52
  sites of in landscape, 96
Maisin, 130
malu, 2, 30, 95
  of Aluni, 96–97
  not interfered with by missionaries, 116
  as resource, 149, 152, 159
Marcus, George, 122
Maring, 149–152
marriage, 35, 37–52
  and courting parties, 38–39
  and bridewealth/brideprice, 39, 45–52
marsupials, 10, 26, 71, 95
Mendi, 18, 66
  violence in, 114–115, 157–158
"Melanesian sociality," 153
metaphor, 70–73
migration, 67–68
mining companies, 96–101
  Bougainville Copper, 109
Mintima, 140
missions, 54–65
  and "founder-effect," 57
  Anglican, among Maisin, 130–131
  see also Christianity
"modernity," as concept, x, 2
  as experience, 133
  contrasted with tradition, 133
  in Tanga, 133–134
  plural modernities, 139
  "vernacular," 142
  and Christianity, 144
  and recessive agency, 145
  among Maring, 149–152

confusion of modernity and tradition in policies, 154
  as multiple, 158–159
  as moving horizon, 160
Modjeska, C. N., 2, 23–24, 34, 35, 36, 55, 59, 64, 110, 164
money (state/introduced), 32, 46
  in bridewealth, 48–49, 51–52
  and wage labor, 67–68
  in compensation payments, 70–83
  in Trobriands, 123
  in Wamira, 124
  incorporation into exchanges in Hagen, 124
  ideas of, in Pangia, 148–149
  and Maring, 150
Moore, Henrietta, 120, 156
moots, 74–77
Mortimer, Rex, 153
Mount Hagen, 13, 16, 18, 42, 43, 67, 84
  history of change in, 108–109
  compared with Simbu, 140–141
  and Melpa people, 164
Mount Kare, 108
Muller Range, 14, 27
Mune, Dick, 114–115
musical instruments, 38

nation, marks of, 167
Nauwa, 25, 27, 49–50
ndekao, 128–129
netbags, 42–43, 72
Nomad, 145
nostalgia, 129–130
numbers, 166

ocher, 52
oil, searches for, x, 2, 19, 20
  symbolic ideas about, 96
  patrols for, 98
  drilling for, at Strickland, 101–102
Ok area, x, 56
  Urapmin in, 63
Oksapmin, 11, 19, 72, 80–81, 102
Ok Tedi mine, 67, 98, 99, 100, 108

omens, 61
Ongka-Kaepa, 133, 166
origin stories, 30, 93
  of Aluni, 95–96
  see also malu
Otto, Ton, 134

pacification, 112
palena, 40, 52, 75, 94, 166
pandanus, fruit, 11, 12–13, 17
pandanus, nut, 11, 27
  pandanus language, 27
  referred to in songs, 43
  and Payame Ima, 95
"pandanus talk," 95
Pangia, 130, 146–149
parakeets, 70–71
parishes, populations of, 26
  composition of, 26–29
  example of Haiyuwi, 30–32
  powers of agnates in, 95
  defined, 163
  names of, 163
pastors, 47, 60, 62
  power of, 63
  at Hagu, 88–89
  power of, 131, 155, 159
Payame Ima (female spirit), 4, 5, 11, 26, 58
  and parakeets, 71
  in origin story, 93–94
  as Hoyape Ima, 94
  as Yuro Ima, 94
  and forest fires, 94
  and pandanus nut trees, 94–95
  and marsupials, 95
  as Papumi and Lukumi, 98
  as Yuro Ima and the Strickland River, 101, 105
  in Yangone story, 103, 104
pigs, as sacrifices, 17
  bride's task to rear, 40
  in bridewealth, 45, 48–49
  in a dispute, 71
  as payments in compensations, 73–83

  theft of, 75
  sacrifices to forest spirits, 85
pikono, 49
  description of, 165
Poli, 93
police, 19–20, 21–22, 65–66, 74, 112–113
politics, national, 88
  provincial, 112
politics of tradition, x, 6
  discussions of, 125–128
  summary on, 136–137
  R. Feinberg on, 137
  J. Clark on, 146–149
polygyny, 76
Ponam, 155
Porgera, 5, 18
Porgera, gold mining company (PJV), 14, 18, 25, 37, 64, 108
  sets up health care centre at Aluni, 67, 112
  site of, 99–100
  SG3 station at Strickland, 99
  Community Outreach section of, 149
Port Moresby, 67
Poyer, Lin, 132
python, 93

Rappaport, Roy, 149
raskol, 109
Rawa, 129–130
reification of custom, 127–128
resistance, among Kwaio, 125–128
  in Southern Highlands, 158
Revelation, Book of, 116
rindi, 91
  and group structure, 164
rindi kiniya, 63–64, 76–77, 84, 92, 111
  in relation to Christianity, 116, 131
ritual, at marriage, 39–40
  at *palena*, 40
  at death, 58–59
  rindi kiniya, 63–64, 76–77, 84

developed in adaptation to
Christianity, 87
to Tindi Auwene, 95
and world's end, 116
see also rindi kiniya, taboos
roads, 65, 108–109
in Aluni Valley, lack of, 109
as mixed blessing, 110
Robbins, Joel, 56, 63, 129
Rohatynskyj, Marta, 132
rumors, 65, 109
Ryan, D'Arcy, 21
Ryan, Peter, 108

sacred stones, 59–60, 61, 62, 92, 97–98, 148–149
sacrifice, to forest spirits, 85
sites of, 91
logic of, 92–93
in Poli story, 93
and Christianity, 146
see also rindi kiniya, ritual, spirits
Sagu, 14
Said, Edward, 122
Sanders, Todd, 120, 156
Sane-Noma, 97–98
Schieffelin, E. L., 147
Schiller, Ann, 132
school, 42
abandonment of, at Aluni, 110
sexual behavior, 44, 75–77
shells, 17, 21
cowries, 21, 46, 70, 92
pearl shells, 17, 21, 72
sickness, 21, 38, 61, 67
and sacrifice, 92
Sillitoe, Paul, 11
on individuals, 164
Simbu, 140–141
Sinclair, James, 19–23, 54, 98
sky beings, 17
songs, 40–43 (for courting), 51, 58
for funerals, 166
sorcery, 72, 115, 128, 144
see also tsome, ndekao
Souter, Gavin, 16, 17

speeches, examples of, 70–73, 85–86, 166
Speer, Albert, 21
spirits (*tama*), 26–28
tini, 40, 58
tsiri, 60, 66
assimilation of, into Catholicism, 64
in stories about the Strickland, 100–105
Stasch, Rupert, 120
Stewart, Pamela J., 11, 16, 17, 18, 20, 21, 22, 24, 32, 57, 59, 63, 70, 80, 85, 92, 95, 97, 103, 114, 120, 125, 129, 130, 148, 156
stone head, of Kopiago, 97–98
Strathern, Andrew, 11, 16, 17, 18, 20, 21, 22, 23–24, 32, 57, 59, 63, 70, 80, 85, 92, 95, 97, 103, 114, 120, 125, 129, 130, 147, 148, 156
Strickland River, x, 10, 11, 13, 16–17, 19, 22, 80, 109
and mining tailings, 99, 100, 101
Strickland-Bosavi, 27
substantivization, 125
suicide, 69, 80

taboos, 27
affinal, 21
observed by new bride, 39
menstrual, 57
adherence to, 156
tama, 26–28, 60
see also spirits
tambaka, 69–72
Tanga, 133
Tangi, 48, 57
Tari, 18, 19, 72
Taylor, James L., 16–17
Telefolmin, 11, 16
theft, 21, 75
Thomas, Nicholas, 123–124, 125, 132, 133, 135, 144

Tindi Auwene, 26, 85, 95–96
  in Yangone story, 103–104, 131
tini, 40, 58, 79, 91
Tonkinson, Robert, 132
trade, 11, 20
  tradestores, 65, 67
tradition, as concept, 6, 16, 55
  "invention of tradition" theories, 125, 128, 132
  conflict between "traditionalists" and others, among Kwaio, 127
  relating to the present, 131
  review of theories of, 132
  inversion of tradition, 132
  dichotomizations of tradition and change, 132
  Ongka's model, 133
  inversion of, 152
  mixed with modernity, 159
Trobriands, 123
  and women's wealth, 123
Trompf, G. W., 93
Tsinali, 27
tsiri, 60, 64, 91, 92, 96
  Tsiri Harola, 97–98
  cowrie-giver, 99
  as trickster, 135
tsome, 80
tsuwake tene, 80–81
Tumbudu River, 20, 65, 109

Village Courts, 66, 74, 82, 112–113
violence, 20
  road holdups, 66
  and guns in Huli-Duna area, 113–114
  in electoral conflicts, 114–116
  among Gebusi, 142–146
  among Duna, 152

wage labor, 67–68
Wagner, Roy, 164
warfare, 21, 22, 113
Weber, Max, 150
Weiner, Annette, 123
wigs, *manda kalu*, 52
Williams, R. Maslyn, 54
Wiru, 147
witchcraft, 4, 21, 22, 26, 51, 61, 62
  Baptists and, 62–63, 64
  autopsies for, 69–70
  perceived lack of "law" on, 74
  accusations of in Aluni in 1991, 75
  failure to protect against, 83
  and SDA church in Aluni, 89
  divination for, 93
  deaths from, in 1996, 96, 118
  and environmental issues, 100–101
  and Christianity, 117–120
  events of 1998 and, 118–120
  comparison with Europe, 119
  other comparisons, 120
  and challenge to pastors, 131
world's end, theme of, 18, 62–63, 64, 116

Yangone, 20, 25, 70
  narrative about oil drilling among, 102–104
yekeanda, 38–39, 76, 166
Yeru, 11, 16, 19, 25, 26, 80
Yokona, 100

Zimmer-Tamakoshi, Laura, 137

This page intentionally left blank

This page intentionally left blank

GPSR Compliance
The European Union's (EU) General Product Safety Regulation (GPSR) is a set
of rules that requires consumer products to be safe and our obligations to
ensure this.

If you have any concerns about our products, you can contact us on

ProductSafety@springernature.com

In case Publisher is established outside the EU, the EU authorized
representative is:

Springer Nature Customer Service Center GmbH
Europaplatz 3
69115 Heidelberg, Germany

www.ingramcontent.com/pod-product-compliance
Lightning Source LLC
LaVergne TN
LVHW011824060526
838200LV00053B/3898